Unique Meeting, Wedding, and Party Places

IN GREATER WASHINGTON

Unique Meeting, Wedding, and Party Places

IN GREATER WASHINGTON

Historic Homes, Art Galleries, Ballrooms, Gardens, Inns,
Conference Centers, Riverboats, Museums,
and Other Distinctive Settings for Events Large and Small

Fifth Edition

Elise Hartman Ford

HOWELL PRESS

Charlottesville, Virginia

09 08 07 06 05 04 03 02 01 00   10 9 8 7 6 5 4 3 2 1

Howell Press, Inc., 1713-2D Allied Lane, Charlottesville, VA 22903
http://www.howellpress.com

Designed by Carolyn Weary Brandt
Edited by Meghan M. Mitchell

Front cover: Lockesly Manor. Photograph by Clay Blackmore
Back cover: National Air and Space Museum. Photograph by Eric Long

Library of Congress Cataloging-in-Publication Data

Ford, Elise.
  Unique meeting, wedding, and party places in Greater Washington / Elise Ford.
    p. cm.
  Includes index.
  ISBN 1-57427-119-9 (pbk.)
    1. Convention facilities—Washington Metropolitan Area—Guidebooks. I. Title.

TX907.3.W3 F67 2000
647.94753—dc21

                                                        00-063225

Contents

SITES FOR FEWER THAN 100 PEOPLE*

SITES FOR 100 TO 200 PEOPLE

*This breakdown identifies the **maximum** number of people a site can accommodate for any type of event. Refer to the individual site descriptions to determine specific capacity information for a particular type of function.

SITES FOR 500 TO 1,000 PEOPLE

SITES FOR MORE THAN 1,000 PEOPLE

How to use this book

If you know exactly where you want to stage your Washington event, go immediately to the Alphabetic Index and find the page number for the site description. Each of the guide's 153 entries provides facts about capacity, location, food and beverage arrangements, rates, limitations and restrictions, lead time for reserving, and facilities for the physically disabled.

But maybe you haven't made up your mind about a site, or you're ready for some new ideas. Or maybe your ideal setting doesn't meet the specific requirements of your group. If you're just starting to plan your function, you may not yet know what your group's requirements are. Perhaps you have a vague idea of what you want but aren't sure what's available in the area.

So how do you uncover the unique Washington site that's guaranteed to suit your group and its event to a T?

This guide will help. In addition to its ultimate purpose of assisting you in finding the perfect setting for your function, the book may be used, first, as a tool in the event-planning process to help you arrive at answers to basic questions—the same questions you can expect to be asked by the staff at each site. These questions are:

- When is the event taking place?
- How many people will be attending?
- What type of event will it be?
- Do you want it indoors, outdoors, or both?
- What is your budget?
- What are your special requirements? For example, do you have specific music, food or drink, or equipment requirements?

This guide is organized by capacity categories since the one piece of information that meeting and party planners often have from the start is the general number of people expected to attend the function. Please note: The sites included in each section are those whose maximum capacities fall into a particular category. Maximum capacities reflect the total space available, usually including the grounds. If you wish to know how many people can be accommodated indoors alone, within one portion of the site, or for a particular type of event, you should refer to the specific information provided for each site.

Once you've determined which sites can accommodate your group, it's up to you to choose the place you want. A Topical Cross-Reference at the back of the book identifies sites by special interest. If you're keen on throwing a large outdoor picnic, look under the Picnic Sites heading for J. R.'s Festival Lakes, located outside Leesburg, Virginia, or High Point Farm, in Clarksburg, Maryland. If you're holding an overnight event, go down the list of overnight conference centers and inns. Is a ballroom central to the purpose and ambience of your party? You have about fifty site choices, all found under the Ballrooms heading in the cross-reference index.

Perhaps you're not interested in traveling far from your office, hotel, or home; in such a case, you should refer to the Geographic Index to discover the names of those sites in your preferred location.

Certainly the budget factor will figure in your selection of a site. Rate information is provided within each site description, so simply look there to decide whether your budget covers the stated costs. The rates and information quoted herein are those provided by the sites at the time the book was researched, in mid-2000.

In addition to rental costs, there are usually other expenses, some of which can be quite substantial. Take catering, for instance. A three-hour cocktail reception for fifty people is likely to run you at least $1,500. Adding dinner will double that, and if you really want to go down in history, some caterers will gladly help you spend as much as $250 per person. Tent rental is another major expense. Prices start at about $300 for a small tent and go into the tens of thousands for the largest tents equipped with special, but sometimes necessary, items such as lighting, guttering, a dance floor, and heaters.

There are other things you should know as you read this book. The word "reception" used throughout refers to any stand-up event; the word "banquet" refers to any type of sit-down function. The serving of alcohol is permitted at most sites; therefore, the book notes only exceptions or restrictions on the use thereof. For example, Collingwood-on-the-Potomac allows only beer, wine, and champagne; the Corcoran Gallery of Art, like many sites, prohibits red wine because it stains.

Regulations and procedures for serving alcoholic beverages vary from jurisdiction to jurisdiction. Chances are, however, that you won't have to obtain a special liquor permit since most event places are already fully licensed or handle the permit process for you. Staff at each site will provide you with exact information regarding jurisdictional requirements for serving alcohol.

Most facilities ask you to adhere to certain rules when you rent their properties. One site may prohibit smoking, for example, and another may not allow fund-raising. The book lists these rules of usage along with site limitations under the heading Limitations/Restrictions, which is included in each description. The list is not necessarily all-inclusive but is intended to give you an idea of the most important use considerations.

You'll notice the recurring phrase "call for availability" when you come to the Lead Time for Reservations portion of site descriptions. While many places are fairly specific about their reservation schedules, others find their schedules less predictable. These facilities prefer that you go ahead and give them a call, no matter the lead time, in case a cancellation or other unexpected circumstance makes their site available when you need it.

The question "Facilities for the Physically Disabled?" appears at the end of each entry. "Yes" indicates that the site itself and a rest room are accessible to someone in a wheelchair. "No" means that neither the site nor its rest rooms are accessible to someone in a wheelchair. "Some," followed by a brief explanation, lets you know that the site is partially accessible to someone in a wheelchair. All sites recommend that you call ahead when your party includes disabled individuals so that you can find out the details of accessibility and ensure that the staff makes the proper arrangements.

Finally, two special sections at the end of the book tell you how to book group seats at Washington's theaters, arrange briefings on Capitol Hill with congressional members or at the White House with administration officials, and how to schedule private tours of the White House.

So there you have it: 153 meeting places that range from capacious to cozy, quaint to sophisticated, simple to elaborate—and all unique. Whatever your dream setting, Washington offers a lot from which to choose.

AMERICAN NEWS WOMEN'S CLUB

1607 22nd Street, NW

Washington, DC 20008

202/332-6770

202/265-6477 (fax)

www.anwc.org

anwc@syrynet.com

Endearing town house in embassy neighborhood

"The best-kept secret in town," commented a certain doyenne of the Washington scene about the American News Women's Club. Well, now the secret is out: The four-story brick town house near Dupont Circle that serves as headquarters to this sixty-year-old professional organization of women writers, editors, journalists, and publicists happens to hold perfectly lovely rooms for meetings, receptions, and dinners.

The framed faces of the club's past presidents greet you from the foyer wall as you make your way to the wide staircase and up to the three event spaces on the second floor. At the front of the house is the living room, whose walls are a combination of white stucco and paneling. Three sets of French doors open to petite balconies overlooking 22nd Street. Built-in bookcases (filled with books), a fireplace, a podium and raised platform, a Steinway grand piano, and an Oriental rug are some of the features of the room that make it suitable for both wedding receptions and conferences.

Through a connecting room, which has fine moldings and a fireplace, lies the dining room. Brunschwig & Fils wallpaper covers the top half of the walls, white-painted paneling the bottom half. A Regency-style bull's-eye mirror, crystal wall sconces, a glass chandelier, and a bay window with accompanying window seat are some of the room's other decorative elements.

CAPACITY
Meeting: 50
Reception: 100
Banquet: 50 in the living room, 36 in the dining room

LOCATION
On 22nd Street in the Dupont Circle area, near where Massachusetts and Florida Avenues meet, three blocks from the Dupont Circle Metro.

FOOD/BEVERAGE
You may choose your own caterer. There is a full-size professional kitchen with commercial-grade equipment. All clubhouse equipment—chairs, tables, china, silverware, silver service, coffee pots, trays, and other items—is available.

LIMITATIONS/RESTRICTIONS
The club is available to members and nonmembers alike all year-round, any time of day. On-street parking is a little tricky on weekdays but opens up considerably after 6:30 P.M. Smoking is not allowed, but dancing and music (kept to a reasonable volume) are allowed. The club holds renters responsible for returning the kitchen to its original state of cleanliness.

LEAD TIME FOR RESERVATIONS
Call for availability.

RATES
The club charges a flat fee of $500 per event, plus a refundable security deposit of $100.

FACILITIES FOR THE PHYSICALLY DISABLED? Some
An elevator provides access to upper floors of the house, and a portable wheelchair ramp is available for use at the front door.

BILLINGSLEY MANOR

6900 Green Landing Road
Upper Marlboro, MD 20772
301/627-0730
http://www.pgparks.com/places/historic.html

Colonial-style home overlooking the Patuxent

The history of this part of Prince George's County goes way back, and Billingsley Manor proves it. The tidy brick colonial house was built in 1740. Its original owner, Maj. John Billingsley, obtained a land grant from the second Lord Baltimore in 1662.

Of course, the house has been much restored since then, most recently in 1989 by its current owner, the Maryland-National Capital Park and Planning Commission (M-NCPPC). The M-NCPPC oversaw a restoration that spruced up these high-ceilinged rooms, giving them a "clean" look that extends to the white walls and handsome reproduction furniture, which you may use. The house is best for intimate functions. On the first floor are a large living room, a dining room, and a spacious center hall that extends from front door to back. Upstairs are separate bride's and groom's changing rooms and bathrooms.

You may also use the grounds for small events. Billingsley lies on 430 acres, on a bluff overlooking marshland and the Patuxent River. To reach the property, you pass through the gates of the Washington Suburban Sanitary Treatment, whose grounds adjoin. Don't be put off by this odd circumstance—it just means the manor is well secluded.

CAPACITY

Reception: 50 inside, 100 outside
Banquet: 20 inside, 100 outside

LOCATION

Billingsley is located nine miles east of the Beltway, near the intersection of Maryland Route 4 (Pennsylvania Avenue) and US Route 301, in a section of Patuxent

River Park southeast of Upper Marlboro. Call for more exact directions.

FOOD/BEVERAGE
You may choose your own caterer. The house has a small kitchen that may be used for re-warming only.

LIMITATIONS/RESTRICTIONS
The house is available daily except Sunday from 11 A.M. to 4 P.M. Smoking, amplified music, open flame candles, and red wine are prohibited in the house.

LEAD TIME FOR RESERVATIONS
Call for availability.

RATES
Weekend rates range from $400 to $600. Call for weekday rates.

FACILITIES FOR THE PHYSICALLY DISABLED? No

C & 0 CANAL BOATS
The Georgetown: 1057 Thomas Jefferson Street, NW
Washington, DC 20007
202/653-5190
Canal Clipper: 11710 MacArthur Boulevard
Potomac, MD 20854
301/299-3613

A moving experience of the past

Once you set foot on one of these boats you have no choice but to sit back, relax, enjoy the scenery, and take in some history.

The C & O Canal is 184.5 miles long and stretches from Cumberland, Maryland, to Georgetown, but you travel only a small portion of that distance. As

you rest on the wooden benches that line the sides of these long, flat-roofed boats, park rangers in period clothing regale you with stories about life along the canal in the 1870s, when the waterway was in its heyday. You can watch as the rangers hitch up the mules that will lead the boat up the canal along the towpath, and you'll see them work the boat through the lock just as was done decades ago.

Two boats are in service, and each uses a different segment of the restored canal. If you board the *Canal Clipper* at C & O Canal National Historical Park, in Potomac, Maryland, you'll travel past beautiful, dense woods, where you may see geese, ducks, and the occasional jogger or cyclist. The *Georgetown* takes you through the old canal district, past both historic town houses and chic shops.

CAPACITY

Boat party: 80

LOCATION

You board the *Georgetown* on the canal between 30th and Thomas Jefferson Streets, NW, in Georgetown. Foggy Bottom is the closest Metro station. To board the *Canal Clipper*, take Beltway Exit 41 west to the Clara Barton Parkway, heading toward Carderock. At the stop sign at the end of the parkway, turn left onto MacArthur Boulevard, which takes you straight to C & O Canal National Historical Park.

FOOD/BEVERAGE
You make your own food and drink arrangements.

LIMITATIONS/RESTRICTIONS
The boats operate April 1 through October; call for information about hours and days of operation. Smoking and alcohol are prohibited.

LEAD TIME FOR RESERVATIONS
Make reservations as far in advance as possible, starting in January of each year.

RATES
For a one-hour trip: $7.50 per adult (ages 15 to 61), $6 per senior (ages 62 and older), $4 per child (ages 4 to 14).

FACILITIES FOR THE PHYSICALLY DISABLED? Some
The *Georgetown* is wheelchair accessible.

CARLYLE HOUSE HISTORIC PARK
121 North Fairfax Street
Alexandria, VA 22314
703/549-2997
703/549-5738 (fax)
www.carlylehouse.org

Exquisite gardens of 248-year-old country manor

John Carlyle, a wealthy Scottish merchant and a leading citizen of Alexandria, built this gorgeous Georgian structure in 1752 and entertained George Washington and Lord Fairfax here. In Carlyle's time, the Potomac River lapped at the back edge of his property. Though the river has receded a few blocks and now lies out of sight of the estate, the view from the back of the house is still spectacular: The Magnolia Terrace overlooks the lovely gardens and the eighteenth-century-style summerhouse.

The tented Magnolia Terrace is where all events take place, and guests are free to wander through the gardens, which feature historic eighteenth-century plantings and a charming gazebo. In addition, you may tour Carlyle House, which has been restored to its eighteenth-century appearance and is furnished with period pieces. In the most prominent rooms, the original woodwork—graceful swan's neck pediments over the doorways and fine cornices—remains. Other rooms on view include Carlyle's magnificent first-floor bedroom and an unplastered room that exposes in layers the house's constructive and restorative history.

CAPACITY
Reception or banquet: 80 seated, 100 on the tented terrace

LOCATION
A few blocks east of the George Washington Memorial Parkway (Washington Street within Alexandria city limits), in Old Town Alexandria.

FOOD/BEVERAGE
You may choose your own caterer. You must obtain a banquet permit if you're

going to have a cash bar. The kitchen is equipped with a warming oven, micro-wave, and sinks. Food and drinks are not permitted anywhere in the house. Caterers must carry liability insurance.

LIMITATIONS/RESTRICTIONS

Carlyle House may be rented April through October only, from 6:30 P.M. to midnight. If you pay an additional fee of $250 per hour, your event may start at 4:30 P.M. Caterers are allowed in two hours before the event but everyone, including caterers, must be gone by midnight. There are no Monday rentals. Smoking, dancing, and all food and drink are prohibited in the house but are allowed on the terrace. Amplified music is not allowed.

LEAD TIME FOR RESERVATIONS

Call for availability.

RATES

Wedding receptions: $1,695, plus tax; all other events: $1,395, plus tax. These rates cover rental from 6:30 P.M. to midnight; if your event begins before 6:30 P.M., you pay an additional $250 per hour. A $500, refundable security deposit is required to book your event. Half of the total fee is due at the contract signing.

FACILITIES FOR THE PHYSICALLY DISABLED? Yes

THE CENTURY HOUSE

1309 Rhode Island Avenue, NW
Washington, DC 20005
202/745-3963
202/965-1646 (fax)

A tour-de-force showhouse off Logan Circle

It's called the Century House because that's how old it is, but the mansion's current owner is an early-thirty-something molecular biologist bounding with energy and ideas. This home of his is something else: a gracious Victorian that rolls with his twenty-first-century punches.

You may rent all three floors, which are connected by the central, soaring, three-story hand-carved oak staircase. Upon entering the mansion you find yourself in the grand hall, a room of red-painted walls and marble wainscoting, high ceilings, Waterford chandeliers, tile and parquet floors, and a magnificent bay window. Within this nook sits a 1995 Disklavier player grand piano (maybe you've seen the one in Union Station), a remarkable invention that can be played in the normal fashion or programmed to play disks of piano recordings—of which our music-loving host has one hundred, from Gershwin to Roger Williams. The grand hall carries you back to the law library, where backlit, glass-fronted, inset bookcases run ceiling to floor. Both the grand hall and law library have wonderful wood-carved fireplaces and antique curiosities, like the 1920s French stereopticon, the 1875 apothecary kit, and the working 1910 Victrola. Great oak doors can close off the library from the hall.

Up that winding oak staircase to the second floor lie the Gershwin Room, whose walls are a Rhapsody-in-Blue hue, and a state-of-the-art kitchen. Another lap on the staircase gets you to the "rose-blue," walled Joplin Room. Both the Gershwin and Joplin Rooms serve well as dining areas and have beautifully carved fireplaces, intriguing artwork (like the Slovenian beehive doors, which are rough wooden panels with scenes of local fables painted on them), and unfettered views of the neighborhood.

To conclude, there are four thousand square feet of entertaining space, five working fireplaces, a five-zone A/C system, a combination of chandelier and inset track lighting, and a small, enclosed front patio.

CAPACITY
Reception, banquet, or meeting: 70

LOCATION
The Century House is located next to Logan Circle (very close to the Studio Theater), near the Dupont Circle Metro station in downtown Washington.

FOOD/BEVERAGE

The Century House can recommend caterers, but you're free to choose your own, as long as the caterer is licensed and insured and provides references.

LIMITATIONS/RESTRICTIONS

The house is available daily in five-hour time slots. Events must end by midnight. Street parking is limited; valet parking is recommended. Smoking is prohibited inside the house, and white wine is preferred.

LEAD TIME FOR RESERVATIONS

Call at least one month in advance.

RATES

Rates vary by season, day of the week, and time of day, but count on paying $1,000 to $2,000 for an evening event and $700 for a daytime meeting.

FACILITIES FOR THE PHYSICALLY DISABLED? Some

The first floor is wheelchair accessible.

CLARK HOUSE

Historic Properties Rental Services
Fairfax County Park Authority
6332 Barcroft Mews Drive
Falls Church, VA 22041-1237
703/938-8835
www.co.fairfax.va.us/parks/weddings.htm
hprs@co.fairfax.va.us

Victorian standout on Columbia Pike

Speeding down Columbia Pike, you may put on the brakes and do a double take as you pass the Barcroft Mews cul-de-sac. A handsome yellow Victorian house jumps out at you amidst this strip of grocery stores and town houses.

Clark House was built in 1902 as the home for dairy farmer William Clark and his family. The house originally stood in Annandale, crowning more than two hundred acres of farmland, but was moved to its current location in 1990.

The Fairfax County Park Authority restored the exterior of the house to its turn-of-the-twentieth-century appearance—note the generous, wraparound porch and the foursquare architecture. The interior boasts some of the original woodwork, but most has been renovated. On the main floor are a long hall and two assembly rooms with track lighting, wall-to-wall carpeting, and business equipment, such as a projector, a pull-down projector screen, and an easel. The rooms are especially well suited to off-site meetings. When you use the front porch and side veranda with this space, the house does well for more festive events. Also available is a downstairs room, well lit and unfurnished.

CAPACITY
Reception: 65
Banquet: 50
Meeting: 50

LOCATION
From the Beltway (I-495), take the Gallows Road exit (Exit 7) and head east on Gallows Road toward Falls Church, turning left at the light past Hummer Road to pick up the Gallows Road extension. Turn left on Columbia Pike. Turn right into the Barcroft Plaza Shopping Center and make an immediate left onto the service road, which becomes Barcroft Mews Drive. The Clark House will be on your left.

FOOD/BEVERAGE
You are free to choose your own caterer. A full kitchen is located on the first level.

LIMITATIONS/RESTRICTIONS
Clark House is available for meetings Monday through Friday, from 7:30 A.M. to 6:00 P.M., and for social functions on weekdays, from 7:30 A.M. to 11:00 P.M., and weekends, from 7:30 A.M. to midnight. Smoking is prohibited inside the house.

A permit is required to serve alcohol, which is allowed inside the building and on the immediate grounds (bar service must remain in the house). Red wine is discouraged.

LEAD TIME FOR RESERVATIONS
Call for availability; the site accepts reservations up to one year in advance.

RATES
Meetings: $350 (four hours) to $475 (eight hours); $50 each additional hour
Social functions: $400 (Fairfax County residents) or $600 (out-of-county renters) for five hours' use. The site charges an alcohol use fee of $100, a refundable, $300 security deposit, and $100 for each additional hour. Call about dis counted winter and weekday rates.

FACILITIES FOR THE PHYSICALLY DISABLED? Some
There is no inside transfer between floors.

DARNALL'S CHANCE
14800 Governor Oden Bowie Drive
Upper Marlboro, MD 20772
301/952-8010

A chance for partyers and posterity

Once a ramshackle eyesore slated for demolition, this Prince George's County landmark was saved by a 1974 discovery that portions of the house date from 1695. Talk quickly turned from razing the property to raising funds for its restoration. It took eight years for the Maryland-National Capital Park and Planning Commission (M-NCPPC) to appropriate the necessary nine hundred thousand dollars and another five years of research, design, and construction before the house was ready to open to the public.

You may use the first floor of the Georgian brick building for food service and table setup. This level is sparsely furnished with period pieces and includes a large central hall, the dining room, a ballroom, and Mrs. Darnall's bedroom. Upstairs rooms, once bedchambers, now display exhibits recreating dramatic moments in Maryland's life and tracing the history of the Darnall family, Darnall's Chance, and Upper Marlboro. Guests are free to view these exhibits as well as those in the basement. Much of the basement's flagstone flooring is original, as are the walls carving out the big wine cellar, the kitchen with its wide hearth, and a room, now the gift shop, that historians believe may have been slave quarters.

In the backyard lies one of the most intriguing features of Darnall's Chance: a burial vault. The vault appears to be the same one referred to in a 1788 deed conveying ownership of Darnall's Chance from one family to another. The grounds are available for functions and include a brick patio, which is tented April through October.

CAPACITY
Reception: 80 indoors, 125 on tented patio
Banquet: 56 indoors, 125 on tented patio

LOCATION

From the Beltway (I-495), take Pennsylvania Avenue/Route 4 south (Exit 11A) and head seven miles to the Upper Marlboro exit. Turn left on Water Street, right at the first light onto Main Street, and left at the next light onto Governor Oden Bowie Drive. Turn right at the second driveway into the grounds.

FOOD/BEVERAGE

You may choose your own caterer, subject to approval by site management. Connected to the house's main floor is a modern wing housing rest rooms and a catering area.

LIMITATIONS/RESTRICTIONS

The house is available daily, year-round. Smoking is prohibited inside. You can serve but not sell alcohol (unless you get a liquor license). Red wine and red punch are restricted to outdoors.

LEAD TIME FOR RESERVATIONS

Call for availability.

RATES

Sunday through Friday: $600 (Montgomery and Prince George's County residents) or $720 (all others) for seven hours; Saturday: $750 (Montgomery and Prince George's County residents) or $900 (all others) for seven hours. For events that exceed seven hours, the site charges $100 per hour Sunday through Friday and $150 per hour on Saturday. A security deposit of $500 is required.

FACILITIES FOR THE PHYSICALLY DISABLED? Some

The first floor and rest rooms are wheelchair accessible.

ELLA SMITH HOUSE

3rd Street and Maryland Avenue, NE
Washington, DC 20002
703/739-1030

A captivating home on Capitol Hill

Two blocks from the US Capitol, on the Senate side, is this handsome Victorian mansion, built in 1889. Even as you approach the town house, you'll notice several distinctive features: the capacious front courtyard, its beautiful rose garden, and the house's charming turret.

Inside you'll discover an unusually wide center hall with a spectacular, forty-foot curving staircase, complete with the original cherry railing. In addition to the hall, the first floor holds three rooms, each with original fireplaces, plaster cornices, and woodwork. On the turret side of the house is the salon, where plush banquettes fit snugly against the bay window. (When the weather's right, you can see the dome of the Capitol from this window and from those on the upper levels of the turret. This view and the house's other charms make it a favorite "shoot" location for movie and TV producers.) Across the hall is the dining room, with paneled wainscoting and a brass chandelier. Beyond the dining room is the kitchen, where a grill rests upon the century-old brick of what was once the fireplace. The second- and third-floor rooms are available to guests who want to peer at the Capitol from the turret windows.

CAPACITY

Reception: 100 using the courtyard, 70 inside
Banquet: 40 using the salon and dining room, 25 in the salon alone

LOCATION

On Capitol Hill, two blocks from the US Capitol. You can park on the street or, after hours only, at the Supreme Court parking lot, a block away.

FOOD/BEVERAGE
The Ella Smith House works exclusively with one caterer to make your food and equipment arrangements.

LIMITATIONS/RESTRICTIONS
Smoking, amplified music, and dancing are not permitted in the house.

LEAD TIME FOR RESERVATIONS
The site recommends that you book three months in advance, but call for availability.

RATES
A three-hour event costs $450, plus $50 for each additional hour.

FACILITIES FOR THE PHYSICALLY DISABLED? No

ERICKSON HOUSE
437 New Jersey Avenue, SE
Washington, DC 20003
703/739-1030

Art from around the world in a private home

This private home of a retired naval officer sits four blocks from the US Capitol, on the House side. Erickson House is a century-old, painted brick town house filled with an astonishing array of Oriental art and furniture—Vietnamese vases, Japanese woodblocks, Peruvian mirrors, and so on—acquired by the owner during his travels.

Your event takes place in the living room, capacious hall, and dining room. A large bay window, a working fireplace, and sliding paneled doors that can close for privacy add to the living room's charm. Upon the oak floor of the generously sized hall rest more foreign art treasures, like the English inlaid secretary and the

Oriental mother-of-pearl and painted screen. Past the staircase leading to the second floor is the dining room, with its expandable teak table and, crowning a corner, a large harp from Paraguay.

When the weather's pleasant, your party can spill out into the fenced-in front yard. At night, you can look up the street from this spot and get an awesome eyeful of the Capitol building.

CAPACITY
Meeting: 40 using both the living and dining rooms
Reception: 50
Banquet: 12 in the dining room, 30 throughout

LOCATION
Four blocks from the US Capitol, two blocks from the House office building, and a short walk from the Capitol South Metro station.

FOOD/BEVERAGE
Erickson House works exclusively with one catering firm to make your food, beverage, and equipment arrangements.

LIMITATIONS/RESTRICTIONS
Erickson House is available daily, year-round, at any time. Smoking is prohibited. Space constrains dancing and loud music.

LEAD TIME FOR RESERVATIONS
Call at least one month in advance.

RATES
Rates start at $400 but vary depending upon the type of function, number of people, and length of event.

FACILITIES FOR THE PHYSICALLY DISABLED? No

FAIRFAX STATION RAILROAD MUSEUM

11200 Fairfax Station Road
Fairfax Station, VA 22039
703/273-3147 or 703/278-8833
www.fairfax-station.org
fxstn@fairfax-station.org

A caboose and depot on the right track

This trim, gray-frame building, reconstructed from an early-twentieth-century structure, houses a community hall and museum rooms that lay out the history of the City of Fairfax and its railroad station. From displays of time lines, old photographs, framed documents, and Civil War artifacts you can learn a lot. The original Fairfax Station was built in the 1850s by Irish immigrants. It played a role of strategic importance during the Civil War and was used as an emergency treatment center; Clara Barton nursed Union soldiers here. After Confederate troops burned it down, Union troops rebuilt the structure, restoring it to use for another one hundred years.

The community hall, a cozy place of wooden floors, ceiling, and walls where the acoustics are terrific, is the main event space. There are no windows, so all lighting is electric. Fifty brown-cushioned chairs and fourteen rectangular tables are available. You may arrange to browse the museum rooms and the gift shop while you're here, and you can also tour the forty-year-old caboose.

CAPACITY
Reception, banquet, or meeting: 50

LOCATION
From Washington, follow Route 66 west to Route 7100 (Exit 55, Reston/Herndon). Stay to the left and follow Exit 55A to Route 123 (Springfield), which leads to Fairfax County Parkway. Head south on the parkway. Take a left on Burke Center Parkway and another left on Ox Road (Route 123). At the second light, turn left onto Fairfax Station Road. Go a quarter mile; the museum is on the right.

FOOD/BEVERAGE
You may choose your own caterer. The kitchen has two ovens, a refrigerator, and preparation space.

LIMITATIONS/RESTRICTIONS
The museum is available year-round, subject to its own schedule. Smoking is prohibited. Amplified music and dancing are allowed inside.

LEAD TIME FOR RESERVATIONS
Call at least a month in advance.

RATES
The site charges $100 for three hours' use Friday through Sunday, plus $25 for each additional hour, and $75 Monday through Thursday for three hours. Wedding receptions cost $200 for five hours. The museum also stages children's birthday parties for up to eight kids, charging $125 to cover site rental, party favors, food, and games in the caboose.

FACILITIES FOR THE PHYSICALLY DISABLED? Some
The museum has a ramp at its entrance and a rest room with a wide door.

FRIENDSHIP FIREHOUSE MUSEUM

107 South Alfred Street
Alexandria, VA 22314
703/838-4994

Restored building honors centuries of fire fighting

This narrow, two-story brick building was built in 1855 to replace an older firehouse that had been destroyed by—guess what—a fire. The firehouse served until the late 1900s as the base for Alexandria's oldest fire-fighting organization, the Friendship Fire Company, which was established in 1774. Its members met in pubs and people's houses until the first firehouse was constructed.

A charming cupola with a firefighter weathervane caps the museum's nineteenth-century Italianate exterior. Inside the straight-up structure are the first-floor engine room and the second-floor meeting room. The brick-floored engine room, sure enough, displays an 1851 engine (which took sixteen to twenty people to operate, although it's a fraction of the size of contemporary fire engines), along with old buckets, axes, hoses, and other apparatus.

The meeting room is a formal space that's furnished with green leather sofas, a board table, and chairs. Desks on raised platforms and fluted columns flank a central podium. Glass cases around the room show off parade uniforms, silk parade banners, capes, helmets, and old photos. This room's ceiling is high and the windows long and narrow. A smaller room behind the meeting room may be used as well.

CAPACITY

Reception: 60
Banquet: 30
Meeting: 12 at the conference table; more when you use benches and folding chairs

LOCATION

On the south side of Washington Street in Old Town Alexandria, between King and Prince Streets. Street parking is usually plentiful.

FOOD/BEVERAGE

You may choose your own caterer. A small room on the second floor holds a wet bar with a sink, microwave, and refrigerator.

LIMITATIONS/RESTRICTIONS

The museum is available weekend evenings after 4:00 P.M. and anytime Monday through Thursday, year-round. Smoking is prohibited.

LEAD TIME FOR RESERVATIONS

Allow four weeks to reserve the site.

RATES

The museum charges $100 per hour.

FACILITIES FOR THE PHYSICALLY DISABLED? Yes

GARRETT PARK TOWN HALL

10814 Kenilworth Avenue
Garrett Park, MD 20896
301/933-7275

Century-old hall with modern features

Wedged in between the bustling metropolises of Bethesda, Kensington, Wheaton, and Rockville, the community of Garrett Park holds onto its small-town America feel. Its tree-lined roads, rambling old houses with wraparound porches, and tiny town center, where the community's five-hundred-odd families come to collect their mail, help keep Garrett Park an enclave unto itself. Just as quaint is the Garrett Park Town Hall, a building that started as an Episcopal chapel when it was erected in 1897.

The gray clapboard hall sits back on its artfully landscaped lawn on a quiet, shady street. An entry area leads you left, into the hall's main room, which is painted white and has windows on all sides. The room has recessed lighting, gray carpeting on pine floors, a descending projection screen, and remnants of its past: an altar/stage area and three pews set against the walls. Beyond the first room lie three interconnecting spaces that are furnished with track lighting, a grand piano, and more gray carpeting. French doors at the back take you out to a tree-shaded patio and garden.

The town hall is used frequently for area art shows and official town business but is available otherwise to party throwers from any neighborhood.

CAPACITY

Reception, banquet, or lecture: 75

LOCATION

Heading north on Rockville Pike, take a right on Strathmore Avenue, then right again onto Kenilworth Avenue.

FOOD/BEVERAGE

You're free to choose you own caterer. The kitchen holds an oven, dishwasher, refrigerator, and counter space. A limited supply of tables and chairs is available.

LIMITATIONS/RESTRICTIONS

The hall is available on a first-come, first-served basis, subject to the town's own schedule. Events must end by 11:00 P.M. Amplified music is not allowed. Dancing is allowed but may restrict the number of guests you're permitted.

LEAD TIME FOR RESERVATIONS

October through December, eight to ten months; January through September, six months.

RATES

The rate for use from 8:00 A.M. to 11:00 P.M. is a flat $400. A nonrefundable deposit of $25 confirms your reservation; an additional, refundable deposit of $25 is required for cleanup.

FACILITIES FOR THE PHYSICALLY DISABLED? Yes

LEE-FENDALL HOUSE

614 Oronoco Street
Alexandria, VA 22314
703/548-1789

House at Lee corner

You're sure to learn two things by renting the Lee-Fendall House: Alexandria is indeed an old town, and the Lees were one of the town's more prominent founding families. This house was built in 1785, and the Lees lived here continuously until 1903. George Washington, along with his friend and Revolutionary War hero "Light-Horse Harry" Lee, liked to drop in for a visit from time to time.

Receptions, lunches, dinners, teas, and meetings take place in the dining room, central hallways (upstairs and down), sunporch, and garden of the white clapboard structure. The garden is an especially attractive setting in spring, when azaleas, roses, and begonias bloom amidst the ancient ginkgo and chestnut trees. The interior is alluring all year-round and is furnished as it was in Victorian times. Almost everything you see, from the baby carriage under the stairs to the 1840 Chickering piano in the drawing room, is a Lee family heirloom.

An intimate dinner in the antique-filled dining room can be an elegant candlelit affair conjuring up the spirits of the thirty-seven Lees who have lived here. The large hallways are perfect for receptions; when you need a break from mingling you can simply slip off to one of the surrounding rooms to peer at period furnishings. (You can't walk through these rooms, but you can view them from the roped-off area just inside the door.)

Docents are available to answer your questions about the Lees and the house. If you ask about the elevator, for example, you'll learn that it was installed by labor leader John L. Lewis when he lived here.

CAPACITY
Reception: 60 inside, 150 using the garden
Banquet: 20
Garden party: 150
Meeting: 20

LOCATION
In Old Town Alexandria, at the corner of George Washington Memorial Parkway (Washington Street within Alexandria city limits) and Oronoco Street.

FOOD/BEVERAGE
You must use a caterer from the site's approved list. A kitchen equipped with a stove (but no refrigerator or freezer) is available.

LIMITATIONS/RESTRICTIONS
Events must end by 11:00 P.M. Smoking is prohibited inside the house. Amplified music is allowed, but not DJs.

LEAD TIME FOR RESERVATIONS
The site accepts reservations years in advance; call for availability. April, May, September, and October are the most popular months.

RATES
The Lee-Fendall House rents for a flat fee of $200 per hour.

McCRILLIS GARDENS
6910 Greentree Road
Bethesda, MD 20817
301/929-6509
www.mncppc.org (click on Montgomery County, then Parks, then McCrillis Gardens)

Five acres of gardens, two gazebos

Are the driveway and its concentric garden plot truly heart-shaped? Yes, the gardener and I concluded, they are. Spiraling off from the heart are five acres of lawn interspersed with 750 varieties of azaleas, planted alongside such ornamental trees and shrubs as dogwoods and mountain laurel. Come May, the gardens are at their peak.

A wood-chip trail winds through the property, and pretty wooden benches sit here and there. There are two gazebos, both of which incorporate into their design wooden ramps that make them thoroughly accessible to wheelchairs. The newest gazebo is almost a pavilion, it's so big; the lawn in front makes for a perfect tenting spot. The other gazebo is more traditional and has steps leading down to a modest lawn area. There's a handsome house on site whose bathroom and kitchen—but no other rooms—are available to you during your function.

CAPACITY
Reception: 100
Banquet: 100

LOCATION
From the Beltway (I-495), take the Old Georgetown Road exit and head south one mile to Greentree Road. Turn right and follow Greentree Road to the gardens, on your left. You may park in the school parking lot across the street on weekends.

FOOD/BEVERAGE

You may choose your own caterer. A small kitchen is available in the mansion.

LIMITATIONS/RESTRICTIONS

The site is available on weekends, April through October, between noon and 8:00 P.M. Since your party will have no place to take cover in bad weather, you're strongly encouraged to rent a tent for your event.

LEAD TIME FOR RESERVATIONS

The site starts booking reservations on December 1 for the coming year.

RATES

The Maryland-National Capital Park and Planning Commission, which owns and maintains the gardens, charges $1,500 for a six-hour rental, plus a $500, refundable security deposit.

FACILITIES FOR THE PHYSICALLY DISABLED? Some

The gazebos are completely accessible, and the grounds are fairly level, but rest rooms are not specially equipped to handle wheelchairs.

MONTPELIER MANSION

On Muirkirk Road, off Route 197
Laurel, MD 20708
301/953-1376
301/953-7572 (fax)
www.pgparks.com/places/historic.html
montpelier_mansion@pgparks.com

Meet in the wings, mingle in the garden

You can't spend the night at Montpelier, as George Washington did two hundred years ago on his way to and from the Constitutional Convention, but you can hold meetings and social events here. When you do, you'll find the mansion the same "large, Hndsome [sic], Elegant House" that Abigail Adams did in 1800.

Before you go indoors, however, you're going to be captivated by Montpelier's splendid garden. Surrounding the mansion is a beautifully maintained presentation of two-hundred-year-old boxwoods, sugar maples, Japanese maples, red maples, old magnolias, white ash trees, sprawling dogwoods, and hollies. The lawn is available with the use of the house for outdoor functions or just for strolling.

There are five parts to the Georgian-style, symmetrical building: the central portion, two hyphens (that is, the passages connecting the house to its wings), and the east and west wings. Two unfurnished wing rooms are the indoor rental areas. Peach-colored and hexagonal in shape, they have nonworking fireplaces and doors leading to brick terraces.

You have access to the rest of the house for a walk-through tour while you're here. The roped-off rooms, including the formal dining room with its ornately carved fireplace and an original corner hutch, are furnished according to the styles of the 1830s.

Montpelier was built by Maj. Thomas Snowden, a Revolutionary War officer and descendant of a wealthy Welsh family that had arrived in Maryland in the mid-1600s.

CAPACITY
Reception: 100
Banquet: 100
Garden party: 100
Meeting: 50

LOCATION
From the Beltway (I-495), take the Baltimore-Washington Parkway north exit and travel on the parkway to Route 197. Take a left on Route 197 and go left again at the traffic light onto Muirkirk Road.

FOOD/BEVERAGE

You may choose your own caterer, as long as the caterer is licensed and insured. A warming/cooling kitchen is available.

LIMITATIONS/RESTRICTIONS

The mansion is not available for rent on Sundays. Smoking is prohibited. Live and recorded music is allowed, but there are volume and location restrictions.

LEAD TIME FOR RESERVATIONS

Call one year ahead for events in April, May, June, September, and October; six months ahead for events scheduled in other months. Always call for availability.

RATES

Weekday meetings: $40 per hour for a minimum of three hours, plus $40 for use of the kitchen; Monday through Thursday evening meetings (after 5 P.M.): $250 for a maximum of three hours (no kitchen charge). Special event rates start at $700 Monday through Thursday and go up to as much as $1,150 on Saturday evenings, with discounts given to residents of Montgomery and Prince George's Counties.

FACILITIES FOR THE PHYSICALLY DISABLED? Some

Portable ramps are available, and the rest rooms are wheelchair accessible.

MURPHY HOUSE

203 3rd Street, NE
Washington, DC 20002
703/739-1030

Old town house thoroughly modernized

Located on Capitol Hill, this turn-of-the-twentieth-century, four-story town house has been opened up to staggered effect. Look up from the living room on the first floor and you see the balconied second floor; stand at the back of the house on this level and the English basement opens to view below you. These are the charming digs of a young Washington professional whose flair for decorating makes this an excellent small meeting and reception site.

Clever impulses have created a handsomely cozy atmosphere. Huge, attractively framed mirrors rest nonchalantly upon fireplace mantels. (The four fireplaces, one on each floor, are all usable.) A tiny library with leather chair and reading lamp, table, and built-in bench seat/bookcase sits in its own second-floor nook overlooking Constitution Avenue. The basement kitchen has a terra-cotta-tiled floor, walls of stone, and a brick hearth. Sliding inset doors separate the living room from a small bar area, a staircase to the basement, and the deck (with hot tub). Up the skylighted stairs is a second-floor den with an "Evita" balcony, as the owner has dubbed this perfect speaking spot for party hosts and hams, and a Chippendale table that expands to seat eight. Another flight takes you to an office/study and the master bedroom.

CAPACITY
Reception: 50
Banquet: 26

LOCATION
On Capitol Hill, two blocks from the US Capitol. You can park on the street or, after hours only, at the Supreme Court parking lot, half a block away.

FOOD/BEVERAGE
The Murphy House works exclusively with one caterer to handle your food, beverage, and equipment arrangements.

LIMITATIONS/RESTRICTIONS
The house is available for functions anytime. There are no specific limitations; discuss your requirements with management.

LEAD TIME FOR RESERVATIONS
Call for availability.

RATES

A three-hour event runs $300 to $400, plus catering costs, which average $45 per person for a cocktail reception.

FACILITIES FOR THE PHYSICALLY DISABLED? No

NORRIS HOUSE INN

108 Loudoun Street, SW

Leesburg, VA 20175

800/644-1806 or 703/777-1806

703/771-8051 (fax)

http://norrishouse.com

inn@norrishouse.com

In the heart of historic Leesburg

The oldest portion of the handsome Norris House Inn dates from 1760. A parlor was added in 1833, a northern wing in 1885, and other rooms appended after the Civil War. But the construction is seamless—the house hangs together beautifully.

The site offers three areas for events: the inn's first-floor dining room, parlor, sunroom, and library; its veranda and gardens; and the Old Stone House, bordering the garden. You may rent one or all of these spaces.

As befits an old house, the inn is decorated with antiques. Wainscoting, working fireplaces, and lots of windows are other features. Your party can spill out onto the covered porch and the half-acre of gardens, which include a centuries-old walnut tree, a magnolia tree, seasonal plantings, and a shade garden. The Old Stone House, across the lawn from the inn, is a tearoom with white-washed walls and a homey ambience. Though generally used on a daily basis for individually reserved teas, the Stone Room is also available to groups for teas, as well as for meetings.

The inn's six lovely bedrooms are furnished with antique brass, canopy, or feather beds; three rooms have working fireplaces.

Across the street from the Norris House Inn, and owned by the same family, is the Thomas Birkby House, which is also available for special events; see the separate listing for the Birkby House on page 212.

CAPACITY

Reception: 40 in the inn, 80 in the inn and gardens

Banquet: 6 in the inn's parlor, 80 using both the inn and gardens

Meeting: 6 in the inn's parlor, 30 in the Old Stone House

Lodging: 6 bedrooms sharing 3 baths

LOCATION

The inn is located fourteen miles from Dulles International Airport and less than an hour's drive from Washington. From the Beltway (I-495), take the Dulles Toll Road (Route 267) to the Dulles Greenway, which terminates at the Route 15 bypass. Take the bypass west. Exit on King Street, and then go north on King Street to Loudoun Street to the property.

FOOD/BEVERAGE

The inn has a list of preferred caterers but will allow you to choose your own, as long as the caterer meets the owners' insurance and licensing requirements. Caterers may use the small service kitchen in the Old Stone House.

LIMITATIONS/RESTRICTIONS

The Norris House Inn is available for functions year-round. When you have a weekend event there, you should expect to book the guest rooms as well. Smoking is allowed outside only. Music is not allowed past 10 P.M.

LEAD TIME FOR RESERVATIONS

Call for availability.

RATES

Rental of the Norris House Inn for two days and nights costs $3,250, with each additional hour over forty-five hours billed at $250 per hour. Garden rental for up to four hours is $20 per person; $150 is charged for each additional hour. Bridal teas in the Stone House start at $200 ($20 per person for a minimum of ten guests). Lodging rates range from $70 to $125 per night.

FACILITIES FOR THE PHYSICALLY DISABLED? No

OLD TOWN TROLLEY TOURS OF WASHINGTON

2640 Reed Street, NE
Washington, DC 20018
202/832-9800
www.historictours.com

Set your meeting in motion

You may not accomplish much business aboard the Old Town Trolleys, but that's not the point.

Painted green and orange and modeled after trolleys that ran in the early 1900s, the vehicles wind their way around Washington affording you a chance to unwind, socialize, and sightsee, all at the same time. Even if you're a native Washingtonian, you may learn a thing or two about the capital from the narrated tour.

These stylized trolleys don't run on a track; they're set on a truck chassis. They travel in all weather. The interior of each car is furnished with brass fixtures and comfortable, green-cushioned seats. You can choose the standard seventeen-stop route, which travels to the National Cathedral, Georgetown, and Capitol Hill, among other places. Or you can charter one or more trolleys for a customized tour of the area—to Mount Vernon, for example, or to Old Town Alexandria. Either way, you can pretty much call your own shots. If you want to decorate the interior, play music, be entertained, and enjoy refreshments—it's all possible.

CAPACITY
Reception: 35 per trolley. A total of 20 trolleys are available.

LOCATION
Stay where you are! Old Town Trolley will come to you if you're located in the greater Washington area.

FOOD/BEVERAGE
The charter consultant can arrange for refreshments, or you may do it yourself.

LIMITATIONS/RESTRICTIONS
Smoking and alcohol are prohibited. The trolleys are not air-conditioned.

LEAD TIME FOR RESERVATIONS
From April through August, call two to three months ahead; call two weeks ahead September through March.

RATES
A fully narrated, two-hour tour runs $255 per hour per trolley, with a two-hour minimum, plus $175 for each additional hour. You may also reserve a trolley to

transport your group, without a narrated tour, for $150 per trolley per hour, with a three-hour minimum, plus $110 for each additional hour (this option is available after 6 P.M. only). Or you can book your group of fifteen or more aboard the trolley's regularly scheduled tours, for $21 per person.

FACILITIES FOR THE PHYSICALLY DISABLED? Yes

PEN ARTS BUILDING

1300 17th Street, NW
Washington, DC 20036
703/739-1030

Former home of Robert Todd Lincoln

A Washington Opera star built this house in 1887, when its turret, bay window, decorative ironwork, and sprawling good size bespoke the Victorian age. The National League of American Pen Women owns the building now, permitting rentals of its first floor for receptions.

You enter first a grand foyer, deeply mahogany-paneled in its ceiling, walls, and intricately carved staircase. A drawing room to the left is decorated with a large gilt Empire mirror, ornate mantel, crystal chandelier, and Oriental carpet in shades of mauve, blue, and lilac. A grand piano fits nicely within the room's turreted nook. Off the drawing room is a sort of memorial chamber to sculptress and league member Vinnie Ream, known best for her sculpture of Lincoln, which stands in the rotunda of the US Capitol. Ream's room is paneled and cozy, with an antique sofa and framed photos of the artist. Returning to the front of the house takes you to the bright dining room, whose center dining table, sideboard, and circular, carved-mahogany side table were donated by members.

CAPACITY

Reception: 100
Banquet: 50
Meeting: 60

LOCATION

The Pen Arts Building is located in downtown Washington, not far from the
Dupont Circle Metro station and about a quarter mile north of the White
House. Parking is on the street or in nearby parking garages.

FOOD/BEVERAGE

The site works exclusively with one catering firm to make your food, beverage, and equipment arrangements. There is a small kitchen off the dining room.

LIMITATIONS/RESTRICTIONS

The air-conditioned mansion is available all year, whenever the league is not holding a function here. Smoking inside the mansion and amplified music are prohibited.

LEAD TIME FOR RESERVATIONS

Call for availability.

RATES

Rates range from $550 to $1,250, depending on the size and type of your function. A refundable, $500 security deposit is required.

FACILITIES FOR THE PHYSICALLY DISABLED? No

RIVERSDALE

4811 Riverdale Road
Riverdale, MD 20737
301/864-0420
http://www.pgparks.com/places/historic.html

A Belgian's legacy to America

You won't see many mansions like Riversdale in the United States. Its 1801 architecture is a rare combination of Belgian (or more accurately, Flemish) and early-nineteenth-century American features. The Flemish influence is most evident in the first-floor parlor rooms, which were patterned after owner Henri Joseph Stier's château near Antwerp. Overall, the five-part, stucco-covered brick mansion is of Georgian design, one created by Stier himself.

The spaces available to you when you rent the house are the east wing, the west wing, and the connecting hallway. The east wing has salmon pink walls, a teal carpet with salmon accents, brass sconces, and three large windows. At the other end of the house is the west wing (once the carriage house), with its twenty-two-foot-high ceiling, wood floor, blue walls (on which hang large framed portraits of George Calvert's ancestors), and a huge crystal chandelier. A double door in this ballroom leads to a brick patio and the grounds, which you are free to roam or to tent as part of your event.

As you travel the connecting hallway between the two wings you pass by three large rooms that are roped off but absolutely worth viewing. Wide entryways link these chambers, which makes it seem as if you're in one large salon. Sixteen-foot-high ceilings with finely carved cornices grace each room. Rounded, floor-to-ceiling, triple-sashed windows in this former orangery lead to the Tuscan-columned, marble-floored south portico and the mansion's back lawn. Before you venture out, though, notice the arched motif set in the walls; these spaces were intended to frame works from Mr. Stier's collection of old masters' paintings, including some by Peter Paul Rubens, to whom he was related. Though this central salon is also roped off, a section of it may be used in limited fashion for a receiving line, picture-taking, signing of the guest book, or place-ment of the gift table.

Stier and his wife, who had immigrated to the United States to escape the French Revolution, lived at Riversdale for less than a year before returning to Antwerp. In their place, the aristocrat's daughter Rosalie and her husband, George Calvert, a descendant of Lord Baltimore, occupied Riversdale. Owner-ship of the estate passed from the Calvert family in 1887 to a number of other proprietors until, in 1949, the Maryland-National Capital Park and Planning Commission bought it. The commission's ongoing restoration of the house attempts to present its rooms as they originally appeared.

A docent/manager will be on site during your celebration and can answer questions about the history of Riversdale. If you want to arrange a formal tour of the premises, be sure to mention this to staff in the course of planning your event.

CAPACITY

Reception: 100

Banquet: 100. The east wing can accommodate 50 and the west wing 80, but the maximum allowed for the entire house is 100.

Meeting: 60 theater-style in the east wing, 100 theater-style in the west wing

LOCATION

From the Beltway (I-495), take Exit 23 (Route 201, Kenilworth Avenue) south. Continue for about three miles and turn right on Riverdale Road. Proceed .5 mile to the mansion on your left. Parking lots are available on the property, or you can park on the street.

FOOD/BEVERAGE

The caterer you choose must be licensed and insured and provide references. A commercial-grade kitchen is located in the east wing and has a double sink, all-convection oven, icemaker, hot plate, and counter space. Food and drink are not permitted in the period rooms. One hundred metal folding chairs, two rectangular tables, and ten round tables are provided.

LIMITATIONS/RESTRICTIONS

Riversdale is available for events Monday through Saturday at any time. There are no Sunday rentals. Events must end by 1:00 A.M. Smoking is not permitted inside or within a six-foot radius of the mansion. Red-staining substances, such as red wine, tomato sauce, and cranberry juice, are prohibited, as is keg beer. Dancing is allowed in the west wing. Music must not go beyond sixty-five decibels between 7:00 A.M. and 10:00 P.M. and fifty-five decibels at other times.

LEAD TIME FOR RESERVATIONS

Call as far in advance as possible.

RATES

Social events held by Prince George's or Montgomery County residents cost $650 Sunday through Thursday and $800 on Friday and Saturday; those outside the county pay $750 Sunday through Thursday and $960 on Friday or Saturday.

These rates cover a seven-hour period; extra hours are $150 each. Half the rental fee confirms the reservation. The balance, plus a refundable security deposit, is due no later than thirty days before the event.

Daytime business meetings cost $30 per hour, breakfasts and luncheons cost $40 per hour, and evening meetings cost $40 per hour. There is a two-hour minimum, regardless. A refundable, $50 security deposit is required.

FACILITIES FOR THE PHYSICALLY DISABLED? Yes

SNOW HILL MANOR
13301 Laurel-Bowie Road
Laurel, MD 20706
301/725-6037
http://www.pgparks.com/places/rental.html

1798 manor house on fifteen acres

This is another, and the newest, of the Maryland-National Capital Park and Planning Commission's rental sites. Snow Hill is a two-story brick house dating from 1798. An inscription in an exterior brick, "GW 1786," is said to have been carved by George or Martha Washington.

The manor's first-floor room, a long center hall, and dining, living, sitting, and music rooms feature deep-set windows, high ceilings, and, in all rooms, fireplaces with cast-iron hearths. The real plus of this site are the large front and back lawns; opening the doors at either end of the center hall creates an easy flow for a party. You are allowed to tent portions of the fifteen-acre lawn. The house alone is best for stand-up functions.

CAPACITY
Reception: 60 indoors. Tenting the lawn allows for more people and seated functions, but check with the staff about the size of your party.

LOCATION

From the Beltway (I-495), take the exit for the Baltimore-Washington Parkway, and from the parkway, take Route 197 north (Laurel-Bowie Road). At the third light (Route 197 and Contee Road), make a right. You'll see a brick wall at the entrance to Snow Hill's driveway, which is lined with cedar trees.

FOOD/BEVERAGE

You may choose your own caterer, but the caterer must have liability insurance. The site has a small kitchen equipped with a convection oven, two-door refrigerator, ice machine, microwave, and hot plates.

LIMITATIONS/RESTRICTIONS

The site books two events on Saturdays. The first ends by 5:00 P.M., and the second begins no earlier than 6 P.M. and ends no later than 1 A.M. Smoking, red wine, and other red-colored beverages are not allowed.

LEAD TIME FOR RESERVATIONS

Six months to a year is recommended, but always call for availability.

RATES

Fridays, Sundays, and holidays: Residents of Montgomery or Prince George's County pay $600, nonresidents pay $720.

Saturdays: Residents of Montgomery or Prince George's County pay $750, nonresidents pay $900.

Weekdays, daytime events: county residents $30, nonresidents $40; evening events (after 5:00 P.M., with a seven-hour minimum): county residents $500, nonresidents $600.

FACILITIES FOR THE PHYSICALLY DISABLED? Yes

SWANN HOUSE

1808 New Hampshire Avenue, NW
Washington, DC 20009
202/265-4414
202/265-6755 (fax)
www.swannhouse.com
stay@swannhouse.com

Stunning Victorian near Dupont Circle

Set diagonally, prominently, and elegantly on a corner near Dupont Circle, this bright brick Victorian mansion upstages its neighborhood. Its façade encompasses a large arched front porch with a balcony overhead. On the main level of the house lies twenty-five hundred square feet of space spread throughout a turreted living room, columned sitting room, sunroom/wet bar, long central hall, and huge dining room. Old (twelve-foot-high ceilings, fluted woodwork, thick crown moldings, and parquet floors) complements new (modern art, some of which is for sale, and furniture; recessed lighting; French doors opening to a deck and pool).

A baby grand piano nestles within the living room's turret, and a tremendous crystal chandelier dangles from the dining room ceiling. The owners have done much to renovate, and decorating has been done on a grand scale. The place has panache.

The mansion functions as a B and B and has nine lovely guest rooms, each with private bath, five with fireplaces, two with Jacuzzis, and so on.

CAPACITY
Reception: 75
Banquet: 30
Lodging: 3 suites and 6 bedrooms, each with private bath

LOCATION

At the corner of New Hampshire Avenue and Swann Street, NW, a short walk from Dupont Circle.

FOOD/BEVERAGE

You must choose a caterer from the site's approved list of catering firms. There is a charming wraparound kitchen on the main level.

LIMITATIONS/RESTRICTIONS

The house is available year-round for weddings, receptions, luncheons, meetings, and other special events. Amplified music is prohibited and smoking is allowed outdoors only, on a porch or deck.

LEAD TIME FOR RESERVATIONS

Call for availability.

RATES

Daytime rates start at $100 an hour; four-hour receptions cost $2,750. A refundable, $1,000 security deposit is required. Lodging runs $125 to $275 per night, depending on the room.

FACILITIES FOR THE PHYSICALLY DISABLED? No

WAKEFIELD CHAPEL

8415 Toll House Road
Annandale, VA 22003
703/938-8835
www.co.fairfax.va.us/parks/weddings.htm
hprs@co.fairfax.va.us

Mailing address: Historic Properties Rental Services
Fairfax County Park Authority
6332 Barcroft Mews Drive
Falls Church, VA 22041-1237

For wedding ceremonies

You might say that Wakefield Chapel has been born again. Built in 1899, the white clapboard structure functioned as a community church until 1951, when it fell into disuse. In 1979, the Fairfax County Park Authority renovated the chapel, and it has been used ever since for wedding ceremonies and the occasional community meeting.

Wakefield Chapel sits on a small rise along a residential street. The chapel is narrow, and its steeple ascends higher than the building is wide. Inside, slender pine paneling covers the walls and ceiling in a diagonal pattern, giving the interior a thoroughly modern feel. Blue-green wall-to-wall carpeting and recessed lighting enhance the feeling.

Although church services are seldom held here, the chapel retains a tranquil, religious character: The raised altar area remains, as do the arched windows and six sets of pews. Downstairs, a small tile-floored basement can serve as a bridal changing area.

CAPACITY
Wedding: 99 (including bride, groom, attendants, and celebrant; can seat 92)

LOCATION

From the Beltway (I-495), take Exit 6 west (Little River Turnpike). Turn left on Wakefield Chapel Road and left again on Toll House Road. Wakefield Chapel is on the left.

FOOD/BEVERAGE

Only cake-and-punch receptions are permitted. You make your own arrangements for food and beverage, but your caterer must provide a business license, a health department certificate, and proof of insurance. There is no kitchen or reception facility.

LIMITATIONS/RESTRICTIONS

The chapel is available from 8:00 A.M. to 9:30 P.M. daily throughout the year. Parking is available only at Chapel Square Elementary School, behind the chapel. Smoking and alcohol (except for a small amount of ceremonial wine) are not permitted. The chapel is heated and air-conditioned.

LEAD TIME FOR RESERVATIONS

Up to one year.

RATES

Rates are $300 (Fairfax County residents) or $500 (all others) for three hours, with an additional hour available for $100. The site charges a $300, refundable security deposit. Call about package deals that enable you to use Wakefield Chapel in conjunction with another Fairfax County Park Authority historic rental property.

FACILITIES FOR THE PHYSICALLY DISABLED? No

WASHINGTON DOLLS' HOUSE & TOY MUSEUM

5236 44th Street, NW

Washington, DC 20015

202/244-0024 or 202/363-6400

202/237-1654 (fax)

Charming collection enlivens the past and parties

If you're looking for a site that offers an icebreaking atmosphere and a social history lesson on the side, this is the place. Try as you might to stick to business, you'll find it hard to resist peering at the miniature furnishings and clever playthings on display here. These are antiques, and the collection gives you a fascinating glimpse of past trends in architecture, decorating, fashion, and pastimes.

A cluster of seven rooms on the first floor and a second-floor Edwardian tearoom compose the available rental space. Because most of the lighting for the downstairs area emanates from the display cases lining the walls, these rooms have an intimate feel about them. Potted palms and antique ice cream tables cheerily decorate the upstairs tearoom.

And everywhere you glance are small treasures: an elaborate 1890 Mexican doll mansion complete with chapel (and priest) and terra-cotta pottery; a mid-nineteenth-century house from Burford, England, featuring early English wallpapers; a 1903 New Jersey seaside hotel; and an 1850s peddler doll hawking such wares as candles, veil pins, and buttons. A staff person attired as an Edwardian waitress conducts daytime events.

CAPACITY

Reception: 80

Banquet: 24

LOCATION

The museum is located in upper northwest Washington, one block west of Wisconsin Avenue, between Harrison and Jenifer Streets.

FOOD/BEVERAGE

You're free to choose your own caterer. The museum has a small kitchen equipped with a refrigerator, freezer, and microwave.

LIMITATIONS/RESTRICTIONS

The museum is available for luncheons, daytime parties, and group tours daily by contract. Smoking is prohibited in the museum.

LEAD TIME FOR RESERVATIONS

At least several weeks, but call for availability.

RATES

The museum can be rented for $75 per hour, with a four-hour minimum. This rate entitles you to use of the entire first floor and the party room on the second floor.

FACILITIES FOR THE PHYSICALLY DISABLED? No

THE ASHBY INN & RESTAURANT

692 Federal Street
Paris, VA 20130
540/592-3900
540/592-3781 (fax)
www.ashbyinn.com
celebrate@ashbyinn.com

A stunning view, cozy quarters, scrumptious food

The Ashby Inn's setting, at the foothills of the Blue Ridge Mountains, is perhaps more Provençal than Parisian in aspect, but the view's delightful. The whitewashed, 1829 inn perches at a bend in a country lane; round it and you come upon the landscaped back lawn and gardens, which extend only so far before giving way to the Virginia hillside and those mountains.

In good weather, you can use the covered slate patio and the back lawn for parties. Inside the quaint inn, you may reserve first-floor rooms: the library, taproom, front and back dining rooms, and glassed-in porch. These are small but gracious areas whose walls are hung with charming paintings by local artists. The more formal front dining room has a fireplace and old heart-pine floors. The back dining room is lined with booths. The taproom was once the dwelling's kitchen and retains a cozy feeling enhanced by chestnut beams, a stone fireplace, and paneled walls. The enclosed porch overlooks the perennial garden through floor-to-ceiling windows.

The inn holds six antique-filled guest rooms; a converted schoolhouse, just down the lane, provides four suites.

The Ashby Inn is known for its restaurant, which serves an ever-changing menu of seasonal dishes.

CAPACITY

Reception or banquet: 150

Meeting: 10 to 20 in one room

Lodging: 6 guest rooms, 4 with private bath, in the inn; 4 suites, each with
    fireplace, private porch, and double bath, in the converted schoolhouse

LOCATION

The Ashby Inn lies sixty miles west of Washington. From the Beltway (I-495),
follow Route 66 west to Exit 23 (Delaplane/Paris). Continue 7.5 miles north on
Route 17 and then turn left on Route 701 (Gap Run), which runs into the
village.

FOOD/BEVERAGE

The Ashby Inn handles all of your catering needs and will work with you to
design your meal. Favorites range from black bean soup with cilantro cream to
grilled rockfish with marinated Bermuda onions and red pepper butter to three-
chocolate terrine. The innkeepers will also prepare a made-to-order wedding
breakfast.

LIMITATIONS/RESTRICTIONS

Weddings are limited to daytime. Smoking is allowed only in the library and taproom. Live music is typically limited to four or fewer instruments.

LEAD TIME FOR RESERVATIONS

Call for availability.

RATES

You can rent the inn for a flat rate of $1,000. Call for catering information. Lodging rates range from $130 (dormer rooms in the inn) to $250 (schoolhouse suites).

FACILITIES FOR THE PHYSICALLY DISABLED? No

THE ATHENAEUM
201 Prince Street
Alexandria, VA 22314
703/548-0035 for recorded information
703/660-6678 for further information

A simply grand old hall and garden

It's the grandness that grabs you at the Athenaeum. In a neighborhood of narrow brick town houses, the building dominates with its Greek Revival architecture, majestic columns, and porticoed entrance.

The grandest part of all is the hall itself. The carpenters raised high the roof beams when they built this structure in 1851, and then they topped the main room with a coved ceiling. The hall is large and unfurnished; the walls stretch tall and white, and the windows are many and oversized. Overall, the effect is one of space and light.

In addition to the great hall and its smaller adjoining room, you also have use of the tiny patio and sculpture garden enclosed by a high brick wall in back. If you're interested in exploring historic Old Town while you're here, follow the path that leads from the garden back out to Prince Street. You'll be charmed to find that not only buildings have been preserved, but some of the streets as well. For example, the portion of Prince Street that runs from the Athenaeum to the waterfront is still cobblestone.

When the Athenaeum is not hosting a function, it serves as an art gallery for the Northern Virginia Fine Arts Association, which has its headquarters here. If the site strikes you as a perfect setting for galas and art exhibits, you may be surprised to learn of the building's past uses—first as a bank, then as a hospital, a medicine warehouse, and a church. There are some good stories associated with the Athenaeum's history. Ask the staff person at your function what happened to the bank customers' money during the Civil War.

CAPACITY

Reception: 165
Banquet: 80
Garden party: 50

LOCATION

In Old Town Alexandria, one street south of King Street and two blocks from the Potomac waterfront. There are five parking lots within two blocks.

FOOD/BEVERAGE

You're free to choose your own caterer, subject to approval by the Athenaeum. A small kitchen on the bottom floor of the building contains a microwave and may be used to warm and cool foods. An extra refrigerator allows for early delivery of beverages.

LIMITATIONS/RESTRICTIONS

You may rent the Athenaeum on Saturdays and Sundays after Easter through Halloween (except in August, when it is closed). Live music and dancing are allowed, but DJ entertainment is not. Amplified music is restricted to keyboard music. Red wine is prohibited. Cleanup must be completed one hour after the event has ended.

LEAD TIME FOR RESERVATIONS
Call for availability.

RATES
$250 per hour, with a six-hour minimum.

FACILITIES FOR THE PHYSICALLY DISABLED? No

BELMONT CONFERENCE CENTER
6555 Belmont Woods Road
Elkridge, MD 21075
410/796-4300
410/796-4565 (fax)
www.acs.org/belmont

An elegant, age-old business retreat

Lots of historic homes offer elegant meeting facilities. After a certain hour, however, most places require you to head on home or back to your hotel, whether or not you're truly finished with business. Not so at Belmont.

When you confer at Belmont, you reside here. Although the term "conference center" has a modern ring to it, Belmont is actually an early-eighteenth-century mansion that sits secluded on eighty-two acres of rolling fields and woods leading down to the Patapsco River. And the use of Belmont is not restricted to business functions. The estate, with its sprawling green lawns and flower gardens, also provides an ideal setting for weddings and other special events.

Inside the pale, cream-colored, stucco mansion are sixteen bedrooms, a conference room (complete with audiovisual and other equipment) that seats twenty, a dining room that seats thirty-five, and a drawing room, library, and ballroom for social gatherings.

With the use of another building on the property, known as the Dobbin

House, Belmont can accommodate as many as twenty-one guests for an on-site, overnight stay. In addition, the fully renovated and modernized carriage house is available for nonresidential day meetings.

Belmont looks and feels like a gracious country inn, only there are no other guests when your group stays here. Each room is charmingly decorated in attractive colonial colors and eighteenth-century-style furnishings. Especially lovely are the drawing room, whose overstuffed, floral-patterned sofa and chairs invite you to sink into them, and the ballroom, a mix of mauve, blue, and rose colors, antique furniture, and a working fireplace.

Belmont offers you ways to break from business, or from the party, without leaving the grounds. There are formal gardens, paths through woods and fields for walking or jogging, tennis courts, and a swimming pool. At least 117 species of birds have been sighted here, which should intrigue the ornithologists among you.

CAPACITY

Reception: 75

Banquet: 50

Garden party/wedding: 225

Meeting: 50

Lodging: 21 guest rooms. Belmont can arrange for additional, nearby sleeping accommodations when the number of your party exceeds capacity.

LOCATION

From Washington, go north on US I-95 to Route 100 east (Glen Burnie); exit and travel until you get to Route 1. Take Route 1 north, then go left on Montgomery Road and right on Elibank Drive to Belmont Woods Road. An immediate left on Belmont Woods Road will take you to Belmont.

FOOD/BEVERAGE

Belmont caters all conference meals and will work with your group to plan the menus. For parties of more than one hundred people, you may choose from a list of approved caterers.

LIMITATIONS/RESTRICTIONS
There are no specific limitations; discuss your requests with management.

LEAD TIME FOR RESERVATIONS
Call for availability.

RATES
Manor House: $230 to $275 per person (complete meeting package (CMP), which covers lodging, meals, equipment—the works)

Carriage House: $70 per person for a day meeting

Call for rates for social functions.

FACILITIES FOR THE PHYSICALLY DISABLED? Some
The Carriage House and Dobbin House, but not the Manor House, are wheelchair accessible.

CABELL'S MILL
5235 Walney Road
Centreville, VA 20120-1725
703/938-8835
www.co.fairfax.va.us/parks/weddings.htm
hprs@co.fairfax.va.us

Mailing address: Historic Properties Rental Services
Fairfax County Park Authority
6332 Barcroft Mews Drive
Falls Church, VA 22041-1237

Stone building by a stream

Who says rustic has to be primitive? At Cabell's Mill it certainly isn't.

This sturdy stone building set in a pretty Virginia park dates back at least to 1780, when the water-powered mill ground grain and, later, sumac. Waterwheel and machinery are gone, but the natural setting remains the same: Big Rocky Run flows by, and trees, shrubs, birds, and flowers surround you.

You can hold an event outside, if you like, or you can use the mill. The interior comprises one large upstairs room and a smaller room downstairs. The stone fireplace on each floor works, but the mill is also equipped with heat and air-conditioning. Stone walls have been covered over with plaster inside, and the overall feel here is of a modern facility. The rooms are mostly unfurnished, although a limited number of chairs and tables are included in the rental. Cabell's Mill offers a simple but gracious setting and is especially suited to groups with restricted budgets.

Cabell's Mill and the surrounding park grounds were given to the Fairfax County Park Authority by Ellanor C. Lawrence, whose husband was the founder and publisher of *US News & World Report*. The Lawrences used the building as a guest house for visitors to their nearby Walney Farm.

CAPACITY

Reception: 125
Banquet: 85
Grounds: 150 with tent
Meeting: 65

LOCATION

From the Beltway (I-495), take Exit 9 to Route 66 west; follow Route 66 eleven miles to Exit 53, Route 28 north. At the end of the exit ramp, turn right onto Walney Road and follow it a quarter of a mile to the mill on your right.

FOOD/BEVERAGE

You may choose your own caterer, as long as the caterer can provide a business license, a health department certificate, and proof of insurance. A park liquor permit is required if you're going to serve alcohol. A cooling kitchen on the lower level is equipped with a counter and sink.

LIMITATIONS/RESTRICTIONS

Smoking is prohibited in the mill, and music must be kept to a reasonable volume. You may not use nails, tape, or tacks to hang decorations. Alcohol consumption is permitted inside and outside, on the immediate grounds, but bar service must stay inside.

LEAD TIME FOR RESERVATIONS

Call up to one year in advance.

RATES

Weekday business function rates are $425 for four hours and $625 for eight hours, with $75 for each additional hour. Social function rates are $850 for Fairfax County residents and $1,050 for all others, covering a five-hour period; all renters pay $150 for each extra hour. The site charges a $100 alcohol use fee, and a $300, refundable security deposit.

FACILITIES FOR THE PHYSICALLY DISABLED? Some

Both levels of the mill are accessible to the disabled, but there is no interior access between floors.

CAMPAGNA CENTER

418 South Washington Street
Alexandria, VA 22314
703/549-0111
703/549-2097 (fax)
http://members.aol.com/campagna45
campagna45@aol.com

Providing social services and services for socials

Taking up, as it does, such a substantial part of a Washington Street block, this three-story, pale tan, painted brick building looks sturdy and even fortified.

The center's appearance suits its main function as headquarters for a nonprofit social service organization that dispenses various kinds of support to children and families in greater Alexandria. Inside, its suite of first-floor rooms works admirably as a place to entertain.

In its original incarnation, in 1812, the building was a school. Imagine: a classroom with fourteen-foot-high ceilings and many long windows, hardwood floors, and hanging chandeliers. (Actually, the chandeliers and the modest assortment of antique furniture are recent donations to the center.)

A half-million-dollar renovation completed in 1994 spruced up the center and reinforced the floor for dancing. The overall effect of the three party rooms and central foyer is that of a clean, bright, and spacious club on the homey side.

CAPACITY
Reception, banquet, or meeting: 10 to 175

LOCATION
Three miles south of National Airport and a couple of blocks south of King Street, in Old Town Alexandria.

FOOD/BEVERAGE
You may choose a caterer from the center's approved list of licensed and insured caterers. On the same floor as the party rooms is a first-class kitchen equipped with double commercial refrigerators, electric ovens, a microwave, and other gizmos.

LIMITATIONS/RESTRICTIONS
Events must end by midnight on weekends and by 11:00 P.M. on weekdays. Red wine and other red-staining beverages are prohibited, as is smoking.

After 5:00 P.M., the center can offer you eighteen on-site parking spaces. Otherwise, you park on the street.

LEAD TIME FOR RESERVATIONS
Call as far in advance as possible.

RATES

Rates vary according to space rented, type of event, and the organization renting.

FACILITIES FOR THE PHYSICALLY DISABLED? Yes

CHRISTIAN HEURICH MANSION

1307 New Hampshire Avenue, NW
Washington, DC 20036
202/785-2068
www.hswdc.org

Victorian castle in downtown Washington

It's safe to say that there isn't an unadorned space in all of Christian Heurich Mansion. There are allegorical paintings on the ceilings, decorative brass grilles hiding the radiators, intricately carved wood panels encasing the fireplaces, and gilding on the bathroom tiles. What you're seeing is the home of a wealthy German brewer whose decorating tastes were influenced by the customs of his native and adopted country, trends in those Victorian times, and his own indomitable personality.

Whether you throw a reception throughout the available first-floor rooms or reserve the conservatory and garden for a banquet, you won't lack for conversation. Decorated as it is with a standing coat of armor, mosaic floor, and silvered plaster medallions on stucco walls, the foyer recalls a medieval castle. The other first-floor areas include a reception room, which is an experience in crimson; the "museum rooms"—the formal front parlor, drawing room, and music room, with an overhanging musicians' gallery; and a dining room, whose walls, ceiling, and furniture are carved of oak.

The conservatory, behind the dining room, presents an image entirely different from that of the rest of the house. This is the room frequently used for events, and no wonder—the terra-cotta and turquoise-colored tile floor, red-paned windows, bark-like wall coverings, and small fountain create a pleasant and relaxing atmosphere.

The Victorian garden, too, is splendid for dinner parties and receptions. Spacious and split attractively in the middle by hedges, it features a brick patio that's a perfect spot for setting up the bar.

The Christian Heurich Mansion serves as the headquarters for the Historical Society of Washington, DC.

CAPACITY

Reception: 130 in the house, 350 in the house and tented garden
Banquet: 50 in the house, 150 in the house and tented garden
Meeting: 60

LOCATION

At Dupont Circle in northwest Washington, within walking distance of the Dupont Circle Metro station.

FOOD/BEVERAGE

The site provides a list of preferred caterers who meet the historical society's insurance requirements. Caterers can use a basement kitchen and a first-floor pantry for food preparation.

LIMITATIONS/RESTRICTIONS

Wedding receptions and political fund-raisers may not be held in the Christian Heurich Mansion. Smoking is allowed only in the garden. Amplified music is not allowed. The mansion is not air-conditioned. Tents are required in the garden when the number of your party exceeds 130.

There is parking on the premises for the disabled only; the mansion includes in its information portfolio the locations and hours of nearby parking garages.

LEAD TIME FOR RESERVATIONS

At least two to three months.

RATES

A $5,000, tax-deductible contribution entitles you to one-time use of the house and garden for a four-hour period.

FACILITIES FOR THE PHYSICALLY DISABLED? Yes

COLLINGWOOD-ON-THE-POTOMAC

The Collingwood Library and Museum on Americanism
8301 East Boulevard Drive
Alexandria, VA 22308
703/765-1652
703/765-8390 (fax)

As a library and museum on Americanism, Collingwood is fascinating. As a meeting site, it's delightful. Both floors of the white Federal Palladian structure are open to you. The downstairs library is painted sky blue and is furnished, as you might imagine, with many bookcases, display tables, and cozy chairs placed here and there. You're free to walk around and peruse the materials, but food and drink are prohibited in the downstairs rooms.

The upstairs museum rooms offer a fine reception and banquet area. There is one large room and three adjoining smaller ones, all of which are filled with artifacts of American heritage: state and military service flags, Revolutionary War mementos, a Hopi kachina doll, and an Alaskan totem pole, to name a few. Other than the museum pieces, the rooms have little furniture, leaving plenty of space for setup tables and mingling.

One of the remarkable things about this site is its location—literally on the Potomac. You can walk out the side door and down the long, sloping green lawn right to the river. The combination of nine green acres and a riverfront location makes Collingwood one of the nicest places to have an outdoor affair.

Collingwood was once part of George Washington's river farm. The oldest part of the mansion dates from 1785; Washington built the dwelling for one of his farm managers. Besides being a museum and library on Americanism, it is headquarters to the National Sojourners, a group of veterans who are also Masons.

CAPACITY
Reception: 100
Banquet: 60
Garden party: 150, but special arrangements can be made to host larger parties
Meeting: 90

LOCATION
Four miles south of Old Town Alexandria. From Washington, take the George Washington Memorial Parkway (Washington Street within Alexandria city limits) to the Mount Vernon Memorial Parkway. Exit at Collingwood Road, turn left onto East Boulevard Drive, and then turn right onto the Collingwood property.

FOOD/BEVERAGE

You may choose your own caterer, subject to approval by Collingwood's directors. A kitchen is available for food preparation but not cooking.

LIMITATIONS/RESTRICTIONS

The site is available year-round, except between December 20 and January 5. Smoking is prohibited inside the building. Alcoholic beverages are limited to wine, beer, and champagne.

LEAD TIME FOR RESERVATIONS

Call for availability.

RATES

Wedding receptions start at $1,100. Call for other rates, which vary depending on the type of function, type of organization renting, and number of guests.

FACILITIES FOR THE PHYSICALLY DISABLED? Some

The first floor of the building, including the rest rooms, is wheelchair accessible. There is an elevator to the second floor.

THE CONGRESSIONAL CLUB

2001 New Hampshire Avenue, NW
Washington, DC 20009
202/332-1155
202/797-0698 (fax)

Amazing mansion built as a clubhouse for congressional wives

It took an act of Congress in 1908 to create a club for the spouses of congressional members. This was before women even had the right to vote, so the organization was really called the Congressional Wives Club. The club has continued to this day, only now its members include not just the wives and

daughters of congressmen, senators, cabinet members, and Supreme Court justices, but congresswomen as well. (The husbands of these members are admitted as associate members.) The president's wife is an honorary member.

The magnificent clubhouse was built specifically for the club in 1914, and members over the years have decorated it with their own silver, rugs, china, glassware, and art. Two floors are available for functions. The first floor is broken up into smaller spaces and is very much like a museum. Among the seven or so rooms through which you're free to wander are the Archives Room, with its pictures of past club presidents and antique furnishings; the First Ladies' Museum Room, which displays mannequins dressed in exact copies of an inaugural or special gown of each first lady since Mrs. Lincoln; and the International Doll Museum, which exhibits foreign dolls from more than sixty countries donated by the wives of ambassadors to the United States. Really, your partygoers will not lack for conversation as they browse among these bibelots and treasures.

Up the grand staircase dominated by an enormous Waterford chandelier lies the main event area, the ballroom—a most amazing space. This is one large, high-ceilinged chamber. Lots of very tall windows and antique sconces upon the walls fill it with light. There's a hardwood floor, working fireplace, and usable

1890 Steinway piano. Two dining rooms adjoin the ballroom, seamlessly serving as an extension of that space. A large mahogany table in one of the dining rooms may be used for a buffet or whisked away.

CAPACITY

Reception or banquet: 200. With a seated dinner and dancing, the ballroom area holds a maximum of 175.

LOCATION

Poised on the diagonal at the corner of 16th Street, NW, and New Hampshire Avenue, NW, to the right as you travel north on 16th Street.

FOOD/BEVERAGE

An in-house catering service handles all meals and will work with you to plan your menu. You may provide the alcoholic drinks, in which case the club charges a $2 per person corkage fee, or you can have the club take care of all that. The club provides chairs, tables, glassware, flatware, and china, all included in the rental rates.

LIMITATIONS/RESTRICTIONS

The club is available daily. Anyone may rent it, but you must be sponsored by a member; if you don't know a member, the club is happy to help you obtain sponsorship. Events must end by midnight. Smoking is not permitted.

LEAD TIME FOR RESERVATIONS

If you would like to book the club for a wedding, try to call six months to a year in advance, but always call for availability.

RATES

Monday through Thursday evenings: $1,200 for four hours; Friday nights, Saturday, and Sunday: $1,500 for eight hours; weekdays: $200 to 500 for four hours.

FACILITIES FOR THE PHYSICALLY DISABLED? No

THE DANDY AND NINA'S DANDY

Potomac Party Cruises
Zero Prince Street
Alexandria, VA 22314
703/683-6076
703/683-7442 (fax)
www.dandydinnerboat.com

For a dandy old time

You could say that the *Dandy* and *Nina's Dandy* are Washington's versions of the Parisian riverboats that cruise the Seine. The *Dandy* has cruised the Potomac for more than twenty years, gaining renown as a floating restaurant/ballroom/tourmobile/meeting site. Its sister, *Nina's Dandy*, came along in 2000 to further satisfy the booming desire among Washingtonians for fine dining on the water.

Both boats are climate-controlled, all-weather, glassed-in cruise vessels. The *Dandy's* interior features mahogany woodwork, plush carpeting, tones of burgundy and pink, and framed prints of Monet, Beraud, and Renoir works on the walls. In the middle is a marble dance floor. Interior features of *Nina's Dandy* include a 460-square-foot marble dance floor, a marble stage, an ebony grand piano, burgundy velvet drapery, a huge pull-down screen for presentations, and a 3,750-square-foot outer upper deck for dancing and strolling.

A candlelit, three-hour evening cruise offers you a sumptuous five-course dinner, followed by dancing to music played over the boat's superb sound system. Cold-weather cruises can be especially fun; guests like to gather around the *Dandy's* working antique wood-burning stove and drink hot toddies and ciders. Both vessels are designed to go under the bridges, affording you a close-up view of the monuments, Georgetown, the Kennedy Center, and other Washington sights.

Private charters are available to groups for special events, including breakfast, midday, and midnight cruises.

CAPACITY

Dandy: Although Coast Guard–certified to carry 200 passengers, the owner recommends parties of no more than 180 for receptions, banquets, and meetings. *Nina's Dandy*: Although Coast Guard–certified to carry 300 passengers, the owner recommends parties of about 250 for receptions, banquets, and meetings.

LOCATION

You board both boats at the Prince Street pier, between Duke and King Streets in Old Town Alexandria. Follow the George Washington Memorial Parkway (Washington Street within Alexandria city limits) to Duke Street and follow Duke Street to the waterfront. There are several parking lots near the pier. Prince Street is one block north of Duke Street.

FOOD/BEVERAGE

The *Dandy* and *Nina's Dandy* are restaurants that offer full-course meals and a fully stocked bar.

LIMITATIONS/RESTRICTIONS

There are no specific restrictions, but review your requirements with management. Smoking is prohibited on the *Dandy* and allowed only on the outer deck of *Nina's Dandy*.

LEAD TIME FOR RESERVATIONS

Call for availability. Large groups should plan further ahead than small ones, since the boats can accommodate more than one small group at a time.

RATES

Evening dinner/dance cruises: $64.27 (*Dandy*), $70.54 (*Nina's Dandy*) per person Sunday through Thursday; $68.97 (*Dandy*), $75.24 (*Nina's Dandy*) per person Friday; and $77.85 (*Dandy*), $84.12 (*Nina's Dandy*) per person Saturday, plus beverage charges.

Lunch cruise rates range from $31.87 per person (weekdays on the *Dandy*) to $37.10 per person (for a Saturday lunch on *Nina's Dandy*).

Call for charter rates.

FACILITIES FOR THE PHYSICALLY DISABLED? Some

The *Dandy* has a gangplank but not a rest room that can handle a wheelchair. *Nina's Dandy* is fully accessible to the disabled.

DRANESVILLE TAVERN

11919 Leesburg Pike

Herndon, VA 20170

703/938-8835

www.co.fairfax.va.us/parks/weddings.htm

hprs@co.fairfax.va.us

Mailing address: Historic Properties Rental Services

Fairfax County Park Authority

6332 Barcroft Mews Drive

Falls Church, VA 22041-1237

Stop in and stay awhile

Folks in earlier times never had it as good as you can today at Dranesville Tavern. Built in 1825 as a "drover's rest"—a stopping place for people on their way to market—the public house provided food, drink, and a place to sleep. When you stop in these days, you can cater your own food and drink, but the tavern offers you the historic atmosphere and charm of its restored rooms, as well as such modern amenities as central heating and air-conditioning.

You can use all seven rooms of the two-story tavern. There are few furnishings, but you do get little glimpses into the past. Small interior windows set in the wall reveal layers of the structure. Restored pieces of painted woodwork wear the squash and blue-green colors in vogue more than 150 years ago. Low ceilings and doorways bear witness to the days when Americans stood shorter.

You are welcome to use the open grounds that surround the tavern.

CAPACITY
Reception or banquet: 99
Garden party: 150 with tent
Meeting: 35 in one room

LOCATION
From the Beltway (I-495), take Exit 10B (Tysons Corner, Route 7) and follow Route 7 west for ten miles. Turn left on Dranesville Manor Drive. Make an immediate right onto the Dranesville Tavern driveway.

FOOD/BEVERAGE
You may choose your own caterer, as long as the caterer has a business license, a health department certificate, and proof of insurance. A kitchen on the premises is equipped with outlets, a sink, and a refrigerator. A banquet license is required if you're going to serve or sell alcohol.

LIMITATIONS/RESTRICTIONS
The tavern is available year-round, from 7:30 A.M. to 11:00 P.M. on weekdays and from 7:30 A.M. to midnight Friday through Sunday. Alcohol is permitted in the building and on the immediate grounds, but bar service must be in the building. Smoking and candles are prohibited inside.

LEAD TIME FOR RESERVATIONS
The site books most reservations one year in advance, but call for availability. The tavern's busiest months are April, May, June, September, October, and December.

RATES
Meetings: $350 (four hours) to $475 (eight hours); $50 each additional hour
Social functions: $550 (Fairfax County residents) or $750 (out-of-county renters) for five hours' use; $125 each additional hour. Call for reduced weekday and winter rates. The site also requires a refundable, $300 security deposit and a $100 alcohol use fee.

FACILITIES FOR THE PHYSICALLY DISABLED? No

DUMBARTON HOUSE

2715 Q Street, NW
Washington, DC 20007
202/337-2288, ext. 230
victoriahostin@dumbartonhouse.org

The Colonial Dames open their doors

Historic Dumbarton House, built in 1799, is the headquarters for the National Society of the Colonial Dames of America, which owns the property and is responsible for having restored it (and more than one hundred other important sites). The dames haven't always allowed the public to rent Dumbarton. The reason they do so now is because they've created a new space for special events on the lower level of the mansion.

Dumbarton House is situated on a hill above Rock Creek Park. The organization excavated beneath the house to form the Belle Vue Room and its outdoor courtyard. The Belle Vue Room is paneled in shades of pale yellow and has an oak floor, a thirteen-foot-high, white coffered ceiling, and lofty Palladian windows and doors leading to the flagstone patio. The assembly room measures twenty-six by forty feet; the patio, thirty-two by forty feet. The courtyard faces a semicircular garden plot backing up against a brick wall; behind it, the splendid hulk of Dumbarton House rises up.

As pleasant as the party space is, you must tour the wonderfully restored mansion. You may enjoy cocktails (though not food) on the first and second floors as you take in the seventeenth- and eighteenth-century antique furnishings, the curved bays, room-size hallways, exquisitely carved mantelpieces, and other architectural features that let you know you've traveled to another place and time.

CAPACITY

Reception or banquet: 175 using both the assembly room and courtyard

LOCATION

Between 27th and 28th Streets, NW, just above Rock Creek Park in Georgetown.

FOOD/BEVERAGE

You must choose a caterer from the site's list.

LIMITATIONS/RESTRICTIONS

The house is available for corporate functions anytime, subject to the site's own schedule, and for weddings on a limited basis. Events must end by 11:30 P.M. Smoking is prohibited. Red wine is not allowed as a cocktail but may be served with dinner. Residential street parking is all that is available.

LEAD TIME FOR RESERVATIONS

The site books events as far in advance as you like.

RATES

Rates range from $2,800 to $5,000, but most events hover near the $4,000 mark for four hours' use. Additional hours cost $350 each. A percentage of the rental fee is required in advance, as security deposit.

FACILITIES FOR THE PHYSICALLY DISABLED? Yes

FONDO DEL SOL
Visual Art and Media Center
2112 R Street, NW
Washington, DC 20008
202/483-2777

A celebration of America's varied cultures

You don't have to travel all the way to South or Central America to enjoy yourselves in true Latino fashion. Hold an event at Fondo del Sol and you can

tango Argentina, sway to salsa and reggae, admire Hispanic-oriented art, and feast on such exotic foods as pollo asada and ceviche.

You know you've found Fondo del Sol when you spot the red banner displaying a golden sun that hangs over the entrance to the white Victorian town house. Four rooms on two floors, the entrance hall, and a small garden are available for use. The front room on each floor features a windowed bay that seems suitable as a setup spot. Overall, the interior is plain, directing your attention to the multicultural art displayed throughout. Half of the gallery's exhibitions showcase the works of Latino artists; the other half feature the works of Native Americans, African-Americans, ethnic Americans, and others.

Fondo del Sol specializes in making events come alive through festive presentations of music, dance, and unusual dishes. This is the sort of place where parties often spill into the street. To make sure the good time lasts forever, Fondo del Sol will also videotape your event for you.

Founded in 1973, Fondo del Sol is the nation's second-oldest Latino multicultural museum.

CAPACITY
Reception: 150 to 200
Banquet: 75 per floor
Meeting: 50 per gallery
Garden party: 80

LOCATION
In the Dupont Circle area of northwest Washington, a seven-minute walk from the Dupont Circle Metro station at Q Street, NW.

FOOD/BEVERAGE
Fondo del Sol will cater your event for you with Caribbean or standard American food. Or, you may make your own arrangements. A small kitchen is available.

LIMITATIONS/RESTRICTIONS
The center is available Monday through Saturday from noon to midnight, and on Sunday by special arrangement.

LEAD TIME FOR RESERVATIONS
At least a month.

RATES
From $600, for a simple cocktail party using one floor, to $5,000, for use of the entire center and provision of music, food, and video services.

FACILITIES FOR THE PHYSICALLY DISABLED? Some
A ramp is available for wheelchair access.

FOREIGN SERVICE CLUB

2101 E Street, NW
Washington, DC 20037
202/342-3400
www.3citron.com
info@3citron.com

A handsome salon near the State Department

A catering outfit manages this one-room site, conveniently located near the State Department, George Washington University, and the Kennedy Center. An awning marks its entrance; otherwise, the building keeps a dignified profile. You enter into a small vestibule, where there is a cloakroom. From here, you find a straightforward space: one long room, carpeted in royal blue, with yellow walls and a dark wood bar in the back corner. Old photos of past Foreign Service Club members, as well as travel posters featuring exotic places where members have been stationed, decorate the walls.

CAPACITY
Reception: 180
Banquet: 99

LOCATION
Right next to the State Plaza Hotel, at the corner of E and 23rd Streets, NW, abutting the campus of George Washington University. Parking is on the street or at two nearby parking garages.

FOOD/BEVERAGE
The catering firm that manages the site, 3 Citron Caterers, is headquartered here, caters all events, and will work with you to plan your meals.

LIMITATIONS/RESTRICTIONS
The club is available every day for every type of function, from weddings to

corporate dinners. There are no restrictions.

LEAD TIME FOR RESERVATIONS
Call for availability.

RATES
You can rent the club for a flat $400 on weekdays and $600 on weekends. The fee covers the provision of tables, chairs, and house linens.

FACILITIES FOR THE PHYSICALLY DISABLED? Some
The entrance and club are accessible to someone in a wheelchair, but the bathrooms are not.

GREAT FALLS GRANGE AND SCHOOLHOUSE
9818 Georgetown Pike
Great Falls, VA 22066
703/938-8835
www.co.fairfax.va.us/parks/weddings.htm
hprs@co.fairfax.va.us

Mailing address: Historic Properties Rental Services
Fairfax County Park Authority
6332 Barcroft Mews Drive
Falls Church, VA 22041-1237

Multipurpose space in a park

There are no hidden treasures here; what you see is what you get. If your main requirement is plenty of space, read on.

Built in 1929, the Grange is a two-story, redbrick building with long sets of concrete steps leading up from either side to the main entrance. Inside are two large halls. The upstairs hall is plain but pleasing with its high, vaulted wood ceiling and new hardwood floor. Six windows line each side wall, letting in lots of light during the day. A large raised platform at one end of the room makes a great bandstand or stage for theater productions and presentations. The ground-floor hall is just as roomy but lacks ornamentation. A recent renovation provided new floors, a kitchen, and fresh paint.

Next door to the Grange is a white frame schoolhouse that dates from 1890. This building has been completely renovated, so it really doesn't show its age. There are two bare rooms inside with hardwood floors and globe fanlights.

Both the Grange and the Schoolhouse lie in a small park setting that includes softball and soccer fields, a picnic pavilion, and playground. They are available for rental together or separately.

CAPACITY

Reception: 200 in the Grange, 49 in the Schoolhouse
Banquet: 120 in the Grange, 49 in the Schoolhouse
Picnic: 200
Meeting/performance: 130 in the Grange

LOCATION

From the Beltway (I-495), take Exit 13 (Georgetown Pike, Route 193) west and go six miles to the park entrance on the right.

FOOD/BEVERAGE

You arrange your own catering and beverage service. A fully functional kitchen on the lower level of the Grange holds a refrigerator, stove, microwave, and butcher-block counters.

LIMITATIONS/RESTRICTIONS

Smoking is prohibited. You may not use nails, tacks, or tape to hang decorations. A permit is required to serve alcohol, which is allowed inside the building and outside on the immediate grounds. Bar service, however, must stay inside.

LEAD TIME FOR RESERVATIONS

Up to one year in advance.

RATES

Grange: $425 for a four-hour meeting and $625 for an eight-hour meeting, plus $50 per extra hour. Social function rental rates are $700 for Fairfax County residents and $900 for all others for five hours, with overtime charges of $125 per hour.

Schoolhouse: $300 for a four-hour meeting and $375 for an eight-hour meeting, plus $35 for each extra hour. Social function rental rates are $350 for county residents and $550 for all others for five hours, plus $75 for each extra hour.

Both Grange and Schoolhouse: $575 for a four-hour meeting and $775 for an eight-hour meeting, plus $75 for each extra hour. Social function rental rates are $900 for county residents and $1,000 for all others for five hours. County residents pay $150 for each hour after five hours; all others pay $250 per extra hour.

Other charges include a $100 alcohol use fee and a $300, refundable security deposit. Be sure to ask about weekday and winter discount rates.

FACILITIES FOR THE PHYSICALLY DISABLED? Some
The Schoolhouse is fully accessible, but the Grange is not.

H. H. LEONARDS'S MANSION ON O STREET

2020 O Street, NW
Washington, DC 20036
202/496-2000
202/659-0547 (fax)
www.erols.com/mansion
mansion@erols.com

Off-the-wall art in a Victorian home

You'll probably feel as if you're in someone's private home when you hold an event at H. H. Leonards's fine arts mansion. That's because it is a private home—

H. H. and family actually live in this furnished, five-story Victorian. Unlike a party at a friend's house, however, you don't have to covet a furnishing silently or ask the host where she purchased it. You can buy it. Everything you see here is for sale, from the paintings in the bathrooms to the bed on which H. H. sleeps.

Rambles around the entire house come with the rental of the site. Art and antiques lovers will be in ecstasy over the more than ten thousand objects on view, including paintings, sculpture, glasswork, pottery, chandeliers, china, and furniture.

The house itself might be considered a work of art. Actually, there are three houses here, although you'd never guess it. The original mansion was built in 1891 and features twelve fireplaces, an authenticated Tiffany window, and Teddy Roosevelt's billiard room. Cherry paneling frames a big picture window in the front drawing room, and oak paneling embellishes the entranceways, walls, and fireplaces.

On either side of the 1891 dwelling are five-story companion spaces, each built and designed by Leonards and showcasing his range of interior designing styles, from Victorian to avant-garde. Twenty thousand square feet contain 8 office/conference areas, 10 full kitchens, at least 12 bedrooms, 28 far-out bathrooms, 180 phones, 100 televisions of all sizes, and countless other communications gizmos.

The place is unbelievable. If you really want to be blown away, take a detour from your event to check out the log cabin loft suite.

The mansion is available for multilevel meetings, receptions, news conferences, seminars, private parties, and overnight stays. It is a registered bed-and-breakfast, as well as a museum featuring rotating exhibits.

CAPACITY

Reception: 200
Banquet: 150
Meeting: 4 to 125
Lodging: 12 bedrooms, some of which are suites

LOCATION

In the Dupont Circle area of Washington, half a block from the Dupont Circle

Metro station.

FOOD/BEVERAGE
H. H. Leonards Associates handles all your catering needs.

LIMITATIONS/RESTRICTIONS
Street parking is limited; a number of parking garages and lots lie within a few blocks. Valet parking is available. Consider taking a taxi. Otherwise, there are no specific restrictions. Call to discuss your requirements.

LEAD TIME FOR RESERVATIONS
Call for availability.

RATES
Rates range from $10 to $250 per person, depending upon the type of event you're planning. What do you get for $250? Well, what do you want? Lodging ranges from $125 to $1,000 a night. Nonprofit groups receive special rates.

FACILITIES FOR THE PHYSICALLY DISABLED? Yes

HISTORIC DUVALL HOUSE
305 Cameron Street
Alexandria, VA 22314
703/548-6611
www.alexandriacity.com/party/duvall.htm
elalcazar@webtv.net

A house of many lives

This Old Town Alexandria town house has been many things in its 250-year lifetime: a tavern where George Washington was feted; the first chartered bank in Virginia; the residence and office of Alexandria's first collector of customs, Charles Lee; and, now, the El Alcazar Antiques shop. In its current incarnation, the owners have put the house to yet another use by offering it as a site for small parties, weddings, and meetings.

Seven public rooms on two floors are available for functions. Each is furnished with antiques, furniture, and paintings. Though everything is for sale, furnishings are arranged as they would be in a home. In addition to high ceilings and original eighteenth-century floors and woodwork, the town house features a fireplace in each room. Behind the building is a small, charmingly landscaped, brick-paved garden.

CAPACITY
Reception: 120
Banquet: 65

LOCATION
A few blocks east of the George Washington Memorial Parkway (Washington Street within Alexandria city limits) and one block north of King Street in Old Town Alexandria.

FOOD/BEVERAGE
You may choose your own caterer, though Duvall House is happy to provide you with a list of caterers who have worked at the site. A full kitchen is available.

LIMITATIONS/RESTRICTIONS
Smoking is allowed only in the garden. Dancing and amplified music are not permitted.

LEAD TIME FOR RESERVATIONS
Call for availability.

RATES
For most functions, you can rent Duvall House for $150 per hour, with a four-hour minimum. For weddings the site charges $235 per hour, with a four-hour minimum. A $200 deposit is required to reserve your date.

FACILITIES FOR THE PHYSICALLY DISABLED? Some

A side entrance allows wheelchair access to the first floor.

HOLLIN HALL

Mount Vernon Unitarian Church
1909 Windmill Lane
Alexandria, VA 22307
703/765-5950

Grand estate on highest site in Fairfax County

In the mid-eighteenth century, George Mason, author of the Virginia Declaration of Rights (see Gunston Hall entry), built a house here for his son Thomson and called it Hollin Hall. That one burned down in 1827. The current Hollin Hall dates from 1916, though its surrounding nine acres hint at the past: There are 175-year-old boxwood gardens, old stone walls, slender allées, and stately holly, magnolia, and maple trees.

The grounds offer choice spots for parties. A magnolia-lined, brick walkway leads through cypress gates and vine-clad brick archways to a tall and circular brick-walled garden. A ring of boxwoods hugs the inside of the wall and further encloses a round expanse of lawn. Nearby is a curved brick walkway set among flowering trees, a favorite photo-shoot location. If you retrace your steps you arrive at the Unitarian meetinghouse's large flagstone terrace, which can be tented.

The meetinghouse, though used for services, is available for rentals. This contemporary building's design includes a vast cathedral ceiling with skylight, exposed oak beams, and brick walls. As useful as this space is, the manor house has more character. At its front door is a circular driveway surrounding a great lawn. You enter into a black-and-white, marble-floored foyer and step left into the clay-colored drawing room, where there are Japanese teak floors, a paneled fireplace flanked by French doors, built-in bookcases, deep-set windows, and more French doors leading to a wisteria-wrapped pergola. This delightful area travels back into a boxwood maze and garden, and to a side yard from which you can see you're at the summit of Fairfax County.

Three rooms in the house have yet to be mentioned. The sunporch, off the drawing room, has brick flooring and picture windows on three sides; the dining room has walls painted with a delicate landscape mural and its original oak floor, lightly embellished with scroll-painted flourishes; and the garden room is a "lettuce-green" hue and has French doors leading outside to the arbor.

Hollin Hall was the 1994 Alexandria Decorator Showhouse; many of its decorative elements are the handiwork of area artisans.

CAPACITY

Reception: 125 (in the house) to 200 (in the meetinghouse or walled garden), with total capacity not to exceed 200

Banquet: 90 (in the house) to 200 (in the meetinghouse), with total capacity not to exceed 200

Meeting: 200

LOCATION

Four miles south of Old Town Alexandria. From Washington, take the George Washington Memorial Parkway (Washington Street within Alexandria city limits) toward Mount Vernon. Turn right onto Morningside Lane, right onto Fort Hunt Road, and left onto Mason Hill Drive. Turn right onto Windmill Lane and drive up the hill to the property. The parking lot accommodates 110 cars.

FOOD/BEVERAGE

Mount Vernon Unitarian Church manages facility rentals and asks that you choose a caterer from its approved list; if you prefer to use a caterer not on the list, you must choose one that is licensed and insured. A kitchen is available for food preparation but not cooking. The site can provide at least one hundred chairs and twenty-one round tables.

LIMITATIONS/RESTRICTIONS

Hollin House is available anytime any day, except on Sunday, when its rental hour starts at 2:00 P.M. Alcohol is limited to beer and wine. Events must end by 10:30 P.M., with everyone, including caterers, gone by 11:30 P.M. Smoking is prohibited.

LEAD TIME FOR RESERVATIONS

The site accepts reservations as much as a year in advance; call as soon as you know your date.

RATES

Rates range from $600 for a two-hour wedding ceremony to $2,500 for a seven-hour period for a wedding and/or reception, depending on which buildings are rented. A security deposit is required.

FACILITIES FOR THE PHYSICALLY DISABLED? Yes

HUNTER HOUSE

9601 Courthouse Road
Vienna, VA 22181
703/938-8835
www.co.fairfax.va.us/parks/weddings.htm
hprs@co.fairfax.va.us

Mailing address: Historic Properties Rental Services
Fairfax County Park Authority
6332 Barcroft Mews Drive
Falls Church, VA 22041-1237

A landmark site and recreational facility

Tennis, anyone? Yes, if you want, you can play tennis, baseball, soccer, volleyball, or basketball, follow an exercise trail, or simply take a hike—in addition to holding a gracious affair at the mansion here.

Hunter House is a yellow, white-trimmed frame structure that lies within the eighty-four-acre Nottoway Park. A ground-floor hall and a large room that opens onto a screened-in side porch are the spaces available to you inside the mansion. White walls, high ceilings, recessed lights, and polished oak floors add luster to unfurnished rooms.

A flagstone path leads from Hunter House's back door to its secluded lawn, a tree-shaded area bordered by gardens and shrubs. The park's recreational facilities are just far enough away so that rebel yells and cheerleading don't disturb your function.

Now the property of the Fairfax County Park Authority, Hunter House was built in 1890 and served first as a residence for Scottish immigrant John Hunter and later as part of a winery.

CAPACITY

Reception: 75 inside, 200 with a canopy on the back lawn

Banquet: 50 inside, 200 with a canopy on the back lawn

Garden party: 200

Meeting: 35

LOCATION

From the Beltway (I-495), take Exit 9 or 9A (Route 66 west). Go right on Route 243 (Nutley Street), left on Courthouse Road, and left again into the park.

FOOD/BEVERAGE

You may choose your own caterer, as long as the caterer can provide a business license, health department certificate, and proof of insurance. The newly renovated kitchen offers stainless steel counters, a sink, and a thirty-five-cubic-foot refrigerator.

LIMITATIONS/RESTRICTIONS

Smoking is prohibited inside the house. A liquor permit is required if you plan to serve alcohol; an alcohol use fee is charged. Alcohol is permitted inside the house and outside on the immediate grounds, but bar service must stay inside. You may not use nails, tape, or tacks to hang decorations.

LEAD TIME FOR RESERVATIONS

Up to one year in advance.

RATES

Weekday business functions run $350 for four hours and $475 for eight hours, with a $50-per-hour overtime charge. Social function rates are $700 for Fairfax County residents and $900 for all others for five hours, with a $125-per-hour overtime charge. The site also charges a $100 alcohol use fee and a $300, refundable security deposit. Ask about weekday and winter discount rates.

FACILITIES FOR THE PHYSICALLY DISABLED? Yes

KENTLANDS MANSION
320 Kent Square Road
Gaithersburg, MD 20878-5726
301/258-6425

Old manor within a modern village

Enter the gates of what appears to be a vast estate, drive along streets with names like Leeke's Lot and Inspiration, past one comely house after another, skirt around a park and a lake, and then you'll arrive: at the one-hundred-year-old mansion that sits at the core of this model Smalltown USA community.

Kentlands Mansion outdates its neighbors by about ninety-five years. Although the house has been renovated, certain winning features betray its age: its high ceilings, wide doorways, and long windows; the fireplace in the parlor; the doorbell pipes in the Music Room; and the crown moldings.

The entire first floor and two conference rooms on the second floor are available for functions. From a spacious central hall with a Steinway piano tucked neatly beneath the staircase, go right into the Yellow Room, so named for its lovely, yellow-sherbet-colored walls. The largest space in the house, the Yellow Room is unfurnished except for a pendulous crystal chandelier, dangling from a fine plaster ceiling medallion, and white silk swags upon the five windows. Adjoining is the mahogany-paneled Music Room, whose many windows and glass-paned door fetch in a lot of light.

On the other side of the hall are more intimate chambers—the paneled parlor and the dining room, each furnished with reproduction furniture and Oriental carpets. Upstairs you'll find a handsome conference room, with deep-seated leather chairs around an oblong table, and the more casual and cheery classroom, which doubles as a bride's room for weddings. The huge upstairs hallway may be used as a breakout space for meetings.

Outside, there are small garden areas and front and back terraces that may be tented.

CAPACITY

Reception: 120
Banquet: 10 to 12 in the dining room, 64 using the Yellow and Music Rooms
Meeting: 10 in the conference room, 16 (with tables) to 24 (without tables) in the classroom

LOCATION

From the Silver Spring direction, take the Beltway (I-495) west to I-270 north (Exit 34); from Northern Virginia, take the Beltway (I-495) north to I-270 north (Exit 38). Follow I-270 to Route 28 west (Exit 6B) and continue on Route 28 about 4.5 miles, until you reach Rachel Carson Elementary School. Turn right through the gates and follow the signs to Kentlands. Parking is available adjacent to the mansion and at the end of the green.

FOOD/BEVERAGE

The caterer you choose must be insured and provide references. The mansion holds a good-sized kitchen equipped with an ice maker, refrigerator, small microwave, dishwasher, sink, and table. Eight round tables, fourteen rectangular tables, and ninety mauve upholstered chairs are available at no extra cost.

LIMITATIONS/RESTRICTIONS

The mansion is available in seven-hour blocks (two hours for setup, an hour for cleanup, and four hours for the event) that may be scheduled any day of the week, for any time period. Events on Sunday through Thursday must end by 10:00 P.M.; those on Friday and Saturday must end by midnight. You may be able to arrange for a longer event, but this must be done ahead of time. Smoking is prohibited inside the mansion. You may not nail decorations to the walls.

RATES

Seven-hour rentals on Saturday and Sunday cost $900 for Gaithersburg residents and $1,200 for nonresidents. If your party lasts longer than seven hours, the additional hourly charge is $200. The mansion requires a $250, refundable deposit to secure your reservation.

You may rent the Steinway piano, along with other equipment; call for these rates and for special weekday and Friday rates.

FACILITIES FOR THE PHYSICALLY DISABLED? Yes

THE LODGE AT LITTLE SENECA CREEK

14500-A Clopper Road
Boyds, MD 20841
301/299-5026

A king-size log cabin by the side of a country road

You're tooling along, thinking you must have missed it, when there it is at a bend in the road: a lodge if ever there was one. It's large, too. One look and you know you're going to be able to lodge a lot of people in that there lodge.

The Lodge at Little Seneca Creek is not some centuries-old little house in the big woods, but an exaggerated replica of one. Built in 1989 and now owned by the Maryland-National Capital Park and Planning Commission, this eighteen-hundred-square-foot structure is meant for entertaining. Besides its size, other features recommend it: the polished oak floor, the natural wood cathedral ceilings, and the immense—I mean immense—flagstone fireplace at one end.

Otherwise, the place is unfurnished. Banks of windows line the walls, and sets of glass doors lead to a great deck off the back. From there you can descend steps to fields, technically not belonging to the lodge but usually available for your use anyway.

The lodge is air-conditioned for warm weather and provides firewood for the hearth for cold days. (It is centrally heated, as well.) Hanging metal lamps provide most of the lighting.

The question is: Where the heck's the creek?

CAPACITY

Reception: 175

Banquet: 120

Meeting: 80

LOCATION

From the Beltway (I-495), take I-270 north to Exit 15B (Route 118, toward Germantown). Follow Route 118 2.1 miles to Route 117 (Clopper Road), where you turn right. Travel 1.4 miles to the lodge on your left. There's parking for eighty-five cars.

FOOD/BEVERAGE

The M-NCPPC has a list of seventy approved caterers from which you must choose. The lodge has a large kitchen equipped with a refrigerator, oven, sinks, and counter space. Five eight-foot rectangular tables, 12 five-foot round tables, and 130 chairs are available for events.

LIMITATIONS/RESTRICTIONS

The lodge is available any day anytime, but events must end by 1:00 A.M. Smoking is prohibited inside. You're not allowed to tack or nail decorations onto the walls.

LEAD TIME FOR RESERVATIONS

The lodge books six months to a year in advance for spring, summer, and early fall events, but call for availability.

RATES

Weekend rentals are for seven-hour periods. Friday and Sunday rates are $800. On

Saturdays, the lodge rents for $1,000. Each additional hour costs $200. Weekday and weeknight rates are lower; call for those fees.

FACILITIES FOR THE PHYSICALLY DISABLED? Yes

THE LYCEUM

201 South Washington Street
Alexandria, VA 22314
703/838-4994
http://ci.alexandria/va.us/oha
lyceum@ci.alexandria.va.us

A meeting place then and now

Back in the 1840s, you might have gathered at the Lyceum with fellow Alexandrians to observe scientific experiments, to listen to concerts and debates, or to hear speeches by the likes of John Quincy Adams. The Lyceum serves equally well today as a place to gather for receptions, banquets, meetings, and performances.

"An ornament to our town," declared the *Alexandria Gazette* about the Lyceum shortly after it had been constructed in 1839. The massive brick and stucco building is of Doric temple design, fronting Old Town's busiest street with four impressive columns. The interior, however, is very modern.

You can rent both floors of the Lyceum, although most groups find that the grand second-floor lecture hall best suits their purposes. The hall boasts a very high ceiling, in which many recessed lights are lodged. Green wall-to-wall carpeting and gold crown molding above each window are among the room's elegant flourishes. A piano, a platform stage, a projection booth, a descending screen, and controlled lighting are available if you need them.

Three galleries on the first floor house exhibits related to Alexandria's rich heritage and serve well as a reception area.

CAPACITY
Reception: 140
Banquet: 90
Meeting/concert: 100

LOCATION
Three miles south of National Airport, on the George Washington Memorial Parkway (Washington Street within Alexandria city limits) in Old Town Alexandria.

FOOD/BEVERAGE
You may choose your own caterer. A small kitchen has two refrigerators but no heating equipment.

LIMITATIONS/RESTRICTIONS
Smoking is prohibited in the building. Dancing is allowed under limited conditions; renters must rent their own dance floor.

LEAD TIME FOR RESERVATIONS
Call for availability.

RATES
Rental fees range from $25 for one hour to $1,200 for six hours, depending on the function. A security deposit is required. Limited audiovisual equipment and folding tables are available for an additional fee.

FACILITIES FOR THE PHYSICALLY DISABLED? Yes

OAKLAND GREEN FARM BED AND BREAKFAST

1912 Oakland Green Road
Leesburg, VA 20175
540/338-7628
540/338-5922 (fax)
www.vabb.com (then click on Inn Listings, Oakland Green)
oaklandbb@aol.com

Family farmhouse for eight generations (250 years)

The words "charming" and "cozy" are too often used these days, perhaps, but in describing Oakland Green none are more apt. You have to traverse quite a bit of deep forest to reach the property, whose eighteenth-century farmhouse blends in with its woodland and garden surroundings.

The house was built in four sections, all joined. The oldest part is the 1730 log house, which serves as a two-level bed-and-breakfast suite. Oakland Green has four sleeping rooms that can accommodate eight people.

Parties and meetings larger than twenty-five or so take place on the lawn, a green expanse backing up against tall, century-old evergreen trees. Even if yours is an outdoor function, you should take time to explore the public areas of the Brown family homestead, whose first floor is available for small gatherings. The dining room is wonderfully warm and inviting, with its well-worn, heart-maple floor, huge hearth, and deep-set windows; it opens to a covered porch. Trees felled on the property provided the maple boards for the floor and walnut wood for the long dining table. The parlor, which was built in the 1790s, reflects Federal influence in its carved mantel, woodwork, chair rail, and window treatments. A homey kitchen is a 1978 addition but fits nicely with the rest of the house because of its wide pine flooring, pine beams, old chestnut cabinets, and hand-braided rugs. Off the kitchen is a screened-in porch, which also may be used.

Its old architecture accounts for much of the character of Oakland Green Farm, but the Brown family's furnishings add enchantment, telling you a good bit about how Americans have lived through the centuries. Old ice skates, cooking utensils, a late-nineteenth-century music box (still working), and family portraits are just some of the interesting items on display.

CAPACITY
Reception: 50 inside, 130 when you tent the lawn
Banquet: 24 inside, 130 when you tent the lawn
Meeting: 24
Lodging: 4 sleeping rooms, 2 1/2 baths

LOCATION
Six miles south of Purcellville, Virginia, and eight miles west of Leesburg; call for detailed directions.

FOOD/BEVERAGE
You may choose your own caterer, subject to the owners' approval. Caterers may use the full kitchen here.

LIMITATIONS/RESTRICTIONS
Oakland Green is available year-round. Parties must end by 11:00 P.M. The site requires that you rent a tent when your party numbers more than fifty. Smoking and dancing are not permitted inside.

LEAD TIME FOR RESERVATIONS
Call six months ahead to reserve the site.

RATES
Weddings cost $1,700; lodging, $80 to $125 per room, plus tax. Call for other rates.

FACILITIES FOR THE PHYSICALLY DISABLED? No

OLD CAFRITZ HOUSE

5001 16th Street, NW
Washington, DC 20011
202/829-1388

A Mediterranean-style dwelling on Washington's "Gold Coast"

Even in its falling-down days, the Old Cafritz House must have shown grand potential, with its thirteen-foot-high ceilings, abundance of wrought-iron fixtures, and unusual Mediterranean-style layout. In 1991, before it fell all to ruin, an enterprising young man came along and resurrected the dwelling from a shambles into a showcase.

The exterior is stucco, painted a creamy butternut squash color. The generously sized garden includes a stone patio and is beautifully landscaped with flowering plants and trees. On one side of the house is a fifty-foot-long pool and areas for lounging and sunbathing, including a twenty-by-twenty-foot deck.

When you enter the house, you step into the vestibule, whose floor is laid with its original, earth-toned Spanish tiles. To your left is the most magnificent room in the house—the one-thousand-square-foot Grand Salon. Paved also with Spanish tiles, the salon's other features include a blocked-beamed ceiling, white stucco walls, and three archways that decorate more than divide the room. Lots of windows—nineteen, in fact—provide natural light during the day; two wrought-iron chandeliers illuminate at night.

Back to the foyer and up two steps is the oversized dining room. Here the floor is oak and the chandelier crystal. Through French doors lies the sunroom, which has arched windows and soft-green-colored walls. One other spot on the main level is a small sitting room, with quail-toned stucco walls and a combination of Spanish and Empire furniture; French doors from this room lead to the poolside deck. Built in 1926, the house seems newly to have come into its own.

CAPACITY

Reception: 125
Banquet: 90 inside, 125 inside and out

Meeting: 80 in the Grand Salon

LOCATION
On 16th Street, NW, about two or three miles straight up from the White House and within a stone's throw of Carter Barron Amphitheater. Street parking is plentiful.

FOOD/BEVERAGE
You may choose from the owner's list of caterers.

LIMITATIONS/RESTRICTIONS
The house is available all year long, any day. Smoking is permitted outside only.

LEAD TIME FOR RESERVATIONS
Call at least thirty days in advance.

RATES
Rates range from $2,000 to $3,100, depending upon the number of people, type of function, and type of organization renting. (Nonprofit organizations receive special rates.)

FACILITIES FOR THE PHYSICALLY DISABLED? No

OLD TOWN HALL
3999 University Drive
Fairfax, VA 22030
703/385-7858 or 800/368-8323

Mailing address: John C. Wood Complex
3730 Old Lee Highway
Fairfax, VA 22030

On a stretch of street that includes unassuming office buildings and shops, you can't help noticing the Old Town Hall. There are the pillars, for one thing: four great white Tuscan order columns standing guard at the building's entrance. The rest of the hall is mostly neoclassical in design—it resembles a temple—with Federal-style details that include the fanlight over the front door and the round-headed dormers.

Old Town Hall offers you the use of both floors for functions. The first floor is a wide-open space broken up by six wooden pillars. There are large windows set in all four walls, so the room is light-filled. Add to this the high ceiling, and you have a radically roomy space in which to hold a meeting, banquet, or reception.

One-time ambassador to Spain Joseph Willard served as lieutenant governor of Virginia and built Old Town Hall in 1900. The building has served as a center for Fairfax City social life.

CAPACITY
Reception: 175
Banquet: 150
Meeting: 150

LOCATION
From the Beltway (I-495), take the exit for Route 66 west and travel to Route 123 (Chain Bridge Road). Follow Route 123 south to Main Street. Go left on Main Street and left again on University Drive. Old Town Hall is at the corner of Main Street and University Drive.

FOOD/BEVERAGE
You may choose your own caterer. There's a kitchen equipped with a refrigerator, microwave oven, counter space, ice machine, and warming unit.

LIMITATIONS/RESTRICTIONS
No smoking is allowed in the building.

LEAD TIME FOR RESERVATIONS
Call for availability. The hall accepts reservations two years in advance. Saturdays are most popular.

RATES
Rates range from $50 for a two-hour, weekday meeting to $750 for a five-hour social event hosted by a nonresident of Fairfax City.

FACILITIES FOR THE PHYSICALLY DISABLED? Yes

PRESIDENTIAL HOUSE
313 East Capitol Street, SE
Washington, DC 20003
202/547-0500
202/547-5900 (fax)

A showcase for political memorabilia

No one thought Harry Truman would win the presidential race back in 1949, so few people bothered to save Truman campaign material. What exists is hard to find. The Presidential House displays some of these rare items, such as a photograph signed by Harry, framed cartoons by political cartoonist Thomas Nast, and other prized mementos reflecting the country's political and presidential history.

The Presidential House, fittingly located a stone's throw from the US Capitol, is an 1889 brick Victorian town house filled with political Americana, all of which is for sale. It's also a private home (the owner of the Political Americana stores lives here), so the collections are arrayed tastefully on the walls and in curio cabinets throughout the three stories. There's a great bay window and a (usable) fireplace in the living room, a creamy-beige-toned dining room, and a long side hall that parallels these rooms and leads to the good-sized, wood-floored kitchen. Out back is a large green lawn. Although your event must be staged on the first floor, guests are welcome to roam the second and third floors to view memorabilia.

CAPACITY
Reception: 100 to 120
Banquet: 38
Meeting: 40

LOCATION
On Capitol Hill, on the southeast side of East Capitol Street, within walking distance of the US Capitol and House and Senate office buildings. Parking is on the street.

FOOD/BEVERAGE
You may choose your own caterer to make food, drink, and equipment arrangements.

LIMITATIONS/RESTRICTIONS
The house is available for events anytime, day or night. Smoking is not allowed inside.

LEAD TIME FOR RESERVATIONS
Presidential House recommends that you call three months in advance.

RATES
Rates run from $425 for a breakfast to $475 for a dinner. A refundable, $100 security deposit is required.

FACILITIES FOR THE PHYSICALLY DISABLED? No

RIVER FARM

American Horticultural Society
7931 East Boulevard Drive
Alexandria, VA 22308
703/768-5700, ext. 114

"Gentleman's home" and horticultural haven on the Potomac

George Washington owned this twenty-seven-acre Potomac River farm property, although he never lived here. His tenants cultivated Kentucky coffee trees, walnut trees, and an Osage orange, along with the usual assortment of crops, like corn and wheat. Prowl the grounds and look for these stately trees—they're at least descendants of those he planted, if not the very same. The Osage orange tree, located in the Shade Garden and thought to be one of the largest in the country, grew from a cutting believed to be a gift from Thomas Jefferson.

There are other reasons to wander around. As headquarters for the Ameri-

100

can Horticultural Society (AHS), the place is bursting with landscaped lawns and interesting little gardens—and the Potomac River beckons from the bottom of the meadow. Look for the children's gardens, the arbor for Chinese wisteria, the ornamental roses, the boxwoods that date from Lincoln's time, the water garden, and the dahlia, azalea, lily, and other beds supported by various plant societies.

The "gentleman's home," so designated by the Fairfax County Historical Society, stands on the foundation of the eighteenth-century brick farmhouse, at the center of the property. A gentleman named Malcolm Matheson Sr. bought River Farm in 1919 and erected the house you see today. Upstairs rooms are AHS offices, but downstairs, renters may use the large, formally furnished parlor overlooking the river, a dining room opening onto a broad, covered brick terrace, and the forty-five-by-twenty-foot, light-filled ballroom/gallery.

Certain features make the house quite inviting: eighteenth-century-style, white painted paneling throughout each room, a handsome front hall, deep-set windows, floral-themed artwork, the sweeping views of river and lawn, and the tented flagstone garden terrace, to name a few.

CAPACITY
Reception: 125 and up
Banquet: 60 to 80
Meeting: 60 to 80 in the ballroom

LOCATION
Four miles south of Old Town Alexandria. From Washington, take the George Washington Memorial Parkway (Washington Street within Alexandria city limits) toward Mount Vernon. Turn left at the sign onto East Boulevard Drive and follow the signs to River Farm.

FOOD/BEVERAGE
You must choose a caterer from the site's approved list. A warming kitchen is available.

LIMITATIONS/RESTRICTIONS
The site is available Monday through Thursday for events involving no more

than sixty guests and Friday through Sunday for events of any size. River Farm allows a limited number of large parties—500 people—and an unlimited number of the 125-person (standing) or 60-person (seated) size. Events must end by 10:00 P.M. Smoking is not permitted anywhere on the grounds.

Parking is restricted to on-site designated parking areas (no parking on East Boulevard Drive). If your event involves more than 125 guests, you must arrange for parking attendants and supplementary toilet facilities.

LEAD TIME FOR RESERVATIONS
River Farm books as far as a year in advance; call as soon as possible.

RATES
Rates start at $300 for a four-hour, weekday meeting and spiral upward from there. A typical eight-hour function for 125 people at River Farm, including use of the tented terrace, costs $5,500. A refundable security deposit of $250 is required to book your event.

FACILITIES FOR THE PHYSICALLY DISABLED? Yes

ROCKWOOD MANOR PARK
11001 MacArthur Boulevard
Potomac, MD 20854
301/299-5026

Camp cum conference center

Mention Rockwood to a Girl Scout and she'll tell you it's a Girl Scout camp. That's what it used to be—a national campsite that welcomed fifteen thousand to twenty thousand Scouts yearly. So it may surprise you to learn that the park has taken on a new life as a classy conference center after a major renovation by its new owner, the Maryland-National Capital Park and Planning Commission.

A rambling brick manor house and three overnight cabins, all situated in a private and carefully maintained park, are available for rental. The house comprises seven multipurpose rooms and ten guest bedrooms.

The first thing you notice about the interior of the manor is that it is decorated throughout in shades of blue and purple. The smallest of these blue rooms is the Girl Scout Room, which accommodates fifteen, theater-style. Brooke Hall, an informal dining room with a carpeted floor, paneled vaulted ceiling, and brick fireplace, is the largest room, accommodating one hundred for conferences and fifty for banquets. Right next door to Brooke Hall is the blue-carpeted Great Falls Room, which can handle forty for presentations and sixty for banquets.

Loveliest of all is the Hoover Room, which seems best suited for receptions. This high-ceilinged space is empty but for its grand chandelier, working fireplace, and mauve carpet. French doors close off the room on one side; when they are left open, the room becomes an upstairs gallery overlooking the sunporch area, known as the Rapadan Retreat.

Overnight accommodations vary from bright, homey bedrooms with private baths to dormitory dwellings with bunk beds and central bathrooms. Rockwood is an ideal setting for small corporate retreats and provides audiovisual equipment for presentations.

CAPACITY
Reception: 150
Banquet: 100 (with 60 in one room and 40 in the adjoining room)
Meeting: 8 to 100
Lodging: 116

LOCATION
Near C & O Canal National Historical Park and within walking distance of the C & O Canal in southwestern Montgomery County, Maryland.

FOOD/BEVERAGE
You must choose a caterer from Rockwood's approved list. Alcohol is permitted, but you must obtain a license if you plan to sell it.

LIMITATIONS/RESTRICTIONS
Amplified music is prohibited outside. Parking is limited to eighty-five spaces.

LEAD TIME FOR RESERVATIONS
The site accepts reservations one year in advance, but call for availability.

RATES
Conference room rates range from $125, for rental of the smallest room, to $1,000, for rental of all conference rooms and lounges, including Brooke Hall. Lodging rates range from $60 per night for a single room to $1,500 per night for all ten guest bedrooms, plus the use of the conference rooms and lounges. Dormitory rates run $8 to $10 a person for one night.

FACILITIES FOR THE PHYSICALLY DISABLED? Yes

ROSSBOROUGH INN
University of Maryland
Route 1
College Park, MD 20742
301/314-8012

A place to eat, meet, and be merry

As you cruise down Route 1 toward the Rossborough, you may question whether there really is a historic, Federal-style mansion mixed in among the fast-food joints and record stores. Keep going. This 1804 inn belongs to the University of Maryland and lies at the gateway to the campus.

Once you enter the Rossborough, you know you're in the right place. An air of history and hospitality pervades.

On the main floor is an elegant parlor where Lafayette once dined. A dark green carpet, maize-colored walls with seafoam green trim, brass chandeliers, and handsome table settings create a refined meeting area. Across the antique-laden hallway is the rustic taproom, a casual combination of old-fashioned bar, pegged wooden floor, and pub-style lighting fixtures.

Up a wide, green-carpeted staircase you find five smaller rooms named for people connected with the inn or the university. The Ross Room, for example, is named for the original owner of the home, and the Calvert Room is named for a later owner who sold the inn to the state of Maryland at the end of the nineteenth century. These rooms were once bedrooms at the inn. Each offers variations on the same Federal-style decor.

Connected by a covered walkway to the inn is a carriage house. With its worn brick floor, working fireplace, and exposed beams, this one-room building is a natural for informal social gatherings.

If you're planning a spring or summer fling, you'll also want to know about the inn's garden and courtyard. Large hedges shield three sides of the English garden, with the fourth side opening to a charming courtyard and its views of the campus.

CAPACITY
Reception: 175 inside, 200 outside
Banquet: 120 inside, 200 outside

LOCATION
Seven miles from the US Capitol, on Route 1 across from the Ritchie Coliseum.

FOOD/BEVERAGE
The inn caters all functions and provides a catering guide upon request. Or, take a peek at it online at www.inform.umd.edu/muc.

LIMITATIONS/RESTRICTIONS
The Rossborough Inn requires you to order food and beverage for your event. A minimum of twenty-five guests is required for weekday functions, seventy-five guests for Saturday functions, and one hundred guests for Sunday events.

LEAD TIME FOR RESERVATIONS
At least two weeks. Large receptions should be booked one month in advance.

RATES
Taproom, $200; parlor, $250; carriage house, $250; garden and courtyard, $350; entire house, garden, and courtyard, $750. Menu rates start at $14.50 per person for a stand-up event and $18.95 per person for a sit-down function.

FACILITIES FOR THE PHYSICALLY DISABLED? Yes
The inn was recently renovated to provide access.

RUSSIAN CULTURAL CENTRE
1825 Phelps Place, NW
Washington, DC 20008
202/265-3840
202/265-6040 (fax)
www.russianculture.org
rcci@erols.com

Exquisite Russian craftsmanship and art shine within a Kalorama mansion

The yellow brick mansion at 1825 Phelps Place, NW, does not stand out within the Kalorama landscape. On a street lined with stately embassies and charming houses, the splendid 1895 building behind a graceful wrought-iron gate is of a piece with its neighbors. The Russian flag flying from a second-floor balcony above the entrance is a quick clue to what awaits you inside, and as you draw closer, you'll note the words "Russian Cultural Centre" carved in stone below the flag.

Russian embassy craftsmen labored ceaselessly for nearly two years to transform the defaced interior into an elegant center for the promotion of Russian culture. One way of introducing Americans to Russian culture and encouraging cross-cultural communication, the center believes, is to open the mansion for events. This way, people can view the intricate models of Russian cathedrals on display in the Moscow Room and the life-size portraits of Peter the Great and Catherine the Great in the Great Hall.

Events take place throughout the ceremonial first floor. From the oak-paneled entrance hallway with its grand swerving staircase, the rooms flow one into the next through oversized doorways that hide sliding pocket doors. The Moscow Room is the most decorative, with ivory-colored walls and gold-leaf accents, intricate moldings, high ceilings, a ten-foot mantelpiece over the fireplace, and the display of model cathedrals. Across the foyer is the Great Hall, with many gilded mirrors, those compelling portraits of the czar and czarina, and a Steinway piano that may be rented for your party. The last salon is the Russian-American Room, paneled in African mahogany, with the words "That Our Two Nations Never Again Polarize" engraved on the walls. Doors lead to a shaded balcony on one side of the room and to the Dacha Terrace, a covered side garden, on another. All rooms in the house have their original oak floors, magnificent Russian-style chandeliers, and Russian artwork.

CAPACITY
Reception: 160 inside, 250 using the house and terrace
Banquet: 100

LOCATION
Near Connecticut Avenue, NW, at the corner of Leroy Place and Phelps Place, in the Kalorama neighborhood.

FOOD/BEVERAGE

The site has a list of approved caterers from which you must choose. You can rent tables, chairs, the piano, and other items from the center.

LIMITATIONS/RESTRICTIONS

The center encourages events associated with Russian culture but doesn't refuse other rentals. Political and religious events are not allowed. Daytime events must conclude by 4:00 P.M. or the evening rate will go into effect. All events must conclude by 11:00 P.M. Smoking is not permitted indoors. Valet parking is a must.

LEAD TIME FOR RESERVATIONS

Call for availability.

RATES

Rates for daytime events start at $1,500. Rates for evening events start at $3,000.

FACILITIES FOR THE PHYSICALLY DISABLED? Yes

ST. LUKE SERBIAN ORTHODOX CHURCH HALL

6801 Georgetown Pike
PO Box 178
McLean, VA 22101
703/790-1005

Church hall of cheery proportions

Yes, this is a church social hall, but no, it's not dark and somber, and no, it's not limited to church socials. St. Luke's found itself unable to fill the hall, built in 1977, so the church decided to share its wealth.

St. Luke's hall is a bright, white stucco structure located amidst million-dollar homes on a picturesque stretch of Georgetown Pike in McLean. The facility consists of one large, forty-by-eighty-foot hall, a bar area, and a complete commercial kitchen. Expansive windows and glass doors run the length of the room on both sides. The view on one side is of the attached colonnade and the hall's private lawn; through the glass doors on the other side lies a partly covered, spacious patio area. The room itself is white, from linoleum floor to acoustic-tile ceiling. Simplicity is the watchword here. To remind partygoers where they are, the hall's back wall displays an assortment of pictures of Serbian monasteries.

CAPACITY
Reception: 200
Banquet: 175

LOCATION
On Georgetown Pike (Route 193) in McLean. Ample on-site parking is available.

FOOD/BEVERAGE
You're free to choose your own caterer. The full kitchen boasts a commercial refrigerator, convection and conventional ovens, a walk-in freezer, and a dishwasher.

LIMITATIONS/RESTRICTIONS
The hall is available all year-round, any day, anytime, but events must end by 11:00 P.M.

LEAD TIME FOR RESERVATIONS
The site accepts reservations a year in advance, but call for availability.

RATES
The rate is $750 for four hours. You get three free hours of setup time.

FACILITIES FOR THE PHYSICALLY DISABLED? Some
The entire facility is at ground level, but the rest rooms are not specially equipped for a wheelchair.

SPRINGDALE COUNTRY INN

Lincoln, VA 20160
540/338-1832

Best of the old, along with the new

Wishing you could whisk your employees off on a scheduled company retreat, but afraid to stray too far from a fax machine? Or maybe you're a bride searching for a wedding reception spot that has it all: character, history, gorgeous grounds, distinguished interiors, and accommodations for some of the wedding party. In either case, you may find what you're looking for at Springdale Country Inn.

The dwelling dates from the 1830s, when it was a Quaker boarding school for girls. Since then, Springdale has been put to a number of uses, among them stints as a Civil War hospital, underground railroad refuge, and weekend getaway for Lyndon Johnson and Sam Rayburn, who played poker here when the house was owned by the head of the Interstate Commerce Commission. In 1989, the manor opened as an inn/special event/meeting facility.

Springdale is located on a paved country road about ten miles outside of Leesburg, forty-five miles from Washington, and eighteen miles from Dulles Airport. The inn sits back on six acres of beautiful land that include terraced gardens, a springhouse, stone walking paths, and bridges crossing babbling brooks.

On the main floor of the white frame structure, you find four rooms stemming off a long central hall. These rooms have oak floors, working fireplaces, built-in bookshelves, and lots of nooks and crannies. They are handsomely furnished in keeping with the spirit and history of the house. Because the building has been renovated and rewired, Springdale is able to offer guests the use of such office amenities as VCRs, computers, a microfiche reader, copy machines, a fax machine, telephones, and a modem. The first-floor sunroom converts into a bedroom with a private, wheelchair-accessible bath for individuals who are unable to manage stairs.

Upstairs are eight bedrooms and four baths, including a three-room suite, outfitted with antiques from the Empire, Federal, and Victorian periods. If your party exceeds the capacity of Springdale for an overnight stay, the inn can arrange for four nearby bed-and-breakfasts to accommodate the overflow.

CAPACITY
Reception: 100 inside, 150 using the house and grounds
Banquet: 75
Meeting: 50
Lodging: 20 in 9 on-site rooms, 35 in 19 rooms when area inns are used

LOCATION
From Washington, follow Route 7 west ten miles past Leesburg, to the Purcellville exit at Route 287. Go .5 mile south on Route 287, then west for .5 mile on Main Street. Turn left on Route 722, Maple Avenue. Springdale is two miles down the road on your left.

FOOD/BEVERAGE
The inn prefers that you use its in-house caterer but will allow you to stock your own bar. Springdale's chef often serves teas and customizes menus from two-hundred-year-old recipes. The kitchen is a fully equipped, commercial facility.

LIMITATIONS/RESTRICTIONS
Smoking and open flames are not permitted. Amplified music is limited to one room on the first floor. A tent is required when your party exceeds the inn's indoor capacity. A fifty percent deposit is required to confirm your reservation.

RATES
For a social event, first-floor party areas and grounds can be rented for $2,000. Lodging for such functions costs $1,000. Meeting room rates range from $125 for four hours to $200 for eight hours, depending upon the amount of space, time, and service needed. Use of the commercial kitchen costs $150. Food service runs an average of $60 to $70 per person per function. Lodging fees are $125 per room per night; group rates start at $48 per person per night.

FACILITIES FOR THE PHYSICALLY DISABLED? Yes

THE STONE MANSION
3900 Stoneybrooke Drive
Alexandria, VA 22306
703/938-8835
www.co.fairfax.va.us/parks/weddings.htm
hprs@co.fairfax.va.us

Mailing address: Historic Properties Rental Services
Fairfax County Park Authority
6332 Barcroft Mews Drive
Falls Church, VA 22041-1237

Contemporary space in an old house

If you've grown accustomed to renting a room in a mansion for your events, or a great hall or garden, why not rent a public park? That's what you can do at the site of the Stone Mansion.

The Stone Mansion lies on a fourteen-acre lot that includes woods, a playground, a picnic pavilion, tennis courts, and grounds. Although this is a county park, the gates will be closed to the public if you rent the mansion and outside areas.

Of course, you can rent the mansion by itself, if you want. Commodore Walter Brooke built this house in 1777 and settled here, on his four-hundred-acre plantation, following his service in the Virginia navy. The large dwelling is now thoroughly modern inside, and its first-floor rooms are for rent. There's a spacious entry area, a lounge featuring an 1872 rectangular grand piano, a buffet/meeting room, and a kitchen. The rooms hold folding tables and chairs.

CAPACITY
Reception: 75

Banquet: 50
Lawn party: 150 with canopy
Meeting: 35

LOCATION

The Stone Mansion is five miles south of Old Town Alexandria. From the Beltway (I-495), take Exit 2S (Telegraph Road) south one mile to a left on the Parkway, which becomes Stoneybrooke Lane after crossing South Kings Highway. Stone Mansion is in Stoneybrooke Park, on the left one block past South Kings Highway.

FOOD/BEVERAGE

You may choose your own caterer as long as the caterer provides a business license, health department certificate, and proof of insurance.

LIMITATIONS/RESTRICTIONS

Smoking is prohibited. Consumption of alcohol is allowed inside the mansion and outside, on its immediate grounds. Bar service must stay inside.

LEAD TIME FOR RESERVATIONS

Call up to one year in advance.

RATES

Weekday business functions cost $350 for four hours and $475 for eight hours, with a $50-per-hour overtime charge. Rates for social functions are $700 for Fairfax County residents and $900 for all others, with a $125 overtime charge for every hour beyond the base five-hour period. A $100 alcohol use fee is required, as is a $300, refundable security deposit.

FACILITIES FOR THE PHYSICALLY DISABLED? Yes

STRONG MANSION

Stronghold Inc.
Sugarloaf Mountain
Dickerson, MD 20842
301/869-7846 (metro area), 301/874-2024 (Frederick)

A dream house in the mountains

When you call for directions to the Strong Mansion, the building superintendent first asks whether you know how to get to "the mountain." This should tell you, if you haven't already guessed, that the estate is at a small remove from Washington. If you're of the opinion that getting there is half the fun and, on top of that, if the day of your event should turn out to be fine and sunny, then you couldn't ask for anything more than this ride though the country that ends up at Strong Mansion.

You'll notice as you pull up to Strong that it's built into a hill. That hill is really the base of said mountain, Sugarloaf by name. Although rental of the mansion entitles you to roam all of its three floors and the grounds, your function will center in the two large and beautiful rooms at the back of the house, both of which open onto the exquisitely landscaped mountainside lawn.

There's the first-floor dining room, magnificent with paneled walls and a teak floor. The room has all the right touches: antique candelabras, gold-framed mirrors, and corner hutches displaying delicate old china. Only stand-up buffets are allowed in the mansion, but you may carry your food outside and sit on chairs set up on the lawn. This peaceful setting presents you with a view of a gazebo, reflecting pool, lily pond, and lots and lots of trees.

On the second floor is the stunning ballroom, which measures twenty-two by sixty feet. The ceiling is sixteen feet high. At one end of the room lies a grand piano, a Hammond organ, and space for dancing; at the other end is a comfortable arrangement of sofas and chairs. Full-length, French casement windows topped by fanlights line the walls.

If you take a walk through the rest of the house, you'll find that most of the other rooms are bedrooms, all furnished with antiques. Strong Mansion was the dream house of a Chicago tycoon named Gordon Strong. He bought Sugarloaf Mountain and started building the mansion in 1912. By the time he died in 1954, only a third of his planned mansion had been completed—the part that stands today.

CAPACITY
Reception: 150
Garden party: 150

LOCATION
About forty miles from the center of Washington. From the Beltway (I-495), take Exit 22 (Hyattstown/Barnesville) off I-270 and head south on Route 109 toward Barnesville. Take a right on Route 95 and follow the road to the mansion. For a more scenic route, follow River Road in northwest Washington all the way to Route 190; take Route 190 past Seneca to Route 109; follow Route 109 to a left on Route 28 and then a right on Route 95.

FOOD/BEVERAGE
You arrange your own catering and bar service. The mansion's commercial kitchen is newly renovated.

LIMITATIONS/RESTRICTIONS
The house is not air-conditioned. You must supply your own tables and chairs. Smoking is prohibited inside.

LEAD TIME FOR RESERVATIONS
Nine to twelve months is recommended, but call for availability. The mansion rents a year in advance for May, June, September, and October, its peak months.

RATES
A flat fee of $1,500 entitles you to use of the whole house for a seven-hour period between 10:00 A.M. and 9:00 P.M.

FACILITIES FOR THE PHYSICALLY DISABLED? Yes

THE TEXTILE MUSEUM

2320 S Street, NW
Washington, DC 20008
202/667-0441
www.textilemuseum.org

Historic houses, historic textiles

Join two mansions together, one designed by the architect of the Jefferson Memorial, John Russell Pope, and the other designed by the architect of the Woodrow Wilson House, Waddy Wood, and what do you have? The answer is the elegant structure that houses the Textile Museum. In terms of reception space, what you have are two rooms and the hall on the first floor of the Pope building, the galleries in the Waddy Wood building, and the combined garden areas of both buildings.

From the museum's grand entrance, in the Pope building, you step directly into the marvelous black-and-white, marble-floored foyer. Flanking the hall at the back of the house are the Myers Room and the Garrett Room. Each is paneled in dark wood and has a fireplace and great furnishings from sixteenth-, seventeenth-, and eighteenth-century Europe. The rooms and foyer open onto the garden through French doors.

The delightful garden features a pebbled path, a fountain sculpture, a large greensward behind the adjoining mansion, boxwoods, magnolias, and a small shaded pavilion.

The Textile Museum, which celebrated its seventy-fifth anniversary in the year 2000, rotates exhibits of historic and handmade textiles and carpets from South America, India, China, Indonesia, Africa, Southeast Asia, and the Middle East. The Pope mansion was originally the home of George Hewitt Myers, who founded the Textile Museum in 1925.

CAPACITY

Reception: 150
Banquet: 50

LOCATION
One block from Embassy Row (Massachusetts Avenue), a fifteen-minute walk from the Dupont Circle Metro station at Q Street, NW.

FOOD/BEVERAGE
The museum must approve your caterer. A kitchen is available for warming and cooling foods.

LIMITATIONS/RESTRICTIONS
The museum is available year-round but does not allow fund-raisers, wedding receptions, or weddings. Smoking, plants, and red wine are prohibited inside. Amplified music is prohibited outside after 9 P.M.

LEAD TIME FOR RESERVATIONS
At least one month, but call for availability.

RATES
Expect to pay $2,500 for a five-hour reception after 5:00 P.M. and $3,000 for a five-hour sit-down banquet after 5:00 P.M. For either type of function, each additional hour costs $250. Meeting space in the museum between 9:00 A.M. and 5:00 P.M. costs $100 per hour.

FACILITIES FOR THE PHYSICALLY DISABLED? Some
There is an elevator at a ground-floor side entrance.

THOMAS LAW HOUSE
429 N Street, SW
Washington, DC 20024
202/554-4844
www.tiberisland.com

Given the importance of the Potomac River to Washington's history, you'd think there would be many eighteenth-century houses still standing along the waterfront, but there aren't. The Thomas Law House is one exception. Built in 1784, this was once the home of Martha Washington's granddaughter.

It sits back on a wide green lawn, a lone but handsome example of Federal architecture. Entering through the elegant, fanlight-topped door, you find yourself in a great center hall, off which lie two rooms, one of which was once a bedroom, the other the main parlor. Both are now suitable for meetings and stand-up receptions. Second-floor rooms include one that leads to a terrace, where you have a wonderful view of the Potomac and the Washington Monument. A modern room on the third floor is available for meetings.

Each of the rooms bears some distinguishing feature that you seldom see anymore: intricate crown molding, black marble Greek Revival fireplaces, rounded inset windows. The rooms have been painted in colors thought to represent the tastes of the period.

The Thomas Law House is part of the Tiber Island Cooperative Homes complex in southwest Washington.

CAPACITY

Reception: 150
Meeting: 40 to 50 in one room

LOCATION

The Thomas Law House lies above the parking lot and across from the pier for the *Spirit of Washington* cruise boat, off the cul-de-sac at the end of Water Street, SW. From Maine Avenue, turn right on 7th Street, then left on Water Street. Follow Water Street to the cul-de-sac.

FOOD/BEVERAGE

You may choose your own caterer.

LIMITATIONS/RESTRICTIONS

The house is available for stand-up receptions and meetings but not for banquets or outdoor functions. Dancing is permitted; amplified music and smoking are not.

LEAD TIME FOR RESERVATIONS

Call for availability.

RATES

Receptions run $1,250 for five hours. Call for meeting rates.

FACILITIES FOR THE PHYSICALLY DISABLED? No

TOP OF THE TOWN

1400 North 14th Street
Arlington, VA 22209
703/387-8696
www.topofthetown.net

The best view in town

Situated in the penthouse of a condominium building called Prospect House, this one-room hall offers the best view in town—a sweeping vista that extends past the Mormon Temple in Kensington, Maryland, to the north, and beyond the Masonic Temple in Alexandria, Virginia, to the south. But front and center, seen through a wall of twelve-foot-high windows and from the terrace, are Washington's main attractions: the Jefferson and Lincoln Memorials, the Washington Monument, the Capitol, the Potomac River, and more. The room itself—with chandeliers, carpeted floor, expandable dance floor, and state-of-the-art sound system—is fine, but the view is everything.

Top of the Town has its own elevator, separate from the one used by residents of Prospect House condominiums. This elevator takes you to a marble foyer and hall, which lead, in turn, to the great room.

CAPACITY
Reception or banquet: 180

LOCATION
Top of the Town is located one block west of the Iwo Jima Memorial, within walking distance of the Rosslyn Metro station. The site has its own private parking lot.

FOOD/BEVERAGE
The staff prefers that you choose from the site's list of approved caterers.

LIMITATIONS/RESTRICTIONS
Top of the Town is available daily from 7:00 P.M. to 11:00 P.M., with additional time available Saturday and Sunday from 1:00 P.M. to 5:00 P.M. You may reserve the site weekdays by special arrangement. Live music is allowed on Friday night, Saturday day or night, and Sunday during the day; recorded music is allowed at other times.

LEAD TIME FOR RESERVATIONS
Call for availability.

RATES
Rates range from $1,700 (Monday through Wednesday nights) to $3,900 (Saturday nights). These fees cover a four-hour period; $500 is charged for each additional hour, except on Friday and Saturday nights after 11:00 P.M., when $1,500 is charged for each additional hour.

FACILITIES FOR THE PHYSICALLY DISABLED? Yes

TORPEDO FACTORY ART CENTER

105 North Union Street
Alexandria, VA 22314
703/838-4199
703/838-0088 (fax)
www.torpedofactory.org
torpedofactoryrentals@juno.com

An artful site on the waterfront

What do you do with a torpedo factory when there's no longer a need for torpedoes? Turn it into a center where artists can work, exhibit, and sell their art—what else?

Built in 1918 to manufacture torpedo shell casings, this large three-story building retains its factory identity, at least in daylight. Exposed pipes, ductwork, and smokestack still stand; bright yellow lighting fixtures are industrial-style, and the walls and mushroom-shaped columns are painted a plain white.

At night, though, the factory takes a magical turn. Spot lighting in the studios replaces fluorescent lighting and draws attention to the artwork. Flowers, music, and good food add their own lively punches.

The intriguing thing about the Torpedo Factory is that its austere design acts as a perfect foil for the rich assortment of arts and crafts displayed in the eighty-three studios and five cooperative galleries housed here. Through the windows of these artists' spaces you'll see work in many forms, including painting, ceramics, sculpture, weaving, jewelry, and glasswork.

You can rent the first floor or the entire building for after-hours events. A balcony that encircles the two-story atrium overlooks the main hall, which is crossed by two catwalks. Whatever space you rent, you're free to stroll out to the enchanting deck area and brick terraces behind the center, where you'll discover yourself face-to-face with the Potomac River.

CAPACITY

Reception: 770 on the first floor, 1,000 in the entire building, 1,300 with one
    tent, 1,450 with two tents
Banquet: 220 on the main floor, 300 in the entire building, 450 with one tent,
    525 with two tents
Theater: 400 on the main floor

LOCATION

Seven miles from the US Capitol, fronting the Potomac River in Old Town Alexandria. Head south on George Washington Memorial Parkway (Washington Street within Alexandria city limits), turn left on King Street, and turn left again on Union Street. The art center will be on your right.

FOOD/BEVERAGE

You choose a caterer from the site's approved list. A small, fully equipped kitchen is available. You must obtain liability insurance.

LIMITATIONS/RESTRICTIONS

The Torpedo Factory is available daily from 5 P.M. to 1 A.M. Hours of use include setup and cleanup. Caterers have access to the kitchen beginning at 4 P.M. Terraces are available for tented events during the day. The center requires and arranges for a security officer and staff person to be present during events.

Smoking is not permitted inside. Alcohol is permitted inside the center and under the tents but not on the outside deck. Red wine may be served only at seated functions. Frying food in hot oil is prohibited, as are open fires used in grilling. No rice, glitter, or confetti is allowed inside the factory.

LEAD TIME FOR RESERVATIONS

Allow six months to a year to reserve the Torpedo Factory for an event taking place around Christmas or during April or May; allow several weeks to reserve the site at other times of the year.

RATES

The Torpedo Factory charges the following flat rates: main floor, $2,000; first and second floors, $2,500; all three floors, $3,000; bricked terraces, $750. A refundable security deposit of $500 is required.

FACILITIES FOR THE PHYSICALLY DISABLED? Yes

WASHINGTON ETHICAL SOCIETY

7750 16th Street, NW
Washington, DC 20012
202/882-6650, ext. 37
www.ethicalsociety.org

Although less grand than its residential neighbors, the Washington Ethical Society's headquarters might dovetail with your requirements just the same—especially if you're looking for a large space at low cost.

It's nothing fancy, but the ivy-covered concrete building holds a hall whose two side walls are all windows overlooking a small but pretty garden area and neighborhood houses and yards. The hall has a good-sized stage with a baby grand piano at its center, wall-to-wall, white-flecked burgundy carpeting, a generously sized entryway, and a high ceiling. Downstairs are a kitchen and a classroom; outside, a modest-sized garden spot.

CAPACITY
Reception: 200
Banquet: 175
Meeting: 200 in the main hall, 40 in the classroom

LOCATION
About four miles up 16th Street from the White House, almost to Silver Spring.

FOOD/BEVERAGE
You choose your own caterer. The kitchen holds a fridge, double stoves, a sink, and limited counter space. The site provides two hundred chairs and twelve six-foot-long tables.

LIMITATIONS/RESTRICTIONS
The hall is available evenings from 4:00 P.M. to 11:00 P.M. on weekdays and from 4:00 P.M. to midnight on weekends. Parking on the premises is limited, so count on parking on the street. You must rent a dance floor if your event includes dancing. Alcohol is restricted to beer, wine, and champagne. Smoking is prohibited inside.

LEAD TIME FOR RESERVATIONS
Call for availability.

RATES

Rates range from $250 to $450 for four hours, depending upon the number of guests. A security deposit of $150 is required to book your reservation.

FACILITIES FOR THE PHYSICALLY DISABLED? Some

There is a ramp into the building, but the bathrooms are not wheelchair accessible.

WASHINGTON VERY SPECIAL ARTS GALLERY

1100 16th Street, NW
Washington, DC 20036
202/296-9100
202/261-0200 (fax)
202/261-0201 (TTY)
www.wvsarts.org

Renovated mansion features very special art for very special events

A century-old mansion at the corner of 16th and L Streets, NW, just a couple of blocks from the White House, is the headquarters for the nonprofit organization Washington Very Special Arts, which rents its space for functions. First-floor areas include a foyer with marble fireplace; the nine-hundred-square-foot, well-lit art gallery, whose gray walls are hung with original works by disabled artists; and an art studio with bandstand. Upstairs rooms include a conference room with crown molding, a fireplace, and French doors overlooking 16th Street and a mahogany-paneled library with another fireplace and stained-glass windows. Both floors are equipped with a sound system that you may use during your function, and hardwood floors on both levels make this a great choice for events that include dancing.

CAPACITY

Reception: 125
Banquet: 50 to 75
Conference: 15 to 20

LOCATION

At the corner of 16th and L Streets, NW, a short walk from the White House and downtown attractions. Parking is on the street and at nearby garages.

FOOD/BEVERAGE

You may choose your own caterer. An art studio on the first floor is available as a staging/prep area for caterers' use.

LIMITATIONS/RESTRICTIONS

The building is available year-round on weekday evenings and on Saturday and Sunday. Smoking is prohibited.

LEAD TIME FOR RESERVATIONS

Call for availability.

RATES

Rates start at $250 for the conference room, $300 for the studio workshop, and $750 for the gallery.

FACILITIES FOR THE PHYSICALLY DISABLED? Yes

WOODEND

8940 Jones Mill Road
Chevy Chase, MD 20815
301/652-9188, ext. 38
www.audubonnaturalist.org (then click on Woodend Rentals)

A stately mansion and wildlife haven

Would you like your group to escape far from the madding crowd? Take refuge in a wildlife refuge. At Woodend, you can commune with nature as well as with each other.

J.R. SCHROEDER

Woodend's stately, redbrick mansion is headquarters for the Audubon Naturalist Society, which operates the estate as a wildlife sanctuary and nature education center. Forty acres of woods, fields, and lawns; twenty-nine species of birds; and all manner of small mammals await those who venture on the nature trails. The hemlock grove provides a dramatic setting for outdoor ceremonies. Sweeping lawns overlook wildflower meadows and towering trees.

If you prefer to gather indoors, the mansion's first-floor rooms satisfy a variety of purposes. All three rooms boast high ceilings, elegant carved fireplaces, and pegged hardwood floors. The Great Hall is a large and open reception area. Three sets of French doors line one wall and open to a stone terrace with a custom-made canopy. A small alcove under the staircase is an ideal spot for setting up a band or refreshment station. Two smaller rooms adjoin the hall: a dining room and a meeting room that leads through French doors to a portico.

If you find yourself admiring the fine design inside and out of the Woodend mansion, there's a reason. Jefferson Memorial architect John Russell Pope designed the house in the 1920s for Capt. Chester Wells, a US naval officer, and his wife, an Australian heiress. The mansion and gardens copy those of Mrs. Wells's family estate in Australia.

CAPACITY

Reception: 125 inside (without terrace), 170 with the canopied terrace

Banquet: 90 inside (without terrace), 170 with the canopied terrace

Garden party: 170 with the canopied terrace

Daytime meeting: 28

LOCATION

From the Beltway (I-495), take the Connecticut Avenue exit south toward Chevy Chase. Turn left on Manor Drive, right on Jones Bridge Road, and left on Jones Mill Road.

FOOD/BEVERAGE

Woodend provides an approved list of caterers. You may make your own beverage arrangements.

LIMITATIONS/RESTRICTIONS

Smoking is prohibited in the mansion. Music and dancing are permitted. Electronic amplification is not permitted outside.

LEAD TIME FOR RESERVATIONS

Call for availability.

RATES

The site prefers that you call for rates, which cover the use of the first floor, canopy-covered terrace, and grounds for an eight-hour period, including setup and cleanup time.

FACILITIES FOR THE PHYSICALLY DISABLED? Yes

Sites for
200 to 500 people

AIRLIE CENTER
Airlie Conference Center
6809 Airlie Road
Warrenton, VA 20187
540/347-1300 or 800/288-9573
540/347-5957 (fax)
www.airlie.com

An island of thought

You have to travel a ways to get here, and that's intentional. In 1959, Dr. Murdock Head founded the nonprofit educational and communication organization known as Airlie Foundation and created Airlie Center. His purpose was to offer conference participants a place free from city distractions and conducive to contemplation—in other words, a veritable "island of thought," as *Life* magazine once called it.

Airlie Center is a beautiful, three-thousand-acre, countryside retreat in the foothills of the Blue Ridge Mountains. The focal point of the center is Airlie House. This elegant, Georgian Revival mansion contains most of the conference rooms, the large banquet hall with its huge picture window, and the administrative offices. A formal garden that lies adjacent to Airlie House and features boxwoods, seasonal plantings, and gazebo provides a lovely setting for a cocktail reception. In an adjoining tree-shaded garden lies a large pavilion (it can accommodate two hundred for a sit-down dinner) overlooking a lake.

Within a minute's walk of Airlie House are the sleeping lodges and quaint VIP guest cottages. Each has its own private bath and additional meeting rooms, and some have working fireplaces.

Airlie's amenities cater to a multitude of needs and interests, among them tennis, swimming, fishing, and hiking. Also at the ready are a sauna and exercise

room, the Whistling Swan Pub for socializing, and the Game Room for friendly contests of billiards or darts.

Airlie Center's latest addition is a twenty-one-workstation computer lab, which facilitates computer training and especially group dynamics in decision-making and consensus-building sessions.

CAPACITY

Reception: 250

Banquet: 200

Garden party: 250

Meeting: 225 theater-style

Lodging: 142 rooms, including some suites

LOCATION

From the Beltway (I-495), take the Route 66 west exit and follow Route 66 to Exit 43A (Gainsville/Warrenton), turning onto Route 29 south toward Warrenton. Go about ten miles on Route 29 until you see the sign for Airlie. Turn right onto Route 605 (Colonial Road, which turns into Airlie Road) and proceed 2.3 miles to the main gate, on the left immediately after a stone bridge. It is possible to fly directly to Airlie—the center has its own 3,250-foot, paved airstrip.

FOOD/BEVERAGE

Airlie Center handles all food and beverage services, including cookouts. The menus tend toward foods that are native to Virginia. Unless you're having a cookout or make some other special arrangement, you eat all three meals in the main dining room.

LIMITATIONS/RESTRICTIONS

Children and pets are not allowed.

LEAD TIME FOR RESERVATIONS

Eight to twelve months, but call for availability.

RATES

Overnight stays run $200 to $240 single occupancy for the complete meeting package, which includes lodging, three meals, two coffee breaks, and use of the conference facilities and standard audiovisual equipment. Day guests are charged $85 for lunch and $115 for lunch and dinner. These rates cover coffee breaks and full-day use of the conference facilities, as well as meals. A half-day meeting with lunch package is available for $32 per person.

FACILITIES FOR THE PHYSICALLY DISABLED? Yes

Airlie House has an elevator, handicapped-accessible rest rooms, three overnight rooms equipped for the disabled, and other structural features designed to provide easy access.

AMERICAN SOCIETY OF ASSOCIATION EXECUTIVES (ASAE) CONFERENCE AND TELEMARKETING CENTER

1575 I Street, NW
Washington, DC 20005-1168
202/626-2799
202/842-1145 (fax)

Confer, then confabulate

You might think something called a conference center would be a place to do business only. But you'd be wrong. Tucked inside the ASAE building in the heart of Washington is a sort of gathering ground for the conference-bound. One minute you're discussing business, the next you're convening for cocktails—all without leaving the room in this comfortable but professional meeting facility.

Three lobby-level rooms make up the center. Each supplies all the technological tools you need to conduct business in the most sophisticated fashion, from audiovisual equipment to telemarketing facilities to videotape machines. The tone set by the center's furnishings makes getting down to business a relaxing proposition.

When you're ready for that break, voilà! You simply pull back the middle dividers to join the three rooms. If you're ready for an even bigger break, just step outside. The ASAE building is only minutes away from the White House, museums, restaurants, and other city sights.

Also available in the building is a twelfth-floor boardroom with high-tech accoutrements and cherry furnishings.

CAPACITY
Reception: 300
Banquet: 200
Meeting: 20 to 25 in the twelfth-floor boardroom

LOCATION
Three blocks from the White House, across the street from the McPherson Square Metro station.

FOOD/BEVERAGE
ASAE handles all rentals and catering. A new, fully equipped commercial kitchen is next to the lobby-level boardroom.

LIMITATIONS/RESTRICTIONS
There are no specific limitations; discuss your requests with management.

132

LEAD TIME FOR RESERVATIONS

One week to one month, but call for availability.

RATES

Rentals run from $400 to $650, depending on whether you're a member of
ASAE.

FACILITIES FOR THE PHYSICALLY DISABLED? Yes

ARTS CLUB OF WASHINGTON

2017 I Street, NW
Washington, DC 20006
202/331-7282, ext. 20

A city site with surprising features

So maybe you think your organization is asking for the moon. You say they
want to hold their function at a historic home in downtown Washington, one
that has a garden and a ballroom, plenty of art and atmosphere? Consider the
Arts Club of Washington.

Located just a few blocks from both the White House and Georgetown, the
club occupies two connecting nineteenth-century town houses. Sure enough,
there's a ballroom, and it has a stage, a Steinway piano, and great wooden doors
opening to the street. Also on the main floor are two elegant banquet rooms
furnished with antiques and Waterford chandeliers. French doors in the back
banquet room lead to a beautiful patio surrounded by a sculpture garden. This
space is surprisingly large and private.

The cozy library and cheerful drawing rooms on the second floor are
pleasant places in which to call a meeting to order or to take tea and make
conversation. There's also an informal meeting place in the dark and mysterious
basement, which is equipped with a setup bar (minus the liquor) and ice cream
parlor chairs and tables.

You'll want to explore all these rooms for several reasons. First of all, the entire property is an art gallery featuring the work of Washington artists. Second, the site is historic. James Monroe lived here in 1817 while he waited for the White House to be renovated following its partial destruction during the War of 1812.

Finally, it's fun. The way the two houses merge is charming. Just when you think you've seen it all you come upon an unnoticed set of stairs that leads to still another level, a door that leads to a balcony, or a hall that leads to who knows where. The Arts Club is a wonderful place to wander.

CAPACITY
Reception: 150 in the house alone, 300 in the house and garden
Banquet: 150 in the house alone
Garden party: 150
Meeting: 25 to 100

LOCATION
Just off Pennsylvania Avenue in downtown Washington, a few blocks west of the White House and east of Georgetown. You can park on the street or in nearby parking garages.

FOOD/BEVERAGE
The Arts Club caters all functions and will work with you to plan your event.

LIMITATIONS/RESTRICTIONS
Music in the house must end by midnight; in the garden, by 11:00 P.M. Red wine is prohibited on the second floor, and smoking is prohibited in the house.

LEAD TIME FOR RESERVATIONS
Eight months to a year for weekend functions and two to three months for functions during the week.

RATES
The club rents for $500 to $2,200, depending upon the day of the week.

FACILITIES FOR THE PHYSICALLY DISABLED? No

THE ATRIUM AT MEADOWLARK GARDENS
9750 Meadowlark Gardens Court
Vienna, VA 22182
703/255-3631, ext. 304

For garden parties, whether in May or December

The Atrium is such a popular wedding site and its weekends booked so far in advance that couples often hold their weddings here on weekdays. The Northern Virginia Regional Park Authority, which owns and operates the Atrium, must be delighted at its success, since the fees you pay to rent the site go not just toward the upkeep of the building, but for caretaking of the spectacular ninety-five-acre Meadowlark Gardens, in which the Atrium resides.

As its name implies, the Atrium is a light-filled space whose main area, the Garden Room, has three walls of windows, a cathedral ceiling, and a two-thousand-square-foot skylight. Plants and potted trees and flowers are everywhere. A little footbridge bends over an indoor stream. Great glass doors lead to a landscaped terrace and to the woodlands and garden beyond. You and your guests are welcome to wander the paved trails through woods, fields, and gardens. If a certain plant or flower catches your eye, you can find out what it is, for everything is labeled. Scattered throughout the grounds are three gazebos, which offer stunning locations for wedding ceremonies.

Though Meadowlark Gardens is located near the Dulles Airport Access Road, you'd never know it. This is a serene and beautiful spot.

Two smaller rooms complete the Atrium: the Iris Room, which opens into the Garden Room and serves well as a space for bar or buffet setups, and the Lilac Room, which often serves as the bride's lounge.

CAPACITY

Reception: 300 using the Atrium and terrace, 230 in the Garden Room with terrace, 80 using just the Iris Room

Banquet: 170 using the Atrium and terrace, 120 in the Garden Room and terrace, 50 in the Iris Room

Meeting: 200

LOCATION

From the Beltway (I-495), take Exit 10B onto Route 7 toward Tysons Corner. Drive five miles west on Route 7, turn left onto Beulah Road, and drive one mile to the park entrance on the right.

FOOD/BEVERAGE

You may choose your own caterer. A preparation kitchen is available.

LIMITATIONS/RESTRICTIONS

Events must end by 1:00 A.M. on Fridays and Saturdays and by 11:00 P.M. on Sunday (except on the eve of a holiday) through Thursday. You may rent a gazebo by itself or in conjunction with the rental of the Atrium. The Iris Room is available on its own, but the Lilac Room is not. The Garden Room by itself is not available on Saturday. The Atrium is available for meetings Monday through Thursday until 4:00 P.M. and Friday until 3:00 P.M., for up to eight hours.

LEAD TIME FOR RESERVATIONS

Call at least one year in advance to reserve the Atrium for a weekend wedding. For other kinds of events and other time frames, allow at least one month.

RATES

Social events: Rates range from $500 for four hours' use of the Iris Room Monday through Thursday to $5,000 for eight hours' use of the entire Atrium, with each additional hour billed at $550 per hour. Tables, chairs, two portable bars, and a dance floor are included. The specified rental period includes setup and cleanup time.

Meetings: Rates range from $200 for use of the Iris Room to $650 for use of the Atrium.

FACILITIES FOR THE PHYSICALLY DISABLED? Yes

THE BALLROOM
5521 Landy Lane
Bethesda, MD 20816
301/913-9810

A private dance studio available for weddings and other special events

Just off busy River Road lies this classic ballroom. The exterior of the building is quite plain, but inside is a suite of elegant rooms, including a handsome reception room set off by columns and the huge ballroom.

If you are looking for a site that can accommodate a large number of people seated all in one room, with space for dancing, consider the Ballroom. Its eighty-eight-by-fifty-two-foot hardwood floor is cushioned underneath to keep guests light on their feet. Waterford chandeliers and sconces light up the main room, the adjoining reception room with fireplace, a circular foyer, and a dining room. The Ballroom also boasts a completely integrated sound system.

CAPACITY
Reception: 300
Banquet: 250

LOCATION
From Washington, go north on Massachusetts Avenue, NW, continuing through Westmoreland Circle. Turn right onto Little Falls Parkway and left at the next light, onto River Road. At the third street, turn right onto Landy Lane. The Ballroom is the first building on the right.

FOOD/BEVERAGE

Site management prefers that you choose from a list of approved caterers. Caterers may use the prep kitchen for warming foods but not for cooking.

LIMITATIONS/RESTRICTIONS

The Ballroom is available daily, with weekday events ending no later than 11:30 P.M. and weekend events ending by 1:30 A.M. Smoking is not permitted. Red wine, cranberry juice, and tomato juice are permitted only at seated meals in the ballroom.

On weekends and after 6:30 P.M. on weekdays, there are 163 parking spaces available.

LEAD TIME FOR RESERVATIONS

Call for availability.

RATES

Weekday rentals run $270 per hour, with a minimum of three hours. For Monday through Thursday nights after 7:00 P.M., expect to pay a flat fee of $2,200; on Friday nights after 7:00 P.M., $4,000. On Saturdays, Sundays, and holidays, the Ballroom rents at a flat rate of $4,000 for eight hours, plus $420 per hour overtime.

FACILITIES FOR THE PHYSICALLY DISABLED? Yes

THE BARNS OF WOLF TRAP

1635 Trap Road
Vienna, VA 22182
703/938-8463
703/255-1896 (fax)
www.wolf-trap.org

If you think about it, you'll realize that a barn just happens to meet many of the requirements for a successful event: it's usually roomy, it's got atmosphere, and you can use it for a variety of purposes. Yeah, you say, but isn't it a little primitive?

Not these barns. There are two of them—the German Barn, dating from 1725, and the English Barn, dating from the 1790s. Both barns are from farms in New York state that were dismantled and reconstructed at Wolf Trap in 1981. The barns were rebuilt using eighteenth-century techniques, so their interiors present you with weathered boarding, hand-cut timbers, oak floors, and pleasant reminders of days gone by.

But just as care has been taken to preserve the beauty of these structures, care has been taken to incorporate modern features for your total convenience. The German Barn is also a theater and has a stage and a balcony with fixed seating. The adjoining English Barn is a little smaller and features a fully equipped, beam-enclosed bar. A lobby next to the English Barn provides additional space.

You can rent one or both barns for any function, from presentations to cocktail parties to black-tie affairs. Included in the rental of either barn, weather permitting, is the use of an open courtyard that abuts both barns.

Down the road from the Barns is the Wolf Trap Filene Center, Washington's summer showplace for concerts, ballets, operas, and other performances. The Filene Center is an outdoor amphitheater surrounded by rolling hills and trees. If you're booking the Barns for business, why not check out the Filene Center's schedule, which runs from late May to mid-September? You might find that Mary Chapin Carpenter, the Kirov Ballet, or perhaps the National Symphony Orchestra is performing the day of your function. If your group wants to attend the show after wrapping up business, contact Group Sales (see How to Book Group Seating for Theater Performances, page 316). Consider purchasing lawn tickets rather than pavilion seats. That way, you can pack a picnic, including champagne, and savor the experience in true Washington fashion.

CAPACITY

Reception: 350 using both barns

Banquet: 220 using both barns

Meeting: 350 using both barns

LOCATION

The Barns are located twelve miles from Dulles Airport and only a few minutes from Tysons Corner. From either the Beltway (I-495) or Route 66, take Route 7 west four miles and turn left on Towlston Road; go 2.5 miles to the Barns, on the left.

FOOD/BEVERAGE

You may hire your own caterer, subject to staff approval, or choose one from Wolf Trap's suggested list. Wolf Trap furnishes all alcohol and bartenders. The site includes a serving kitchen.

LIMITATIONS/RESTRICTIONS

Smoking is prohibited in the Barns. Parking is limited.

LEAD TIME FOR RESERVATIONS

The Barns are available year-round, subject to Wolf Trap's performance schedule. May, June, September, and October are the most popular months, and weekdays are easiest to reserve. Allow at least nine months.

RATES

Weekday meetings: $60 to $150 per hour

Parties: $1,200 (for the English Barn) to $2,000 (for both barns), with a six-hour minimum. Overtime charges run from $125 per hour for the use of the English Barn to $180 per hour for the use of both barns.

FACILITIES FOR THE PHYSICALLY DISABLED? Yes

BRISTOW MANOR

11507 Valley View Drive
Bristow, VA 20136
703/368-3558, ext. 2
www.bristowmanor.com

Southern mansion on the green

The sparkling white Bristow mansion stands at the forefront of an emerald green golf course, and together they make a pretty good setting for a party.

Bristow Manor's one-hundred-year-old façade, fronted by a two-story-high columned portico, is what you see as you approach the property. The house overlooks the first, ninth, and eighteenth holes of the Bristow Manor Golf Club, at which you can play a round, in coordination with your function, as long as you've booked your game in advance.

The interior of the Colonial Revival mansion includes a ballroom, a large front hall, and a front parlor that extends through a dining room to a bar area. Special features include floor-to-ceiling windows—and many of them; fourteen-foot-high ceilings; huge mirrors; original hardwood floors; and great doorways. Upstairs are rooms that may be used for meetings. A large pavilion on the grounds is perfect for outdoor functions and for catching the overflow from parties inside.

CAPACITY

Reception: 150 inside; 250 inside and out, using the pavilion
Banquet: 125 throughout the first floor; 250 inside and out, using the pavilion

LOCATION

From the Beltway (I-495), take I-66 west to Exit 44, Route 234 south. Proceed approximately .4 mile and exit onto Route 28 south, Nokesville Road. Go about 2 miles and turn left at the light, onto Route 19, Bristow Road. Go about 1.5 miles and turn right onto Route 611, Valley View Drive; continue to the manor, on the left. An adjacent lot offers plenty of parking.

FOOD/BEVERAGE

The golf club handles all food and beverage arrangements and provides tables, chairs, china, and other items.

LIMITATIONS/RESTRICTIONS

The site is available year-round, all day long. Dancing is permitted only on the dance floor, which the manor provides. Smoking and open flame candles are not permitted in the house.

LEAD TIME FOR RESERVATIONS

Call nine to twelve months ahead for peak times—spring, summer, and early fall.

RATES

Rates vary from $500 to $1,595, depending upon the day of the week and the time of year. Catering rates average $18 to $38 per person. A refundable security deposit of half the rental fee is required.

FACILITIES FOR THE PHYSICALLY DISABLED? Some

The first floor is wheelchair accessible.

BROOKSIDE GARDENS

1800 Glenallan Avenue
Wheaton, MD 20902
301/962-1404
www.mncppc.org

Delightful places to party within fifty acres of gardens

You can exchange vows in the wedding gazebo, which is strewn with hanging baskets of greenery, then stroll down the holly tree lane to hold your reception in the balmy, flower-filled conservatory. Or maybe you'll choose the fragrance garden, which has its own Victorian-style gazebo, as well as fountains, scented flowers, and herbs. You have many options at Brookside Gardens.

Long available for wedding ceremonies, the site now allows wedding receptions, as well as other kinds of parties, throughout its grounds. Besides the conservatory, fragrance garden, and gazebos, the property has lawns available for tenting; a Japanese teahouse, which overlooks hills, ponds, and trees and is good for small parties; and—its newest offering—a reception hall, built specifically to accommodate the many fans of Brookside Gardens who recognize the place as a kind of paradise and the perfect setting for a celebration. The reception hall lies inside the visitor center and overlooks the azalea garden and aquatic ponds.

The Maryland-National Capital Park and Planning Commission, Department of Parks and Planning in Montgomery County, owns and operates Brookside Gardens.

CAPACITY

Reception: 50 in the teahouse, 125 in the conservatory, 150 in the fragrance garden, 175 in the reception hall, 250 on a tented lawn

Banquet: 20 in the teahouse, 125 in the fragrance garden, 125 in the reception hall, 250 on a tented lawn

LOCATION

Brookside Gardens lies within Wheaton Regional Park. From the Beltway (I-495), take the exit for Route 97, Georgia Avenue north. Follow Georgia Avenue three miles to Randolph Road, where you turn right. Follow Randolph to Glenallan Road and turn right; then turn right again into Brookside Gardens.

FOOD/BEVERAGE

You must choose an approved caterer from the site's list. A small warming kitchen is available in the reception hall. Hard liquor and distilled spirits are not permitted.

LIMITATIONS/RESTRICTIONS

The sites at Brookside Gardens are available daily, except December 25. You may be required to rent a tent for outdoor events. One hundred parking spaces are available.

Brookside Gardens does not close to the public when you have a private function here.

LEAD TIME FOR RESERVATIONS

The staff recommends that you call at least six months in advance to reserve a site.

RATES

Rates start at $350 for a one-hour ceremony in the gazebo and at $2,000 for a seven-hour event in the reception hall. Call for more exact information, including the hours available at each location in the gardens.

FACILITIES FOR THE PHYSICALLY DISABLED? Yes

CAPITOL HILL CLUB
300 1st Street, SE
Washington, DC 20003
202/484-4590
www.capitolhillclub.com

Republicans' hangout on the Hill

You'd never guess that John Wayne and Winston Churchill had anything in common, but they both were once members of the Capitol Hill Club. So were Dwight D. Eisenhower, Spiro T. Agnew, and Gene Autry. In fact, the fifty-year-old club welcomes as a member anyone who has dealings on the Hill.

To rent the club for an event, you must be a member or be sponsored by one. Nine rooms are available, and whether your group numbers fifteen for lunch or four hundred for a reception, there is a space just suited to your event size and type. Each room is decorated tastefully in subdued colors, mostly creams and blue-greens, and furnishings recall colonial Williamsburg. Portraits of Republican presidents hang on the walls throughout the club.

If you're planning a reception for two hundred or so, you'll probably want to rent the lovely Eisenhower Lounge, on the lobby level. Comfortable furniture is arranged in cozy clusters around the room, making it easy for a large crowd to mingle and still carry on private conversations. A display case at one end shows off an impressive collection of decorative elephants.

The Presidential Dining Room, with its many long windows hung with handsome teal curtains, is a handsome banquet area. This room also hides a surprise: Underneath the carpet lies a dance floor. The room accommodates 225 seated guests without the dance floor and 160 seated guests with the dance floor.

Other rooms include three formal but intimate conference rooms and a large, light-filled banquet/reception area that can be partitioned into four separate chambers.

(Democrats, you've got your own hangout—see the National Democratic Club listing.)

CAPACITY
Reception: 400
Banquet: 200
Meeting: 200

LOCATION
On Capitol Hill, directly across from the Capitol South Metro station.

FOOD/BEVERAGE
The club prepares all the food and handles all the beverage arrangements for your event but will work with you to plan your menu.

LIMITATIONS/RESTRICTIONS
To hold an event here you must either belong to the club or be sponsored by a member.

LEAD TIME FOR RESERVATIONS
Depends on the type of event you're planning and the number of attendees; call for availability.

RATES

Call for rates.

FACILITIES FOR THE PHYSICALLY DISABLED? Yes

CARNEGIE INSTITUTION OF WASHINGTON

1530 P Street, NW

Washington, DC 20005

202/387-6400

Behind an imposing façade, a dazzling hall—and then some

Film crews have shot scenes in its boardroom (for *The Pelican Brief*, for example), and embassies regularly throw parties in the Rotunda and reception room. These three rooms, plus a large auditorium and another conference room, are the rental areas within the Carnegie Institution building.

First the Rotunda. Its floor is marble inlaid in shades of gray, brown, and white. A circle of stately Corinthian columns of imitation ornamental marble defines the room and sets off four raised alcoves, inset in the rounded walls. These prove to be ideal spots for flowers, "living statues," and other decorations. The grandness of scale here pulls one's eyes upward to the carved plaster dome three stories above, where a skylight and a sunburst-pattern chandelier spill lighting.

The Rotunda flows directly into the reception room, which you may use in conjunction with the Rotunda or close off with sliding doors. The reception room is large and elegant, with white walls, molding, and columns; a floral carpet; and five double French doors leading to the hallway and on through to the auditorium. Root Hall, named after Elihu Root, a founding trustee and former US secretary of state and secretary of war, has more character than most auditoriums. A mural depicting groups of heroic figures—astronomers, geographers, explorers—gazing upon the skies, lands, and waters covers the side walls. Transparencies of the sun and moon cloak the ceiling. The proscenium stage is all of eight feet, almost an afterthought.

Mahogany-paneled walls, great windows, hanging portraits of Andrew Carnegie and past presidents of the institution, a marble fireplace, a huge board table, Oriental rugs, and maroon leather chairs make the boardroom the ultimate meeting room. Another conference room, the Mayor Room, lies on the other side of the Rotunda and has a high ceiling, wall-to-wall carpeting, floor-to-ceiling windows, and the usual conference paraphernalia, like grease boards and a screen.

Carnegie founded the institution in 1902 "to secure for the United States leadership in the domain of discovery." This grand masonry, with its balustrades, portico, and columns, was erected in 1909 to serve as headquarters for the administration of the institution while its scientists conduct research around the world.

CAPACITY

Reception: 500 in the Rotunda and reception room
Banquet: 250 in the Rotunda and reception room
Meeting: 30 to 50 in the boardroom, 10 to 15 in the Mayor Room
Auditorium: 400

LOCATION

At the corner of 16th and P Streets, NW, about eight blocks north of the White House and within walking distance of the Dupont Circle Metro station.

FOOD/BEVERAGE

You may choose any licensed and insured caterer. A full kitchen lies just off the Rotunda. The institution can provide a number of tables and chairs for your event.

LIMITATIONS/RESTRICTIONS

The site is available and open to anyone anytime, subject to the institution's schedule. Annually, the building closes from December 24 through January 1, is reserved during the months of June and July for a teachers' program, and hosts the institution's trustees meeting during the first week of May. Food, drink, and smoking are prohibited in the board and conference rooms and in the auditorium. Parking is limited, although it may be possible to reserve nearby neighborhood lots for evening events.

LEAD TIME FOR RESERVATIONS
Call as far in advance as possible.

RATES
Use of all the rental space costs $3,000 for an all-day or an evening event ($2,100 for nonprofit organizations; you must provide nonprofit IRS 501(c)3 documentation to receive this rate). Call for rates to use one of the meeting rooms or the auditorium. A thirty percent deposit is required with the signing of the rental contract.

FACILITIES FOR THE PHYSICALLY DISABLED? Some
A ramp provides wheelchair access to the building; an accessible rest room is on the first floor.

THE CHERRY BLOSSOM
Potomac Riverboat Company
205 The Strand
Alexandria, VA 22314
703/684-0580
www.potomacriverboatco.com
prcboats@aol.com

Rollin' on the river

Even before you step aboard the *Cherry Blossom* you recognize that it's no ordinary boat. If, as you stand admiring it, the movie *Showboat* comes to mind, that's because the 1984-built *Cherry Blossom* was modeled after the nineteenth-century paddle wheelers that brought entertainment to ports along America's rivers. The three-deck vessel is painted white, the huge paddle wheel is painted yellow, and a wrought-iron, mahogany-topped rail runs around the outside decks.

The captain perches inside his pilot's house, ready to take you rollin' on the river.

The *Cherry Blossom* was designed specifically for gracious, privately chartered entertaining; nevertheless, the features you find within may surprise you: mahogany paneling, brass fixtures, artfully etched windows, gold- and red-painted tin ceilings, plush wall-to-wall carpeting, scalloped gold and pale green wallpaper, and grand chandeliers. The two enclosed lower decks are equipped with air-conditioning and heating, so the *Cherry Blossom* is ready to roll anytime you are during the year.

You can hold any sort of event on board, from a dance to a fancy dinner. All the while, the *Cherry Blossom* slowly showboats its way along the Potomac, passing the Washington monuments if you go north or the quaint sights of Old Town Alexandria and Mount Vernon if you go south. You can stay inside and see it all from the boat's many windows, venture out to the promenade deck that encircles the enclosed second level, or climb to the open, third-level Hurricane Deck. For the best view of all, go up top with the captain.

CAPACITY

Reception: 400

Banquet: 200

Meeting: 200

LOCATION

You can board the *Cherry Blossom* at her home port in Old Town Alexandria, right behind the Torpedo Factory at the foot of Cameron Street. Or, you can board the boat at a Washington location. Call for further information.

FOOD/BEVERAGE

The *Cherry Blossom* has a list of approved caterers from which you must choose. The boat's galley is fully equipped for cooking and cooling. There are also ice machines on board.

LIMITATIONS/RESTRICTIONS

No specific restrictions.

LEAD TIME FOR RESERVATIONS

A year for spring and weekend events; three to four months otherwise.

RATES

You may rent the *Cherry Blossom* for a minimum of three hours at $1,000 per hour, plus $9 to $18 per person for beverages.

FACILITIES FOR THE PHYSICALLY DISABLED? Some

Ramps provide access to the main deck.

CITY CLUB OF WASHINGTON

Columbia Square
555 13th Street, NW
Washington, DC 20004
202/347-0818
202/393-4682 (fax)

This private club for the city's movers and shakers lies on the concourse level of a downtown building sublimely designed by I. M. Pei and Partners. Centering the structure is a grand, thirteen-story atrium-lobby whose glass walls and skylights pour light upon the granite walls, the terraced gardens, and the dramatic granite staircase that sweeps down to the lower level, where you enter the City Club. The club's façade of glass-paned doors carries in light from the atrium. The club's interior is an elegant spin on the traditional English men's clubhouse, which is not to say that women will feel out of place here: it's simply more handsome than pretty. Dark wood paneling and leather chairs predominate. Marble and glass accent tables and walls. Colors are muted, as is the lighting.

From its entrance, where a magnificent arrangement of flowers crowns a large, round, Italian marble table, the club wraps around to the left, where you come upon a series of cozy sitting areas with fireplaces and a bar. At the back are the main dining room—a gracious space with chandeliers and plush blue carpeting—and several meeting rooms. Along a hall leading back to the entrance is a paneled library with a mural painted upon the ceiling. To your left as you arrive back at the foyer is another tastefully appointed dining room.

CAPACITY
Reception: 300
Banquet: 4 to 140, depending upon the room
Meeting: 4 to 140, depending upon the room

LOCATION
On the concourse level of the Columbia Square building, with entrances from both F and 13th Streets in northwest Washington. The parking garage is accessible from 12th Street; the Metro Center station of the subway line is located outside the F Street entrance to the Columbia Square building.

FOOD/BEVERAGE
The City Club caters all events here, varying menus by season and specializing in Continental and American cuisine.

LIMITATIONS/RESTRICTIONS

Members may reserve the club's rooms for meetings and special events year-round, anytime, and may sponsor friends and business associates who wish to host functions here. The member must guarantee the event; the nonmember is required to pay a deposit.

LEAD TIME FOR RESERVATIONS

You should call at least a week ahead to reserve the club for a private function.

RATES

Members pay no rental fees to hold events here. Nonmembers who have been sponsored by a member pay a minimal fee to reserve the club for an event. Catering charges average $70 per person for a sit-down dinner and $40 to $45 per person for a cocktail buffet.

Membership rates vary, depending on the classification of membership; call for specific information.

FACILITIES FOR THE PHYSICALLY DISABLED? Yes

DECATUR HOUSE MUSEUM AND CARRIAGE HOUSE
1610 H Street, NW
Washington, DC 20006
202/842-0917
202/842-0030 (fax)
www.decaturhouse.org

History and style carry the event

The Decatur House estate has three areas available for special events: two Victorian parlors on the second floor of the historic Decatur House Museum, the courtyard-garden, and the principal space, the Carriage House. You may rent

these areas separately or together.

The Decatur Carriage House is most conducive to events, for it is that rare thing: a thoroughly modern and spacious meeting facility on the site of a historic home. By holding an event here, you can tour a marvelous Washington landmark that's been the home of a vice president, congressmen, and famous others, yet you avoid the usual historic property restrictions regarding food, drink, size, and entertainment.

Situated on the spot where War of 1812 naval hero Stephen Decatur once stabled his horses, the Carriage House offers you one large hall for meetings, receptions, and banquets. You enter the hall through an octagonal foyer, the floor design of which represents a mariner's compass.

An exceptionally pleasing, pale color scheme greets you inside the hall. Exceptional, too, are the room's dimensions. The hall covers twenty-three hundred square feet and has a twenty-foot-high vaulted ceiling. Floor-to-ceiling windows overlook, and French doors lead to, the private garden and brick-paved courtyard. The beautiful garden is floodlit at night and is available year-round. The use of heated tents here can increase the number of your party in winter.

Opposite the Carriage House is the Decatur House Museum. Ground-floor rooms reflect Federal-period decorating and lifestyles. For example, the Sheraton chairs and Chippendale table you see are original to the Decatur family.

Upstairs rooms reflect the Victorian period and appear as they were when the Beales, a prominent California family, inhabited the house from the 1870s to 1956. A magnificent American Centennial glass chandelier hangs in the south drawing room. The ceilings are painted with foliate designs, and an elaborate parquet floor in the north drawing room features an inlaid California state seal. These Victorian parlors are the only two rooms in the house that are available for small parties.

CAPACITY

Reception: 85 in the Victorian parlors within Decatur House, 250 in the
   Carriage House, 500 in the Carriage House and tented garden
Banquet: 70 in the Victorian parlors within Decatur House, 120 in the Carriage
   House, 220 in the Carriage House and tented garden
Meeting: 150 seated theater-style

LOCATION

Across from Lafayette Square and one block from the White House; within walking distance of the Farragut West and Farragut North Metro stations.

FOOD/BEVERAGE

Decatur House requires you to choose a caterer from its approved list.

LIMITATIONS/RESTRICTIONS

All clients must be members of the Friends of Decatur House. The use of a tent in the garden is mandatory if the number of attendees exceeds the capacity of the Carriage House. Dancing and amplified music are prohibited after 11:30 P.M. Decatur House has no parking facility; however, you can arrange to have valet parking or reserve parking garages in the area. Cash bars are not permitted.

LEAD TIME FOR RESERVATIONS

Like most of Washington, Decatur House is busiest from mid-September to mid-December and from March to June. The staff recommends that you call for availability.

RATES

For the Decatur Carriage House and/or the courtyard, weekday rates range from $1,500 for a four-hour daytime meeting to $3,250 for a four-hour private event; weekend rates are $3,250 for a seven-hour period (allowing four hours max for the event itself) or $4,250 for a nine-hour period (allowing six hours max for the event itself).

Weekday and weekend rates for rental of the Victorian parlors range from $5,500 for a standing reception to $6,500 for a seated reception of up to forty people, $7,500 for a seated function of up to fifty people, and $10,000 for a seated function of fifty-one to seventy people. Additional fees include those for overtime ($450 per hour for the event and $100 per hour for extra setup or cleanup time); Friends of Decatur House membership ($200 for corporations, $100 for individuals and nonprofits); and insurance.

FACILITIES FOR THE PHYSICALLY DISABLED? Some

The Carriage House and courtyard, but not the Decatur House Museum, are accessible.

EVERMAY

1623 28th Street, NW
Washington, DC 20007
202/333-8801
202/333-8802 (fax)
www.evermay.org

Historic Georgetown estate in view of the Washington Monument

This is my new favorite place. I have walked along 28th Street in Georgetown and passed Evermay many times, always wondering about the stately mansion visible just beyond the property's brick walls. But Evermay was, and is, a private home, and until recently public entry was not allowed. In the spring of 2000, however, Evermay's owners, the Belin family, decided to open their doors for special event rentals.

Beyond that brick wall lies a four-acre estate set on a hill, with garden levels descending in three stages from the mansion at the top. In all, there are three and a half acres of gardens, which include flat green lawns, gazebos, shaded niches, six fountains, centuries-old trees, holly hedges and boxwoods, rose bush borders, and decorative plantings of all kinds. Tenting is allowed on all three levels. One spot that especially lends itself to tenting is the thirty-foot-wide brick terrace extending off the back of the house; it is from this terrace that you spy the Washington Monument, presenting itself clearly in the distance.

A man named Samuel Davidson purchased this land in 1792, commissioning the same architect to design his house as L'Enfant had chosen to design the layout of the capital. The mansion was completed in 1806, and though it has been much modified since, Evermay retains its Federal characteristics and charm. The Belin family acquired Evermay in 1923.

You have use of two floors and the grounds when you rent Evermay. The first level holds the Orangery, full of plants and with high ceiling, arched windows, and two (working) fireplaces; a paneled drawing room; a long center hall that takes you to the terrace and gardens; and a dining room with jade-colored walls and lots of chinoiserie. Upstairs are bedrooms and bathrooms. Rooms throughout the house are entirely furnished with Belin family belongings; while the owners will move most of the furniture to accommodate your function, they are also happy to leave everything in place. The Belins are intent on providing a warm and gracious home for events—not just the exquisite shell of one.

CAPACITY

Reception: 250 in the house, 500 in the gardens

Banquet: 100 in the Orangery. It is possible to seat more than 100 people in one space on one of the tented terraces.

Meeting: 5 (in any one room) to 125 (seated theater-style in the Orangery)

LOCATION

Evermay is located on the northeast edge of Georgetown bordering Oak Hill Cemetery, on 28th Street between Q and R Streets.

FOOD/BEVERAGE

Evermay works with a list of preferred caterers but will consider others. The house has a great kitchen off the dining room and a side terrace off the kitchen that is perfect for deliveries.

LIMITATIONS/RESTRICTIONS

Rental of Evermay, including preparation and cleanup, is for the entire day, beginning at 8:00 A.M., unless otherwise negotiated. Events must conclude by midnight on Friday and Saturday and by 11:00 P.M. on Sunday through Thursday, unless special arrangements are made. Because Evermay's owners are interested in making you feel at home, they allow things—like smoking and red wine—that other historic houses do not. The one drawback for some will be the lack of air-conditioning in the older parts of the house (the drawing, dining, and upstairs rooms and the hall). Tenting may be required, depending on the size of your event, and you may have to pay two days' rental fees if the assembly of your tent takes place on the day prior to your event (which it probably will).

On-site parking is extremely limited—only ten spaces—so valet parking is recommended for any event of more than seventy-five people.

LEAD TIME FOR RESERVATIONS
Call for availability.

RATES
Rates vary based on the number of guests, space to be used, type of event, and other considerations. Estimates based on single-day use of Evermay for a wedding reception range from $7,500 for fewer than 50 guests to $11,000 for more than 200 guests. Estimates based on single-day use of Evermay for all other events range from $3,500 for fewer than 50 guests Sunday through Thursday to $8,500 for more than 125 guests on a Friday or Saturday.

FACILITIES FOR THE PHYSICALLY DISABLED? No

FOLGER SHAKESPEARE LIBRARY
201 East Capitol Street, SE
Washington, DC 20003
202/675-0324
www.folger.edu

"Go to the feast, revel and domineer"

Gather at the Folger Shakespeare Library and watch as the Falstaffs, Prince Hals, Rosalinds, and Cleopatras among you are revealed. In this Tudor "great house" setting, a meeting can provide high drama, a banquet may seem a royal feast, and a stand-up reception is a merry mingling of actors removing their masks.

Each of the five rooms available is spectacular. As you proceed apace through the Elizabethan Great Hall or into the adjoining Old Reading Room, you'll fancy yourselves in a castle. The two rooms are representative of Tudor banquet halls; each measures an enormous length and sports a towering ceiling. Stand-up receptions and banquets take place in the Great Hall, a handsome room with patterned-tile floor and blocked wall paneling, or in the Old Reading

Room, where Shakespeare's spirit is in beautiful evidence—stained-glass windows depict the Seven Ages of Man described in *As You Like It*.

You see more stained glass, displaying characters from Shakespeare's plays, in the Founders' Room, a space suitable for small meetings and receptions. This is a paneled, Tudor-style room furnished with high-backed chairs and a seventeenth-century refectory table. Other small rooms, the extremely elegant Board Room and the adjoining Tea Room, are also available for receptions or intimate dinners.

The Elizabethan Theatre, which suggests an Elizabethan public playhouse but is fully enclosed, is another great space for an event.

CAPACITY
Reception: 250 in the Great Hall or Old Reading Room, 500 in both halls
Banquet: 180 in the Great Hall or Old Reading Room
Elizabethan Theatre: 250
Dinner: 50 in the Board Room, 40 in the Founders' Room, 50 in the Tea Room

LOCATION
One block east of the US Capitol.

FOOD/BEVERAGE
The library has a list of caterers who have worked here successfully and are familiar with the site. A warming kitchen is available, as well as an elevator.

LIMITATIONS/RESTRICTIONS
Political fund-raisers are not allowed. Loud music is not allowed in the Great Hall when there are performances going on in the theater. Daytime events are restricted to Sundays.

LEAD TIME FOR RESERVATIONS
At least six months, and nine months for December events, but call for availability. April and May are also popular months.

RATES
Rental fees are as follows: Great Hall, $8,000; Elizabethan Theatre, $8,000; Great Hall/Elizabethan Theatre package, $12,000; Old Reading Room, $12,000; Great Hall/Old Reading Room package, $20,000; Great Hall/Elizabethan Theatre/Old Reading Room package, $24,000; Founders' Room, Board Room, or Tea Room, $2,000 each.

FACILITIES FOR THE PHYSICALLY DISABLED? Some
There's back-door access to the elevator and a wheelchair-accessible rest room in the theater. Call in advance.

GADSBY'S TAVERN
138 North Royal Street
Alexandria, VA 22314
703/548-1288

Hot spot in colonial times

As you collect your colleagues around you at Gadsby's Tavern, you're carrying on a tradition that goes back to 1770, when the original tavern was built. Just as you have chosen an unbusinesslike setting in which to discuss the news of the day, work-related or otherwise, so did our founding fathers.

The original tavern building now houses the Gadsby's Tavern Museum. What today operates as Gadsby's Tavern is right next door and was once the City Hotel. Three rooms have been restored to replicate the meeting rooms of the original tavern. Food, serving pieces, furnishings, and costumes recall colonial times.

In the Tap Room, you'll find a barkeep dressed in britches, billowing shirt, and vest dispensing drinks through the window of the wooden bar enclosure in the back corner. The cozy room exudes a convivial atmosphere with its well-worn floor, fireplace, an antique desk or two, hurricane lamps, square wooden tables, and old chairs.

Adjoining the Tap Room are the warm but slightly more formal dining rooms. You'll see the same wide-planked floor and square tables found in the bar, but other touches, such as blue Roman window shades and woodwork painted pistachio green, enhance the decor. You'll chuckle at the Hogarth reproductions hanging on the walls, depicting scenes of drunken revelry.

During the warmer months, a courtyard behind the tavern is also available with the rental of the tavern rooms or for regular dining. This space originally served as the coachyard for the tavern. Three old coach sheds still stand, and one of them may be used as the bar for receptions.

Trees and shrubs and a large white canopy help to make this a shaded and attractive spot for parties.

CAPACITY
Reception: 300 using the entire tavern and an adjacent ballroom
Banquet: 100
Garden party: 100

LOCATION
A few blocks east of the George Washington Memorial Parkway (Washington Street within Alexandria city limits) and one block north of King Street, in Old Town Alexandria.

FOOD/BEVERAGE
The tavern caters all events and features mostly colonial-style food (for example, "colonial seafood pasties," English trifle, and "George Washington's favorite"). Menus are available.

LIMITATIONS/RESTRICTIONS
Only period music is allowed, and amplified music is prohibited in the tavern. (The tavern can help you find musicians who play period music; in fact, such musicians perform there nightly.)

LEAD TIME FOR RESERVATIONS
Four to five days.

RATES
The entire tavern may be rented for a three-hour period, from 2:30 P.M. to 5:30 P.M. on weekdays or from 3:00 P.M. to 6:00 P.M. on Saturdays and Sundays, for $1,000. Individual rooms can be booked any day of the week from 5:30 P.M. to 8:15 P.M. or from 8:30 P.M. on. The average lunch cost is $8 per person; the average cost per plate at dinner is $20.

FACILITIES FOR THE PHYSICALLY DISABLED? Yes

GLENVIEW MANSION AT ROCKVILLE CIVIC CENTER PARK
603 Edmonston Drive
Rockville, MD 20851
301/309-3001
301/294-8073 (fax)
www.ci.rockville.md.us

New use for an old house

Rockville wasn't always the booming metropolis you see today. At the beginning of this century, the area was idyllic countryside dotted with the grand estates of wealthy Washingtonians. The Glenview Mansion was one of these. Built on 150 acres, this stone plantation house, with its first-floor conservatory, dining room, grand foyer, small sitting room, lounge, and library and second-floor servants' quarters and countless bedrooms, once belonged to the moneyed wife of a rich cardiologist.

You can use it any time of the year. The entire first floor is available for social events and the occasional business conference, and six rooms on the second floor are available for meetings.

The central foyer dates from 1838, when a Maryland judge and abolitionist constructed the original building. The mansion was renovated in the 1920s by the Lyon family. The result is a gracious reception area on the first floor that joins the lounge to the foyer to the library. Wide entryways seem to extend the space of one room into the next. Next to the library is the marble-floored conservatory, a great space for dancing; behind the lounge is the walnut-paneled dining room. These rooms are all large and made for entertaining in grand fashion.

The upstairs conference rooms are small and furnished with tables and chairs. They include chambers used by the Rockville Municipal Art Gallery for art shows.

Besides the mansion, you can rent two other facilities on the estate: the five-hundred-seat F. Scott Fitzgerald Theatre and the Social Hall. The theater offers more than just a stage area; there's an orchestra pit, sophisticated sound and lighting systems, a lobby, ticket booth, and dressing rooms. The Social Hall, located on the lower level of the theater, measures ninety by sixty feet and may be rented for meetings, receptions, and dinners.

CAPACITY
Reception: 225 in the mansion, at least 225 in the Social Hall
Banquet: 60 in the mansion, 225 in the Social Hall, 500 in the theater
Performances: 500 in the theater

LOCATION
Near the junction of Route 28 and Rockville Pike.

FOOD/BEVERAGE
The mansion allows only stand-up buffets, but you can choose your own caterer. A kitchen is available in both the mansion and the Social Hall for warming and cooling foods. The mansion's kitchen also has a microwave oven.

LIMITATIONS/RESTRICTIONS
Tents are not permitted outside, and cooking is not permitted inside. You cannot bring additional tables and chairs into the mansion. Smoking and red wine are prohibited in the mansion.

LEAD TIME FOR RESERVATIONS

For social events in the mansion, Rockville residents should call up to fifteen months in advance; nonresidents, not more than twelve months in advance. To book the Social Hall, call twelve months in advance. If you're planning a meeting, call for availability.

RATES

Call for rates.

FACILITIES FOR THE PHYSICALLY DISABLED? Yes

JOSEPHINE BUTLER PARKS CENTER AND MERIDIAN HILL PARK

2437 15th Street, NW
Washington, DC 20009
202/387-9128
202/234-3342 (fax)
www.washingtonparks.net

A community center inside a former embassy, and the national park across from it

The Josephine Butler Parks Center is a work in progress. The Renaissance Revival–style, forty-room mansion that once housed the embassy of Brazil and then Hungary is undergoing a renovation to master its new roles as a center for community-based, nonprofit culture and service organizations and as a rental space for concerts, dances, poetry readings, classes, wedding receptions, and other special events.

Architect George Oakley Totten Jr. designed this house and others in the neighborhood, and the mansion bears his stamp. Its exterior features an elegant entrance, a spacious balcony overlooking Meridian Hill Park (see below), and the use of terrazzo, marble, and glazed terra-cotta. The interior includes classroom spaces, a grand staircase, and an upstairs ballroom with parquet floor that adjoins a gallery and a large hall—space that leads out to that marvelous, shaded balcony terrace.

An organization called Washington Parks and People owns and operates the center, which is named for the community leader who spearheaded the effort to restore Meridian Hill Park. The organization is aiming for Earth Day 2002 as the completion date for the center's restoration. For now, the rooms in the mansion available for functions are in fine shape but perhaps not as polished as they eventually will be.

Meridian Hill Park, on the other hand, is now a shining jewel in the city because of the joint revitalization efforts of the National Park Service and the Friends of Meridian Hill, a nonprofit group of residents and community, cultural, and business organizations. The park is available for concerts, weddings, and all kinds of events. Its twelve acres hold beautifully landscaped gardens, many fountains (including a world-renowned cascading fountain, one of the longest in North America), and remarkable statues of famous figures, from Joan of Arc on a horse to Dante Alighieri and President Buchanan.

Washington Parks and People manages the use of both spaces for events and is happy to help you plan your function.

CAPACITY

The mansion can handle 350 for a stand-up reception, 150 seated in the ballroom and adjoining gallery, and 50 to 200 for a meeting, in either a classroom or the ballroom.

Meridian Hill Park has small groves for small functions but can accommodate thousands overall.

LOCATION

The mansion is at the top of the hill on 15th Street, on the right-hand side of the street as you head north, about half a block past Chapin Street, NW. Meridian Hill Park is between W and Euclid Streets, NW. Its entrance is on 15th Street, just down from the Josephine Butler Parks Center.

FOOD/BEVERAGE

You may choose your own caterer, as long as the caterer has a business license and insurance. The center is equipped with a simple serving kitchen. Alcohol is confined to wine and beer in the mansion and not allowed in the park. Food service in the park is restricted, but park events frequently feature picnic boxes for pickup at the entrance to the park.

LIMITATIONS/RESTRICTIONS

All events must end by 11:00 P.M. in the center and by 9:00 P.M. in the park. Smoking is prohibited in the center.

The mansion has thirty-five on-site parking spaces. Otherwise, you should count on using street parking, the Metro (the closest station is the green line's U Street/Cardozo stop), S2/S4 buses that travel up 16th Street, taxis, or valet parking.

LEAD TIME FOR RESERVATIONS

Call for availability.

RATES

Rates vary, depending on the purpose and length of the function, anywhere from $100 for use of one of the classrooms for half a day by a nonprofit organization to $1,800 for a wedding reception. Permitted use of the park is free, except for wedding ceremonies, for which a $200 fee is payable to the National Park Service.

FACILITIES FOR THE PHYSICALLY DISABLED? Yes

LOCKESLY MANOR

State Route 723
Millwood, VA 22646
540/837-2800
540/837-2801 (fax)
www.lockesly.com
info@lockesly.com

A stately mansion in view of the Blue Ridge Mountains

Drive about seventy minutes west of Washington, heading toward Blue Ridge Mountain country and the little village of Millwood in Clarke County, and, with the right invitation, you will reach Lockesly Manor. The imposing brick manor house lies at the end of a boxwood- and yew-lined drive, surrounded by 104 acres. Designed to resemble an eighteenth-century château—its façade presents an Ionic-columned portico, a balustrade, and French windows with semicircular fans—the mansion actually dates from 1792. Alterations since then (most significantly in 1952) created the structure you see today.

You may hold an event outdoors, tenting the grounds, which offer superb views of the mountains and rolling countryside. The Lockesly estate includes twenty-five manicured acres, landscaped in terraces to produce the appearance of a tree garden. Or you may use the mansion's first floor. Inside are a great hall with double curving staircases; a hand-laid, oak, parquet-floored drawing room, whose paneling once graced the walls of an eighteenth-century French château; a walnut-paneled Hunt Room; and a library. French doors lead from the Hunt Room and the drawing room to flagstone terraces; beyond the Hunt Room terrace is a thirty-five-by-forty-foot tent, which holds a stage and wooden floor—this is where the dancing takes place. Owner and equestrian Anna Lee Horton lives here, and she has painstakingly restored the mansion's interior to reflect its original French-influenced décor and her own interest in horses. Working fireplaces, a French grand piano, crystal chandeliers, and breathtaking views are all part of the package.

CAPACITY

Reception: 300

Banquet: 200 throughout the first floor and terraces

Garden party: 400 using the tented grounds

LOCATION

From the Beltway (I-495), follow I-66 west to Exit 23, picking up Route 17 north. Follow Route 17 north to Route 50 west (a left). Travel five miles on Route 50 until you reach Route 723, where you turn right, then drive one mile to the entrance to Lockesly, on the right. Parking is on the gravel drive at the west end of the manor, not on the grass.

FOOD/BEVERAGE

You may choose a caterer from Lockesly's list of approved caterers. A warming kitchen with commercial freezer, two sinks, refrigerator, and two ovens is available. The caterer or renter provides the alcoholic beverages.

LIMITATIONS/RESTRICTIONS

Dancing is allowed in the tent off the Hunt Room terrace. Smoking is allowed on the lawns only. Red wine and red punch are not allowed. Guests are not permitted on the second floor.

LEAD TIME FOR RESERVATIONS

Call for availability.

RATES

Rates vary based on season, number of people, and type of event, but this should give you an idea: You may reserve Lockesly for eight hours on a Saturday for $3,500 or for the weekend, from Friday at 4:00 P.M. to Sunday at 11:00 A.M., for $7,500. For more precise information about what these rates include, call Lockesly or check its Web site.

FACILITIES FOR THE PHYSICALLY DISABLED? Yes

McLEAN GARDENS BALLROOM

3811 Porter Street, NW
Washington, DC 20016
202/966-9781
http://members.aol.com/mgballroom

A belle of a ballroom

When you enter the McLean Gardens Ballroom, you can feel time slow down and the annoyances of the outside world disappear. Life is warm and wonderful, and everyone present is a gracious and exceptional human being.

How does the ballroom create this atmosphere? Maybe it's the epic dimensions of the room: fifty-four by fifty-four feet, with a forty-foot-high ceiling. Maybe it's the pale, pale yellow of the walls. Maybe it's the tasteful arrangements of Williamsburg-style furnishings. At any rate, this one-room site is at once intimate and elegant.

The ballroom was built in 1942 but completely renovated in 1984. Four huge pillars define it, setting off the center parquet dance floor from the living room setups on either side. Elaborate moldings, working fireplaces at either end, chandeliers, and great swags of peach and gold drapes at the long windows provide finishing touches.

Not to worry—you don't have to dance to hold a function here. The ballroom is available not only for dances but for receptions, dinners, and meetings.

CAPACITY

Reception: 350
Banquet: 110 with a buffet, 150 without buffet
Meeting: 150 to 175

LOCATION

One block off Wisconsin Avenue, NW, within walking distance of the Washington National Cathedral.

FOOD/BEVERAGE

You can choose any caterer who meets the ballroom's insurance requirements. A service kitchen and preparation room are available. You provide your own alcoholic beverages.

LIMITATIONS/RESTRICTIONS

No specific limitations; discuss your requirements with management.

LEAD TIME FOR RESERVATIONS

Call for availability.

RATES

$1,500 Monday through Thursday and $3,000 Friday through Sunday for an eight-hour period. Tables and special event planning services are provided compliments of the site.

FACILITIES FOR THE PHYSICALLY DISABLED? Yes

MARKET FIVE GALLERY AT EASTERN MARKET

North Carolina Avenue and 7th Street, SE
Washington, DC 20003
202/543-7293

Artistic appetites at Eastern Market

Everyone knows about Eastern Market, on Capitol Hill. This is the inside/outside bazaar where greengrocers, butchers, bakers, farmers, artists, craftspeople, florists, and other merchants vend their wares daily (except Monday), but especially on weekends. You can't have events in the indoor food market of the South Hall, but you can rent Eastern Market's Market Five Gallery, a bustling arts and community space on the flip side of the food market. Performing and visual artists, neighborhood groups, political organizations, and fund-raising entities—most nonprofit agencies, actually—are welcome to rent the gallery.

It is what it is: a big old hall with a high ceiling, exposed rafters, and a well-worn, red-painted cement floor. Its age shows, but that may be part of its appeal, for the place definitely has character. There are arched windows on three sides and a stage on the fourth. Art by local talent hangs on walls and partitions. Out front is an expansive brick courtyard.

CAPACITY
Reception: 400
Banquet: 350
Dance: 150
Meeting: 250
Performance: 200

LOCATION
The entrance to the Market Five Gallery is on North Carolina Avenue, SE. The nearest Metro station is two blocks away, the Eastern Market stop. On-street parking is ample.

FOOD/BEVERAGE
You may choose your own caterer. The site can provide some setup tables and some chairs.

LIMITATIONS/RESTRICTIONS
The hall is available year-round Tuesday through Sunday, days and evenings, primarily for cultural, educational, and community events, as well as events sponsored by nonprofit and political groups, but you should call for more specific information. Smoking is permitted.

LEAD TIME FOR RESERVATIONS
About two months.

RATES

Call for rates.

FACILITIES FOR THE PHYSICALLY DISABLED? Some

The rest rooms are not wheelchair accessible, but the building is.

MERIDIAN HOUSE

1630 Crescent Place, NW
Washington, DC 20009
202/939-5592
www.meridian.org/facility.htm

A thoroughly French grand mansion

As the French might say, c'est une maison magnifique! You think of France when you see Meridian House for several reasons. An imposing limestone structure designed in the style of an eighteenth-century estate found in the Île-de-France, it sits on a shady street behind a high stone wall. Antique French furniture, marble busts, brass hardware and lighting fixtures, and lattice parquetry are some of its interior features. Even the garden's linden trees were imported from France.

You can rent the main floor's reception gallery, loggia, library, drawing room, dining room, and, in season, the rear and side gardens. The gallery, loggia, and garden are all in a line down the center of the mansion, forming a natural reception area. Waterford torchères, large blue Chinese temple jars, and mirrored walls distinguish the gallery. The loggia is a spacious and rounded sunroom with long arching windows that frame views of the lovely linden trees and pebbled courtyard.

The library and drawing room adjoin the center areas, expanding available reception space in a delightful way. The library is an unusual jade green color and has built-in bookshelves and map cases. Next door, the drawing room features a silk French carpet, a piano, and pale blue walls.

On the other side of the house is the dining room, ideal for banquets and buffets. A beautiful Flemish tapestry hangs on one wall; its dimensions determined the size of this room and the height of ceilings throughout the house.

Adjacent to Meridian House is the White-Meyer House (see entry page 226), purchased and renovated by Meridian International Center in 1988. The magnificent Georgian-style mansion was designed by Meridian House architect John Russell Pope. Rented together, the two mansions double their individual capacities for meetings and events.

CAPACITY
Reception: 350 inside, 500 in and out
Banquet: 90 to 150
Garden party: 500
Meeting: 10 to 100 in one room

LOCATION
From downtown Washington, head north on 16th Street, NW, to Belmont Road. Turn left and follow the street around as it curves. Turn right on Crescent Place.

FOOD/BEVERAGE
The staff prefers that you choose a caterer with demonstrated experience at

Meridian House. A pantry on the main floor is available for warming and cooling foods but not cooking.

LIMITATIONS/RESTRICTIONS

All red-staining substances, including red wine, are prohibited. Smoking is prohibited inside. Fund-raising is not allowed. Floral arrangements must arrive prepared.

LEAD TIME FOR RESERVATIONS

Call for availability.

RATES

Wedding receptions: $6,000

Daytime events: whole day/whole floor, $1,500; whole day/one room, $1,000; half day/whole floor, $1,000; half day/one room, $500

Evening events: $3,500 for the whole floor

Call for additional information.

FACILITIES FOR THE PHYSICALLY DISABLED? Some

Meridian House has a street-level entrance and an elevator that will take you to the main floor.

MEXICAN CULTURAL INSTITUTE

2829 16th Street, NW
Washington, DC 20009
202/728-1628

Olé! A celebration of Mexico in European-style quarters

When it was built in 1910, this Italian-style building with French and English architectural accents was simply a residence for President Taft's secretary of the treasury. Later, from 1921 to 1989, it served as the Mexican Embassy. In

1990, President Carlos Salinas de Gortari inaugurated the site as the Mexican Cultural Institute, whose purpose is "to enhance the understanding and knowledge of Mexican art and culture among the American people in the nation's capital."

You may reserve one or all three of the institute's floors. On the first level is the dramatic front hall, with a limestone floor and an eighteenth-century baroque altarpiece. Flanking the hall are art galleries displaying modern Mexican art. There is also an auditorium at the back.

A sweeping staircase in the entrance hall showcases an unbelievably colorful and fascinating mural that embraces the staircase wall all the way up to the third floor. On the second floor are the primary reception rooms: a large hall; the ornate Music Room, modeled after one in the Fontainebleau palace outside of Paris and featuring a spectacular organ and a vaulted, painted ceiling; the Golden Room, decorated in French Renaissance style; the huge Dining Room, with its Baccarat chandelier and hand-carved furniture; and its adjoining Atrium, a glass-ceilinged chamber whose walls and floor are entirely covered in vivid Mexican tiles. The third floor houses a library, once used as the ambassador's office, where eighteenth-century Belgian tapestries hang and hand-painted stencils embellish the ceiling.

CAPACITY

From 40 (in one room) to 300 (using the whole mansion), for any type of function. The auditorium can seat 180 people.

LOCATION

Straight up 16th Street, about 1.5 miles from the White House. Adjacent to the institute is a fifty-two-car parking lot; street parking is your alternative.

FOOD/BEVERAGE

You may choose your own caterer. There is a full kitchen on the second level, and caterers can use an elevator to transport food to the reception rooms on the second floor.

LIMITATIONS/RESTRICTIONS
The institute is available for functions Monday through Saturday. Smoking, food, and drinks are not permitted in the galleries.

LEAD TIME FOR RESERVATIONS
Call for availability.

RATES
Rates for use of the special event rooms start at $3,500.

FACILITIES FOR THE PHYSICALLY DISABLED? Yes

MOUNT AIRY PLANTATION
8714 Rosaryville Road
Upper Marlboro, MD 20772
301/856-9656
301/856-4206 (fax)

Maryland hunt country's historic estate

Maryland's founding family, the Calverts, hunted here. George and Martha Washington slept here. John Parke Custis, Washington's stepson, married here. Presidents Taft, Wilson, Coolidge, Hoover, and Roosevelt were all, at various times, entertained here. And now it's your turn.

Up a winding road you go until you come upon this marvelous restored mansion, poised on a summit in the woods. The primary rental areas are the first floor and grounds, although you may arrange to reserve upstairs rooms as well. The house's architecture is a little bit of this and a little bit of that: English cottage, Federal, Georgian, and Greek Revival styles. Somehow, the designs blend together inside to create warm and inviting places for meetings, receptions, and dinners.

The dark-stained, pine-paneled Hunt Room is comfortable and cozy.

Adjoining it is a chamber that dates from 1725, the oldest standing portion of the building. The Lord Baltimore Lounge, as it is called, is furnished with period antiques and reproductions. A huge hearth dominates one wall, and a smaller working fireplace is set in the opposite wall.

There are three light-filled dining rooms. Two are a pleasant ensemble of colonial hues, flowered carpeting, and attractive table settings. Of the three, the garden room is the prettiest. Its ceiling is covered in a creamy muslin fabric that filters the strong light from a skylight, and the room extends directly into the brick-paved pavilion, whose windows combine latticework and glass and overlook the woods and gardens. Window panels along one wall are removable so that the space can spread farther outdoors, onto a terrace that can be tented.

Upstairs rooms are available for meetings, as bridal lounges, and for other uses.

CAPACITY

Reception: 300
Banquet: 225 without a tent, 300 with a tent
Meeting: 30 to 300

LOCATION

From the Beltway (I-495), take Exit 11A and head south on Route 4 about four miles to Route 223. Turn right on Route 223 (Woodyard Road) and continue on this road, whose name will change to Rosaryville after two miles. Travel on Rosaryville Road until you see the sign for Mount Airy; turn left at the entrance and follow the road to the top of the hill.

FOOD/BEVERAGE

A caterer operates and manages Mount Airy and caters all functions here.

LIMITATIONS/RESTRICTIONS

Smoking is not permitted indoors. Parking is allowed only in the lot adjacent to the house and in other designated areas.

LEAD TIME FOR RESERVATIONS

Call for availability.

RATES

Weekdays: $180 per hour per floor, with a three-hour minimum
Weeknights, $900; Fridays, $1,500; Saturdays and Sundays, $2,400. Weeknight and weekend rates cover use of the first floor and grounds for eight hours, with $250 per hour charged beyond the eight hours. You can arrange to use upstairs suites for additional fees.

FACILITIES FOR THE PHYSICALLY DISABLED? Yes

THE NATIONAL AQUARIUM

US Department of Commerce Building
14th Street and Constitution Avenue, NW
Washington, DC 20230
202/482-2826

Clown fish and garfish and sharks, oh my! Green eels, alligators, and deadly piranhas! Yes, they're all here, as well as many other water creatures—the built-in entertainment for your party at this most unusual of all meeting sites in Washington.

Your event goes along swimmingly from the start: You enter the aquarium by descending a flight of stairs awash in blue. The sound of crashing waves can be heard in the background. The staircase leads into the aquarium's long entrance hallway, which is dotted with freestanding tanks, a touch tank, and educational graphics. The hallway in turn leads to the aquarium proper, a circular room whose walls are lined with more than seventy tanks. The illuminated fish tanks provide most of the lighting for both the aquarium and the hallway, and the dim atmosphere reinforces the feeling that you have arrived underwater.

Believe it or not, you can hold not only receptions at the aquarium but banquets, too. Standing or sitting, you'll have quite a view. There are more than twelve hundred fish on display, and it is fascinating to see the variety: transparent fish and colorful fish, fish without eyes and fish that fly, fish that kiss and fish that kill. If you're in the mood to learn a fact or two, you can watch the video about sea life at the aquarium.

The National Aquarium is the oldest public aquarium in the country. It was started in Woods Hole, Massachusetts, in 1873 and transferred to its current location in 1932. It has been run by a nonprofit organization called the National Aquarium Society since 1982.

CAPACITY
Reception: 300
Banquet: 120

LOCATION
In the Federal Triangle (the Federal Triangle Metro station is close by), within walking distance of both the White House and the Washington Monument.

FOOD/BEVERAGE

You may use a caterer on the museum's approved list or choose one not on the list, subject to the aquarium's approval. (The caterer must be insured and provide references.)

LIMITATIONS/RESTRICTIONS

The aquarium is available daily, year-round, from 6:00 P.M. to 11:30 P.M.

LEAD TIME FOR RESERVATIONS

One to two months.

RATES

A $2,500, flat fee entitles you to an evening's use of the aquarium.

FACILITIES FOR THE PHYSICALLY DISABLED? Yes

NATIONAL DEMOCRATIC CLUB

30 Ivy Street, SE
Washington, DC 20003
202/543-2035
www.democlub.net

Democrats' hangout on the Hill

The National Democratic Club is the preferred dining and meeting site of Democratic senators, congressmen, congressional staff, and party officials, as well as those who lobby them.

You can rent one or more of the club's three floors or just one of its five rooms. As you enter the building, you'll notice the 8½-by-11-inch wall photographs of all current Democratic members of Congress, arranged according to their ranking positions.

The clubroom on this floor is large and features a bar and grill and photos of the US Capitol. Against one wall, a fireplace has been converted into an attractive copper and wood wine closet; mirrors cover the other walls. On the second floor is an open reception area with a brass-topped, mahogany bar and a private meeting room that can be partitioned into two spaces. The meeting room's exterior walls are hung with large pictures of the Democratic presidents; inside walls feature mahogany wainscoting and photographs of Democratic first ladies.

The O'Neill Room, a banquet hall on the third floor, has burgundy banquettes, dusky rose walls, and brass chandeliers. (A redecoration is planned for this room.) Glass doors at one end of the room lead to a balcony overlooking Capitol Hill. Adjoining the O'Neill Room is a formal conference room.

(Republicans, see the Capitol Hill Club listing.)

CAPACITY
Reception: 25 (in one room) to 400 (throughout)
Banquet: 100 in one room
Meeting: 5 to 100

LOCATION
Two blocks east of the US Capitol.

FOOD/BEVERAGE
The club caters all functions but will work with you to plan your menu.

LIMITATIONS/RESTRICTIONS
The site is available to members and to nonmembers who are sponsored by a member or reserve a space through their senator or representative.

LEAD TIME FOR RESERVATIONS
One to two weeks, but call for availability. The club accepts reservations up to six months in advance.

RATES

The club does not charge for room rentals but requires a $55 minimum of food and beverage expenses.

FACILITIES FOR THE PHYSICALLY DISABLED? Yes

NATIONAL 4-H CENTER

7100 Connecticut Avenue
Chevy Chase, MD 20815
301/961-2840

A former campus without distractions

The first thing you'll notice about the National 4-H Center is that, with its sweeping front lawn and stately buildings, it looks like a college campus. In fact, from 1903 to 1950, this was the site of Chevy Chase Junior College.

The thirty conference rooms range in size and can be set up to meet the needs of your group. Almost every room carries a name—for example, the Missouri Room or the Oklahoma Room—indicating the state whose 4-H Foundation sponsored its unique furnishings. These rooms also display artwork donated by their 4-H sponsors.

For the most part, the conference rooms are utilitarian meeting areas equipped with tables, chairs, and other tools, such as screens, flip charts, black-boards, and podiums. Audiovisual equipment is available at a nominal charge. Many of the conference rooms also have noteworthy decorative features, how-ever. The Missouri Room, for instance, features brass chandeliers and walnut paneling.

A new wing houses a 550-seat auditorium with elevated stage, and the center also offers overnight accommodations. Different types of bedrooms are available. Most are four-person rooms with two bunk beds and a central or private bath. Other rooms share a bathroom, dormitory-style. All have a TV, a telephone, daily maid service, and linens.

Although this facility is a get-down-to-business sort of retreat, it does provide opportunities for recreation. You can go for walks on its twelve secluded and wooded acres or play volleyball and video games. If you want, the center can arrange off-site educational programs.

CAPACITY
Reception: 50 to 500
Banquet: 425

Meeting: 25 to 550
Lodging: 700

LOCATION
Just outside and north of Washington, on Connecticut Avenue. Metro buses stop right in front of the center.

FOOD/BEVERAGE
The National 4-H Center offers a full-service cafeteria with individually served or buffet-style luncheons and banquets, receptions, refreshment breaks, box lunches, and other special services as requested.

LIMITATIONS/RESTRICTIONS
The National 4-H Center is a division of the National 4-H Council, a nonprofit organization. Its primary purpose is to serve its members, youth, civic and church groups, and other nonprofit organizations. Its facilities are available year-round to groups with similar missions—that is, not-for-profit and educational.

LEAD TIME FOR RESERVATIONS
Most groups reserve eight to twelve months in advance.

RATES
Call for rates. Center staff prefers to discuss this information with individual clients.

FACILITIES FOR THE PHYSICALLY DISABLED? Yes

NATIONAL GEOGRAPHIC SOCIETY

1145 17th Street, NW
Washington, DC 20036
202/828-6616
202/857-5864 (fax)
www.nationalgeographic.com

Lead your next expedition to National Geographic Society headquarters

The three-building complex that houses the headquarters of the National Geographic Society also holds three excellent event spaces: Explorers Hall, the Gilbert H. Grosvenor Auditorium, and the National Geographic Dining Room. You can arrange to arrive at the M Street entrance, walking through the open-air courtyard planted with Bradford pear trees and displaying an intriguing rock sculpture before proceeding into the spacious M Street lobby, where the party often begins. If you have reserved Explorers Hall, you can return to the courtyard and stroll across to the hall, or take the elevator to a lower level to reach the 17th Street building via underground access. Explorers Hall is now scaled back— *Geographica*, the society's interactive geography center, has closed, but the south hall of the building continues as a museum, exhibiting fascinating artifacts and information about widely diverse subjects, whether bears or Australia, from a geographic standpoint.

Back in the M Street building, you may use the Gilbert H. Grosvenor Auditorium for lectures, conferences, or concerts. This highly comfortable hall features soft, green-cushioned seats, state-of-the-art lighting and sound, front projection screen, and other helpful equipment. From there, it's a stroll across the lobby to the spacious dining hall, whose floor-to-ceiling windows overlook the illuminated courtyard. Partitions in this room may be used to apportion the space for small gatherings.

CAPACITY
Explorers Hall: 150 standing
Grosvenor Auditorium: 400

Dining Room: 410 standing or seated

LOCATION
Five blocks from the White House, in the heart of downtown Washington. A maximum of two hundred parking spots in the society's garage may be available at added cost.

FOOD/BEVERAGE
The society's in-house caterer handles all meals and will work with you in planning your function.

LIMITATIONS/RESTRICTIONS
The National Geographic Society's facilities are available Monday through Friday after business hours; the auditorium sometimes, though rarely, may be reserved during regular business hours. The site is not available for rental from December 15 through January 15. Commercial, political, fund-raising, and private social events, including weddings, are not permitted. Smoking and red wine are prohibited.

LEAD TIME FOR RESERVATIONS
Call for availability.

RATES
Rental of any one of the three spaces costs $4,000; use of all three spaces costs $12,000.

FACILITIES FOR THE PHYSICALLY DISABLED? Yes

NATIONAL POSTAL MUSEUM

Smithsonian Institution

1st Street and Massachusetts Avenue, NE

Washington, DC 20013

202/633-9362

www.si.edu/postal

Perfect location for red-letter celebrations

Of all the Smithsonian museums, the National Postal Museum might feel the most personal. Who has not waited breathlessly for a special letter? Or sent off a missive anxiously to a friend far away? The museum tells the story of the mails, touching upon the lives of those who deliver it, those who send it, the methods of dispatch through the centuries, and how our current system has evolved from ancient Egyptian times.

The museum's size is also intimate. Located on a single floor—the lower level of the former Washington City Post Office building—it covers seventy-five thousand square feet and holds more than sixteen million objects. Five exhibit areas branch off from a central atrium, which is capped by a glass ceiling four floors above. The atrium is itself an exhibit, with three early mail planes overhead, a mid-nineteenth-century stagecoach, a progression of US mail trucks, a replica of a railway mail car, various interactive video kiosks (bring your address book so you can mail souvenir postcards to your friends), mailboxes from around the world, and other intriguing artifacts.

The National Postal Museum wants to make it clear that, "while the museum does not rent its space, events related to the museum's mission that are cosponsored with the museum may be held there. In addition, financial contributors to the museum may be invited to cosponsor a special celebratory event at the museum." At such functions, the atrium serves admirably as a food and beverage location. Guests can then wander through the galleries, where they can learn about the history of mail service from pre-Revolutionary through Civil War America, how mail was delivered to expanding urban and rural populations in the twentieth century, the modes of transportation and technology used for mail service, the poignant role of letters in personal communication, and stamp production and collecting.

One floor up from the National Postal Museum is another event site, Postal Square (see entry page 187). It is possible to coordinate the use of both floors. You might, for example, convene for cocktails in the National Postal Museum and move upstairs for a seated banquet.

CAPACITY
Reception: 20 to 400
Banquet: 10 to 100

LOCATION
Next to Union Station, at the corner of 1st Street and Massachusetts Avenue, NE, on the lower level of the Postal Square building. Parking is limited. The closest Metro stop is the red line's Union Station, next door.

FOOD/BEVERAGE
You may choose the caterer, whose insurance policy must meet the museum's requirements. Museum staff will help you coordinate your arrangements with caterers.

LIMITATIONS/RESTRICTIONS
Social events of a personal nature are not allowed, nor are fund-raising, product marketing, or political events. Functions must be cosponsored with the museum; that is, demonstrably related to the museum's mission or hosted by a contributing sponsor of the museum. Smoking is not permitted. The museum must authorize in advance such things as the guest list, printed and promotional materials, and speakers or performers.

LEAD TIME FOR RESERVATIONS
At least six weeks, although events are frequently booked six months in advance.

RATES
The museum cosponsors events in celebration of donations and prefers to discuss

this matter with individual cosponsors.

FACILITIES FOR THE PHYSICALLY DISABLED? Yes

NAVAL HERITAGE CENTER
At the US Navy Memorial
701 Pennsylvania Avenue, NW
Washington, DC 20004
202/737-2300, ext. 720
www.lonesailor.org

A shipshape place below the street

From the plaza anchoring the US Navy Memorial, it's a few short steps into the Naval Heritage Center, and one flight down a wide and curving granite stairway to its main gallery. As you descend, pause to admire the Wave Wall, a series of glass panels whose etched and illuminated profiles of thirty-two ships present a two-century perspective of American naval history.

Below deck (street level) finds you in a reception room whose décor screams US Navy. The custom-made blue carpet quite cleverly evokes a sense of the ocean, and there are pictures of ships on the walls and navy memorabilia enclosed in glass cases. If you're interested in learning more about naval history, the center will turn on the various interactive video kiosks for your guests' use and entertainment.

Off to one side of the reception room is a 247-seat theater with a two-story, fifty-two-foot-wide screen. Behind retractable doors at the end of the gallery is the US Presidents Room, a paneled dining room commemorating the naval service of twentieth-century US presidents.

CAPACITY
Reception: 350
Banquet: 180 in the entire hall, 50 in the US Presidents Room
Lecture: 247

LOCATION

The center is located on Pennsylvania Avenue, NW, between 7th and 9th Streets, across from the US Archives building. The closest Metro station is the Archives/Navy Memorial stop on the yellow and green lines. A public parking garage with an entrance on D Street, NW, provides paid parking for about seventy cars. Other public garages and lots are nearby.

FOOD/BEVERAGE

You're welcome to choose your own caterer. A kitchen equipped with warming ovens and chilling units lies off the paneled dining room.

LIMITATIONS/RESTRICTIONS

The US Presidents Room is available Monday through Friday, year-round, 7:00 A.M. to 11:00 P.M. The gallery deck (main hall) is available year-round in the evenings. Smoking is prohibited. Red wine is permitted only at sit-down dinners.

LEAD TIME FOR RESERVATIONS

Book the center two to nine months ahead of time.

RATES

Rates range from $600, for half-day use of the US Presidents Room, to $2,550, for evening rental of the entire facility.

FACILITIES FOR THE PHYSICALLY DISABLED? Yes

NEWTON WHITE MANSION

2708 Enterprise Road
Mitchellville, MD 20716
301/249-2004
301/249-8009 (fax)
www.pgparks.com

A little bit of the unexpected

You expect a meeting/entertainment site to possess certain qualities—an attractive setting, room to accommodate you, adaptability, a convenient location—that sort of thing. What you can't always count on is personality. The Newton White Mansion delivers on all scores.

You may have seen stone lions or dogs poised at the gateways to other grand estates; here, your arrival is marked by a brick rooster atop one brick column and a brick hen crowning the other, a whimsical touch that stands in sharp contrast to the mansion's proper Georgian façade. Throughout the interior, you'll notice a fine, bleached pine paneling instead of the more common dark wood paneling. Wall murals depicting bucolic farm scenes mix with a stylized art deco design in the dining room. Even the mansion's setting is a surprise—the rolling hills surrounding you are actually part of the adjoining golf course. (Games are on a first-come, first-served basis, if you're interested in playing a round.)

You have the use of the first floor, second-floor changing rooms, and the grounds when you rent the estate. First-floor rooms include the dining room and an adjoining enclosed porch, a long central hall, a study, a large ballroom and an adjoining back room, and an atrium. The glass-enclosed atrium overlooks the golf course and gardens and has a skylight.

In addition to its unusual features, the Newton White Mansion offers you beautiful versions of the usual features. Full-length windows in the ballroom are hung with balloon curtains and overlook the grounds. Crystal chandeliers illuminate this room at night. French doors at the back of each of the first-floor rooms lead to a large, forty-by-sixty-foot brick patio, which may be covered with a tent. Another smaller patio lies off the ballroom. Paneled fireplaces in the ballroom and study are functional.

Built in 1939, this house was once the home of Captain White, the first commanding officer of the World War II aircraft carrier USS *Enterprise*.

CAPACITY

Reception: 360 throughout the first floor
Banquet: 275 throughout the first floor
Garden party: 200 to 300 standing
Meeting: 200 in the atrium

LOCATION

From downtown Washington, take US Route 50 (John Hanson Highway) east to Route 704 north, the first exit beyond I-95 (Washington Beltway). From Route 704, turn right onto Route 450. Turn right onto Route 193 (Enterprise Road) and travel approximately three miles. Turn right onto the grounds.

FOOD/BEVERAGE

You choose your own caterer. The mansion offers a large warming and cooling kitchen equipped with a four-hundred-pound ice machine.

LIMITATIONS/RESTRICTIONS

No specific restrictions; discuss your requests with management.

LEAD TIME FOR RESERVATIONS

The mansion starts accepting reservations one year in advance.

RATES

Weekdays: $150 per hour before 5 P.M. Monday through Thursday evenings: $300 for a three-hour period; $1,200 for a seven-hour period. Friday and Sunday: $2,600 for a seven-hour period. Saturday: $3,000 for a seven-hour period. The site bills extra hours at $325 an hour Monday through Thursday evenings, $350 an hour Friday after 5 P.M., and $380 an hour Saturday and Sunday. A refundable, $500 security deposit is required. Ask about discounted rates for Prince George's and Montgomery County residents and for nonprofit groups.

FACILITIES FOR THE PHYSICALLY DISABLED? Some
There are two permanent wheelchair ramps.

OATLANDS

20850 Oatlands Plantation Lane
Leesburg, VA 20175
703/777-3174
703/777-4427 (fax)
www.oatlands.org
oatlands@erols.com

A grand old Virginia home

Shortly after you arrive here, you start to wonder what it would be like to own Oatlands. Who can resist? The wonderful Greek Revival mansion bursts with character. Its many rooms are furnished with antiques that are not only beautiful but comfortable. The surrounding grounds keep the outside world at a distance while the formal terraced garden keeps you entranced with its unexpected turns, mysteriously hidden enclosures, and endlessly varied flowers, plants, and trees. The only thing Oatlands seems to be missing is occupants, and that's where you come in.

For a reasonable fee, you can rent the grounds, garden, and a rustic carriage house. During your event, you may tour the mansion's second-floor bedrooms and hall, as well as its first-floor octagonal drawing room, large entry hall, dining room, breakfast room, library, and "morning room."

Everything you see is noteworthy. The tall white pillars of the façade, for example, are actually oak-sheathed walnut tree trunks painted to look like plaster.

The capitals at the tops of the pillars were designed by Oatlands's creator, George Carter, great-grandson of famous Virginia plantation owner "King" Carter. Furniture on the first floor is a mix of Louis XIV, XV, and XVI; second-floor furniture is all American.

George Carter started building the house in the Federal style in 1804 and had altered it to the Greek Revival style by 1830. He designed and planted the original garden as well. When William Corcoran Eustis and his wife, Edith, bought Oatlands in 1903, they renovated the mansion and restored and expanded the garden. All of the furniture in the house (except for the dining room's massive sideboard) belonged to the Eustises, and the tea house, bowling green, reflecting pool, and rose garden reflect their handiwork in the garden.

Oatlands is now a property of the National Trust for Historic Preservation.

CAPACITY

Reception: 300 with the use of a tent on the lawn, 120 in the carriage house

Banquet: 80 in the carriage house

Fairs and exhibitions on the grounds: more than 1,000

Meeting: 75 in the carriage house

LOCATION

Approximately six miles south of Leesburg, Virginia, on Route 15. From Washington, take Route 7 west to Leesburg, and then go south on Route 15. Or, take I-66 west to Route 50 west to Gilbert's Corner, and then go north on Route 15.

FOOD/BEVERAGE

Oatlands has a list of six approved caterers from which you must choose. Site management requires that the caterer also handle the rental of tents, tables, and chairs. A kitchen in the basement is available and equipped with a stove, a refrigerator, double ovens, sinks, a freezer, and work tables.

LIMITATIONS/RESTRICTIONS

Oatlands is available evenings from April 1 through December 30. Smoking is prohibited inside. Liquor must be served by a bartender provided by the caterer. Prospective renters must supply a certificate of insurance.

LEAD TIME FOR RESERVATIONS

At least four months.

RATES

Call for rates.

FACILITIES FOR THE PHYSICALLY DISABLED? No

OXON HILL MANOR

6901 Oxon Hill Road
Oxon Hill, MD 20745
301/839-7782
www.pgparks.com.

Meet in grand manner at the manor

Staging an event at Oxon Hill Manor, some ten miles or so from the White House, whets your appetite for the good life. Everywhere you look, inside and out, you see beauty, and that beauty is yours, if only for a few hours.

Before you take possession of the five first-floor rooms available to you within this neo-Georgian house, proceed directly to the partially covered, wide brick terrace that runs along the back and side of the house. From there you find the manor's enormous green lawn sloping down into a woods that meets the Potomac on the horizon. To the side of the house lie lovely gardens and a reflecting pool. You're free to stroll the grounds or to rent them for a tented event in conjunction with the rental of the house.

Back inside, you see that the drawing room, library, and dining room each capture a portion of the breathtaking view through tall French doors that open onto the terrace. Each of these rooms is spacious, high-ceilinged, and possessed of its own distinct character. The rose-colored drawing room, with its huge stone fireplace, finely carved woodwork, and parquet floor, is elegant. This is the place for musical entertainment and dancing. Dark wood paneling and tall built-in bookcases lend the library a warm, snug feeling, making it an inviting place to mingle during cocktail receptions. A choice spot for intimate banquets is the dining room, whose peaches-and-cream-colored walls display large Chinese watercolor murals painted on rice paper.

You may also use the spacious, marble-floored foyer for your event; you may have a bar here and use the room to expand your reception area. Down a long hall and past a grand, sweeping stairway is the tearoom, suitable for small meetings or as a dressing room for the bride-to-be.

You'll never get to see all of them, but Oxon Hill Manor actually houses forty-nine rooms. The manor was built in 1928 for American diplomat Sumner Welles. Welles held many esteemed positions during his career, which included a term as undersecretary of state to President Franklin Delano Roosevelt. Roosevelt was one of the many illustrious visitors to Welles's estate.

CAPACITY
Reception: 300 inside and in the tented garden
Banquet: 210 throughout the first-floor rooms, 300 inside and in the tented garden
Garden party: 300
Meeting: 40 to 80 in one room

LOCATION
From the Beltway (I-495), take Exit 3A south and turn right onto Oxon Hill Road.

FOOD/BEVERAGE
You can choose any caterer who is licensed and insured. The site provides tables and chairs as part of its rental fee.

LIMITATIONS/RESTRICTIONS
The garden can be rented only with the use of the house. Use of the house and walk-throughs are by appointment only. Tenting is not allowed on Saturdays.

LEAD TIME FOR RESERVATIONS
One year for Saturday events and at least six months for other days, but call for availability.

RATES
Friday and Sunday, $2,600 for seven hours; Saturday, $3,000 for seven hours. Call for weekday rates.

FACILITIES FOR THE PHYSICALLY DISABLED? Yes

THE PATTERSON HOUSE

15 Dupont Circle, NW
Washington, DC 20036
202/483-9200

A timeless treasure with a trendy address

The Patterson House has many claims to fame, not the least of which is its use as a temporary White House by Calvin Coolidge in 1927 when the roof of the real White House was undergoing repairs. It was from the mansion's second-floor loggia that Coolidge, his wife, and the triumphant Charles Lindbergh, fresh from his record-breaking transatlantic solo flight, waved to the crowds that filled the circle below them.

The four-story, marble, Beaux Arts–style building was designed in 1901 by the esteemed Stanford White for *Chicago Tribune* owner Robert Patterson. The Pattersons were keen on entertaining, just as you will be once you see the regal rooms within.

You enter a central hall—high ceiling, marble floor—off which stem several rooms. One of these, known as the Members' Dining Room, is a semiformal, carpeted room with Oriental antiques, floral curtains, and mementos on display. Up a grand marble staircase is a suite of three wonderful rooms, again radiating off an elegant foyer. The white-paneled ballroom has a wooden floor, a musicians' gallery, and an impressive tapestry covering a long wall. The ballroom leads to the President's Auditorium, an immense hall added in 1954 and featuring a dance floor, a large stage, fabric-covered walls, and a ceiling nearly, but not quite, as high as the ballroom's. This floor also holds the Patterson Dining Room, exquisitely decorated with family furnishings like the magnificent sideboard and crystal chandelier.

A library and several comfortable sitting rooms may also be available for your use.

CAPACITY

Reception: 500 using both floors, 400 using the second floor

Banquet: 48 in the Patterson Dining Room, 80 in the Grand Ballroom, 200 in
the President's Auditorium, 175 in the Members' Dining Room
Meeting: 50 to 300 in one room

LOCATION
The Patterson House sits on a triangular lot right on Dupont Circle.

FOOD/BEVERAGE
You must choose your caterer from the site's approved list and purchase all
beverages through the site, which has a full liquor license. There is a large, fully
equipped kitchen on the first level. While the site does not provide china, glassware, or silverware, it does offer the use of its twenty-one tables and three hundred chairs.

LIMITATIONS/RESTRICTIONS
The Patterson House is available anytime, except Christmas, New Year's Eve, and
the month of August. Management recommends that you arrange for valet
parking or encourage your guests to arrive by taxi or Metro (the Dupont Circle
station lies just across the circle from the site). Smoking is prohibited. Ballroom
dancing only is allowed in the ballroom; other kinds of dancing and amplified
music are confined to the President's Auditorium. Children are not permitted.

LEAD TIME FOR RESERVATIONS
Call one year in advance.

RATES
$5,000 for rental of the first and second floors, $3,300 for rental of the second
floor alone, $1,700 for rental of the President's Auditorium, $1,400 for rental of
the Grand Ballroom, $1,000 for rental of the Members' Dining Room, and $600
for rental of the Patterson Dining Room. These rates increase by thirty percent
for events held on holidays and holiday weekends. They cover a four-hour period;
an additional, ten percent overtime charge applies for every hour thereafter. A
deposit of $1,500 confirms your reservation.

FACILITIES FOR THE PHYSICALLY DISABLED? Some

The site has an elevator but no ramp or specially equipped rest rooms.

THE PHILLIPS COLLECTION

1600 21st Street, NW

Washington, DC 20009

202/387-2151, ext. 267

www.phillipscollection.org

A feast for the eyes

At the Phillips Collection, you can feast your eyes on Bonnards and Renoirs while you're enjoying your fete. This is Washington's beloved museum of modern art and the oldest such gallery in the United States. You can rent the main building and/or its annex for your event.

The museum was once the private home of the Phillips family, so the setting is as eye-catching as the art. First-floor rooms in the Georgian Revival–style main building feature Oriental carpets, pastel walls, and exquisite, small pieces of furniture. The Jacobean music room on the same floor serves as the banquet hall and lecture room, and it is breathtaking. Heavy wood columns support one end, and dark-stained, quartered oak paneling covers the walls. The high ceiling is polychrome plaster molding.

The rooms upstairs are more gallerylike, with cream-colored walls and little furniture. But the atmosphere of a private home disappears completely in the annex, where the rooms are wide, open, and airy.

But enough about the design of the place; it's the paintings that will most thrill you. You'll view Daumiers and Cezannes, Klees and Braques, Kokoschkas, Gauguins, Sisleys, Morisots—and more.

One other tip: Be sure to look at the fireplaces in the main building; each is unique and a work of art in itself.

CAPACITY

Reception: 250 in the main building, 250 in the annex, 500 in the main building and annex

Banquet: 110 in the main building, 55 in the annex

Lecture: 100

LOCATION

One block west of the Dupont Circle Metro station, at Q Street, NW.

FOOD/BEVERAGE

You may choose your own caterer subject to the approval of museum staff. A catering kitchen with sinks, commercial dishwasher, disposal, and refrigerator is available on the lower level of the main building; a kitchen with stoves is available on the first floor of the annex.

LIMITATIONS/RESTRICTIONS

The museum is available all day Monday and after 5:00 P.M. every other day but Thursday. Weddings and wedding receptions are not permitted. Red wine, tomato juice, and Bloody Mary mix may be served only at seated dinners, not at receptions. Cigarette smoking is prohibited.

LEAD TIME FOR RESERVATIONS

Call for availability.

RATES

A $5,000 membership fee entitles you to one-time use of one building; an additional $3,500 is charged for building use. A $10,000 membership fee entitles you to unlimited use of the museum with a $6,000 charge for use of both buildings or a $3,500 charge for use of one building.

FACILITIES FOR THE PHYSICALLY DISABLED? Yes

POPLAR SPRINGS

9425 Rogues Road
Route 602, Box 275
Casanova, VA 20139
540/788-4600
poplarsp@citizen.infi.net

Fieldstone manor in Fauquier County

Out Warrenton way, deep in the country, at the conclusion of a winding, cedar-lined drive sits this grand manor. The two hundred acres of surrounding farmland, forests, and streams nicely seclude the property—and provide plenty of space for a party.

The mansion, which was built in 1928, has twenty-inch-thick fieldstone walls. Beyond these walls, on the main floor, are the great room, library, dining room, and sunporch. Flagstone terraces adjoin the library and the great room. All of this, plus the never-ending grounds, is available for events.

Arched entranceways lead from room to room, the most splendid of which is the great room. This three-story-high chamber has balconies at the second-floor level, exposed timber beams, working fireplaces, circular stained-glass windows, and original hardwood floors. French doors lead to the terrace and a tiered garden.

Inside walls are bare fieldstone; the sunporch floor is stone, as well. Modeled after sixteenth- and seventeenth-century European manors, Poplar Springs has a decidedly Old England feel about it.

CAPACITY

Reception: 350 inside, unlimited outside
Banquet: 200 inside, unlimited outside
You must rent tents when you anticipate more than 200 guests.

LOCATION

Head west on I-66 from Washington and take the Warrenton/Gainsville exit to

Route 29 south. Follow Route 29 south for ten miles, staying to the left and bypassing the South Warrenton Business District. Take Exit 643 (Meetze Road) and turn left off the ramp. Proceed 4.6 miles and turn left onto Route 616 (Casanova Road). Travel 1.2 miles, passing the town store, and turn right onto Rogues Road. The entrance to Poplar Springs is on the left.

FOOD/BEVERAGE

Poplar Springs contracts with one catering firm to handle food and beverage requirements. The site has a full kitchen off the dining room.

LIMITATIONS/RESTRICTIONS

Poplar Springs is available daily, year-round. The throwing of rice, birdseed, and confetti is not allowed, and smoking is not permitted inside. The house is heated and air-conditioned. Balconies may be decorated, used as perches for musicians and photographers, or the place from which the bride tosses the wedding bouquet.

LEAD TIME FOR RESERVATIONS

The site accepts reservations as many as two years in advance. For dates in May, June, September, and October, call at least one year ahead.

RATES

Monday through Thursday, $250 per hour; Friday after 5:00 P.M. and Sunday, a flat $2,000; Saturday evenings and holidays, a flat $3,500; and Saturday daytime, $3,000. These rates usually cover an eight-hour period. A refundable, $250 security deposit is required.

FACILITIES FOR THE PHYSICALLY DISABLED? Some

A ramp allows wheelchair access to the main floor, but the rest rooms are not specially equipped to handle wheelchairs.

PRINCE GEORGE'S BALLROOM

2411 Pinebrook Avenue
Landover, MD 20785
301/341-7439

Not just for dancing

The Prince George's Ballroom used to be known as the Beaver Dam Golf and Country Club, and the site still has that easy, relaxing, country club feel. Instead of a golf course, though, you'll find great green grounds; instead of a swimming pool, there's a sweeping driveway; and instead of a clubhouse, there's the ballroom.

One long dance hall and an adjoining sunporch compose the ballroom area. The hall measures eighty-five by forty feet, providing plenty of room in which to kick up your heels. A revolving crystal ball and beaming colored lights turn the ballroom into a disco at night. By day or by night, the hall features polished floors, a high, sloped ceiling, and brass chandeliers. An alcove at one end of the room offers a cozy lounge area in front of a copper-covered fireplace.

Through five sets of French doors lining one wall is the sunporch. This room, which is nearly as long as the main hall, is furnished in light gray and white.

Prince George's Ballroom is available for any type of event, from black-tie affairs to casual business meetings.

CAPACITY

Reception: 250
Banquet: 250
Meeting: 270
Patio: 250

LOCATION

From the Beltway (I-495), take Exit 17B to Route 202. Follow Route 202 west two miles to Pinebrook Avenue. Turn left and follow Pinebrook Avenue until you arrive at the ballroom grounds.

FOOD/BEVERAGE

You make your own catering arrangements. The ballroom is equipped with a commercial-grade kitchen, which caterers may use to warm foods.

LIMITATIONS/RESTRICTIONS

Call for specific rules and regulations.

LEAD TIME FOR RESERVATIONS

Up to a year, but call for availability.

RATES

Monday through Thursday, after 5:00 P.M., $540; Friday, Sunday, and holidays, $1,100; Saturday, $1,300. These rates cover a seven-hour period. A $400, refundable deposit is required to reserve the ballroom for a weekend date.

FACILITIES FOR THE PHYSICALLY DISABLED? Yes

RASPBERRY PLAIN

16500 Agape Lane
Leesburg, VA 20176
703/777-1888
703/777-2122 (fax)
www.raspberryplain.com
info@raspberryplain.com

Up a long and winding road lies a manor house

Follow a twisting country road past clusters of lilac bushes and beneath a canopy of hundred-year-old hardwood trees and—voilà! You are rewarded for your journey by Raspberry Plain.

This Georgian, colonial-style mansion was built in the early 1900s on land once owned by Thomson Mason, brother of George Mason (see entries for

Gunston Hall and Hollin Hall). The brick house, with its two-story, columned portico, stands at the center of fifty acres and presides over a large, circular front lawn set off by towering trees. The south lawn, the north lawn, and the formal gardens (featuring a stone pathway, century-old boxwood hedges, stone benches, and plots of seasonal flowers) are part of the rental space. On all sides are breathtaking views of the Blue Ridge Mountains and rolling countryside.

Raspberry Plain has a wonderful center hall, stretching from an arched front entranceway over which loops the landing of the staircase to the north door. To the right lie the cherry-wainscotted, tastefully appointed drawing room, the Victorian parlor, and the terra-cotta, tile-floored Fountain Room, whose French doors lead to the conservatory and the great outdoors. On the other side of the hall are the light-filled dining room and the Governor's Room, which is often used as a dressing room for the bride when Raspberry Plain hosts a wedding. The bride may use the front hall staircase for her grand entrance and, later, as a backdrop for pictures. Working fireplaces, glass-paneled pocket doors, and elaborate ceiling moldings are a few of the other special features.

CAPACITY
Reception: 200 inside, 300 inside and out
Banquet: 200 inside, 300 inside and out

Meeting: 200, split among three rooms

LOCATION
Three miles north of Leesburg and about thirty-three miles northwest of Washington. From Washington, take the Beltway (I-495) south to the Dulles Toll Road exit, which you follow to the exit for the Dulles Greenway (Route 267). From Route 267, take Exit 1B to Route 15 north and proceed to Raspberry Drive, where you turn left. Take the first right onto Raspberry Plain Lane and another right onto Agape Lane.

You can also take the Route 7 west exit from the Beltway and follow Route 7 almost to Leesburg. Take the Route 15 north exit toward Frederick, and then follow the directions above.

FOOD/BEVERAGE
You must choose your caterer from an approved list. Caterers may use the mansion's work space for food preparation and heating but not for cooking.

LIMITATIONS/RESTRICTIONS
The site is available any day, anytime. The mansion is air-conditioned. Smoking is not allowed inside.

LEAD TIME FOR RESERVATIONS
The site accepts reservations one year in advance; call at least one month ahead of time.

RATES
Weekday rates start at $2,000, weekend rates start at $3,300.

FACILITIES FOR THE PHYSICALLY DISABLED? Yes

SEWALL-BELMONT HOUSE

144 Constitution Avenue, NE
Washington, DC 20002
202/546-3989
202/546-3997 (fax)

Historic house/museum featuring suffrage collections

Hold a function at the Sewall-Belmont House and you're on the site that fostered today's women's movement. Not only that, but the mansion is one of the oldest on Capitol Hill, dating from the late 1600s. The redbrick structure is an amalgam of architectural styles, from colonial farmhouse to French Hansard, reflecting the changes made to it over the course of three hundred years.

Two of the mansion's floors and a large, enclosed garden are yours for events. Want to dance? The garden's brick terrace makes a great outdoor dance floor. Want to dine? A tent on the lawn in summer and the sunporch in winter provide perfect banquet areas. Want to confer or simply kick back and gab? The whole house is good for that.

All the rooms are handsomely furnished. Like its architecture, however, the house's appointments represent cross-period styles and the preferences of its various occupants. The best thing to do is have a docent give you the history of both the house and the women's movement. You'll find out, for example, that Albert Gallatin, secretary of the treasury under Presidents Jefferson and Madison, lived here from 1801 to 1813; that Alice Paul, the author of the Equal Rights Amendment, led the early fight for its passage from this house; and that since 1929 the house has served as headquarters for the National Women's Party, which Paul founded.

CAPACITY

Reception: 125 inside and on the bricked terrace, 350 inside, on the terrace, and
    in the tented garden
Banquet: 80 on the bricked terrace, 230 on the terrace and in the tented
    garden

Meeting: 30

The site provides the tent, except during the winter months.

LOCATION
On Capitol Hill, across the street from the Supreme Court building and next to the Hart Senate Office Building.

FOOD/BEVERAGE
The Sewall-Belmont House has a list of approved caterers from which you may choose. The kitchen may be used to warm or cool but not prepare foods.

LIMITATIONS/RESTRICTIONS
Food and beverages are not allowed in the historic part of the house, and the throwing of birdseed or rice is prohibited. Smoking is not allowed inside.

LEAD TIME FOR RESERVATIONS
Call for availability.

RATES
Rates range from $1,400 to $3,950, depending upon the number of guests, plus a $500 security deposit. Special rates apply during January, February, and August.

FACILITIES FOR THE PHYSICALLY DISABLED? No

STRATHMORE HALL ARTS CENTER
10701 Rockville Pike
North Bethesda, MD 20852
301/530-5889
www.strathmore.org

Fine art, refined setting in North Bethesda

Some houses, like some people, have presence, and Strathmore Hall is one of them. Cars whiz past on the road below, and shoppers converge on the sprawling mall down the street; but poised on a hill above it all, Strathmore Hall maintains its pleasant peace.

Notice first the exterior: a turn-of-the-century, redbrick mansion surrounded by eleven green acres that include an English sculpture garden and a stately pavilion. Columned porticoes crown the mansion's entrance and a patio.

Step inside and be equally impressed. You are standing in a marble-floored foyer lit with brass torchères. The ceiling is glass, set in intricate latticework. Go right into the marvelous music room, where a light wood floor contrasts with the dark wood of paneled walls.

Go left from the foyer and you're in the dining area, painted pale pink and cream. A chandelier sparkles above, and a long, built-in plant stand overflowing with greenery extends across a wide front window.

Behind these front rooms are a cozy library; a cheery, peach-tinted main hall leading to the patio; and three galleries exhibiting the works of area artists. All eight of these first-floor rooms, as well as a kitchen, are at your service when you rent Strathmore.

CAPACITY
Reception: 250 inside, 400 with a tent
Banquet: 80 in one room, 120 throughout the first floor
Meeting: 60

LOCATION
From the Beltway (I-495), take the Rockville Pike (Route 355) exit, going north, and travel on Rockville Pike about .5 mile. Strathmore Hall is located next to the Grosvenor Metro station, .5 mile south of White Flint Mall.

FOOD/BEVERAGE
You choose your own caterer. A large kitchen on site is equipped with a warming oven, freezer, refrigerator, double sinks, and lots of counter space.

LIMITATIONS/RESTRICTIONS
Smoking is prohibited in the galleries.

LEAD TIME FOR RESERVATIONS
One year for Saturday and Sunday events; four months for events on other days.

RATES
Monday through Thursday: $2,000 for Montgomery County residents and $2,400 for nonresidents; Friday through Sunday: $3,000 for Montgomery County residents and $3,400 for nonresidents. Fees cover eight-hour rentals.

FACILITIES FOR THE PHYSICALLY DISABLED? Yes

THOMAS BIRKBY HOUSE

109 Loudoun Street, SW
Leesburg, VA 20175
703/779-2933
703/771-8051 (fax)
http://birkbyhouse.com
info@birkbyhouse.com

Nineteenth-century coachmaker's residence, carriage house, and gardens

Across the street from the Norris House Inn (see entry page 32) and owned by the same family is the Thomas Birkby House. Once the residence of a coachmaker, who worked here until 1903, the Birkby House's oldest section dates from 1780. Behind its brick façade lie eight rooms, including a ballroom, front and rear parlors, groom's lounge, bride's room (off which hangs a balcony), library, and boardroom. The boardroom is fully furnished, but other rooms contain a scattering of select pieces: Persian rugs, artwork, hunt tables, and servers. The ballroom holds two working fireplaces; the library another. Also available are a two-story, brick carriage house, which has been completely refurbished as a small conference center/event site, and a stunning half acre of formal gardens.

See the Norris House Inn entry if you are interested in offering some of your guests a place to spend the night.

CAPACITY
Reception: 500 using two tents beside and in front of the carriage house, 300 using one tent, 125 in the Birkby House and on the terrace, 90 using only the carriage house

Banquet: 180 using a tent, 75 in the Birkby House and on the terrace, 60 in the carriage house

Meeting: 2 to 75 throughout the house

LOCATION
The Birkby House is located fourteen miles from Dulles International Airport and less than an hour's drive from Washington. From the Beltway (I-495), take the Dulles Toll Road (Route 267) to the Dulles Greenway, which terminates at the Route 15 bypass. Take the bypass west, exit on King Street, and then go north on King Street to Loudoun Street to the property.

FOOD/BEVERAGE
The Birkby House has a list of preferred caterers but will allow you to choose your own, as long as the caterer meets the owners' insurance and licensing requirements. Caterers may use the kitchen in the main building and/or the kitchen in the carriage house.

LIMITATIONS/RESTRICTIONS
The Birkby House is available for functions year-round. When you book the house for a social event you have exclusive use of the property; no other event will be taking place here at the same time. You must rent a tent when you plan to seat guests on the terrace or in the garden. Smoking is allowed outside only. Music is not allowed past 10 P.M.

LEAD TIME FOR RESERVATIONS
Call for availability.

RATES
Meeting rates range from $200 for use of the rear parlor in the Thomas Birkby House to $900 for use of the carriage house. (The facilities are available weekdays

only for meetings.) These rates include the use of such business equipment as computer, fax machine, copier, VCR, lectern, white board, overhead projector and screen, flip charts, and Internet connections.

Social event rates range from $900 for use of the carriage house on weekdays and Sunday to $3,250 for use of the Birkby House and terrace, carriage house, and gardens on a Saturday or holiday. These rates cover a seven-hour period up to 11 P.M., with extra hours billed at $250 per hour on Saturdays and holidays and $150 per hour on other days. They do not cover tent rental.

FACILITIES FOR THE PHYSICALLY DISABLED? Some
The first floor of the Thomas Birkby House, as well as a rest room there, is accessible to the disabled.

TOWER CLUB

8000 Towers Crescent Drive, Suite 1700
Vienna, VA 22182
703/761-4250
www.tower-tysons.com

A sky-high sanctuary eight miles from the White House

When you stand at one of the seventeenth-floor windows of the Tower Club and gaze into the distance, it isn't hard to pick out certain landmarks, like the Washington Monument or the National Cathedral. What's startling is that they're so tiny. Eight miles really diminishes height and size. Washington and Virginia are just bunches of little villages abutting one another into the horizon, or so it seems from your penthouse perch.

That the view here is interesting but not distracting is fortunate, because the club itself deserves attention. It's an elegant spot with a number of different places for gathering. The Atrium is the area you enter when you step off the elevator. Covered by a rounded glass roof thirty feet high, the room is bright and filled with palm and fica trees. The floor is marble, and there's a stage and an ashen dance floor.

Off to one side of the Atrium is the Commonwealth Room, the club's main dining room, which is filled with tables and tapestry-covered chairs. On the other side are a number of private rooms, including the large Fairfax Room and a series of smaller chambers, each featuring the same general décor: thick wall-to-wall carpeting, sea-green wall coverings, and blinds that work as screens. Behind the Fairfax Room is the George Mason Library, which is partly paneled and cozily furnished with plush blue armchairs in front of a gas fireplace.

A covered balcony encircles the penthouse, and you may step out for a breath of fresh air or to check how traffic is moving on the Beltway, immediately below you.

The Tower Club was founded in 1988 as a private meeting place in which business professionals could dine, do business, and entertain.

CAPACITY
Reception: 2 (using one of the smaller rooms) to 250 (using both the Atrium and Fairfax Room)
Banquet: 10 (in the library) to 150 (in the Atrium or Fairfax Room)
Meeting: 2 (in one of the smaller rooms) to 150 (in the Fairfax Room)
Larger parties are possible during nonmember hours.

LOCATION
On the seventeenth floor of the Tycon Tower I building, at the intersection of Route 7, the Beltway, and Route 123, in Tysons Corner.

FOOD/BEVERAGE
The in-house caterer handles all of your food and beverage requirements.

LIMITATIONS/RESTRICTIONS
The Tower Club is a private club that allows members and sponsored nonmembers to use its facilities for special events.

LEAD TIME FOR RESERVATIONS
Call for availability.

RATES
Nonmembers pay a $750 usage fee and, if applicable, a ceremony fee of $300. Average catering costs are $64.95 to $68.95 per person for daytime weddings and $74.95 to $82.95 per person for evening weddings. Call about rates for other kinds of functions.

FACILITIES FOR THE PHYSICALLY DISABLED? Yes

TUDOR PLACE
1644 31st Street, NW
Washington, DC 20007
202/965-0400, ext. 110
www.tudorplace.org

Home to Martha Washington's descendants for 180 years

Tudor Place is a 5$^1/_2$-acre property occupying one city block in Georgetown. Most of it is open lawn and gardens, but crowning the summit of the sloping South Lawn is the exquisite Palladian mansion designed by Dr. William Thornton, first architect of the US Capitol.

You may tour much of the first floor during your function, with docents on hand to answer your questions. The entrance into the suite of neoclassical rooms makes for one of the grandest arrivals in Washington. Here you will see the central salon, drawing room, dining room, parlor, and study, each furnished splendidly with the belongings of Martha Washington's descendants, the Peter family. Martha Custis Peter, Martha Washington's granddaughter, purchased Tudor Place in 1805 with an eight-thousand-dollar legacy left her by her step-grandfather, George Washington. The Peter family continued to live here until 1984.

The main event areas are outside. If you exit through the clever pull-up window to the domed portico, you find yourself looking out at a sea of green—the South Lawn, which is a perfect place to tent. On the other side of the house is the wonderfully landscaped North Garden, which includes a circle of box-woods in front of the entrance, a grape arbor, a lily pool, and a bowling green, with large collections of period flowers and shrubs and pebble paths connecting it all. The Federal landscape plan has survived these many years, and all the plants, shrubs, and flowers you see are descendants of those sown nearly two centuries ago.

Adjoining the garden is the Dower House, an early Victorian whose double parlor and dining room are available for events.

CAPACITY
Reception: 50 in the Dower House, 350 outside
Banquet: 16 in the Dower House dining room, 200 outside

LOCATION
In Georgetown, in the block bounded by Q, R, 31st, and 32nd Streets.

FOOD/BEVERAGE
You may choose a caterer from Tudor Place's authorized list or use another caterer subject to the site's approval. For lawn and garden parties, caterers must set up a preparation tent outside. Food and drink are not allowed inside the mansion. Food and drink are allowed inside the Dower House, however, and caterers of events there may use its kitchen.

LIMITATIONS/RESTRICTIONS
Tudor Place and Dower House are available daily at any time. Wedding receptions, but not ceremonies, are permitted. Events must conclude by 10:30 P.M. Valet parking is required for groups of more than seventy-five people.

Because Tudor Place is a historic landmark and because the property is located in a residential neighborhood, certain things are not allowed—namely, amplified, taped, or rock music. This applies to Dower House, as well.

LEAD TIME FOR RESERVATIONS

Call at least three months in advance for Tudor Place; two weeks ahead for Dower House.

RATES

Contributions required to hold an event at Tudor Place range from $2,000 to $10,000. A $750 donation entitles you to the use of Dower House. An extra $100 covers a tour of Tudor Place.

FACILITIES FOR THE PHYSICALLY DISABLED? Some

The garden paths are fairly wheelchair accessible.

WALSH-RECKORD HALL OF STATES

National Guard Memorial Building
1 Massachusetts Avenue, NW
Washington, DC 20001
202/789-0031

An elegant hall of impressive dimensions

One block down from Union Station and three blocks from the US Capitol is the headquarters for the National Guard Association of the United States and its quietly dramatic Walsh-Reckord Hall of States. Inside the pink marble rotunda that serves as an entrance to the building, a life-sized, bronze statue of a minuteman reminds you that the National Guard dates from colonial days. You descend a marble, double-wide stairway to the Medal of Honor Gallery, a round room with a marble floor, where you can read about the Medal of Honor and its National Guard recipients.

Just beyond the gallery, through a double set of paneled doors, lies the Hall of States. The hall covers 3,332 square feet of floor, has a ceiling height of 20 feet, and includes a 114-square-foot stage, which is set off by columns. Colorful state flags draw your eyes upward, where you'll notice the magnificent blocked-paneled ceiling. The same paneling encloses sets of columns that run the length of the room on both sides. The floor is carpeted, and recessed lighting keeps the hall discreetly illuminated. A small, unadorned meeting room adjoins it.

CAPACITY
Reception: 250
Banquet: 150
Conference: 70 seated in a U, 250 seated theater-style. The small adjoining room accommodates 10 for a meeting.

LOCATION
One block from Union Station, right next to the National Postal Museum, on Capitol Hill.

FOOD/BEVERAGE
You may choose from one of three approved caterers. A kitchen lies conveniently between the loading dock and the hall.

LIMITATIONS/RESTRICTIONS
The hall is available for business events during the week, subject to the National Guard Association's own schedule. A parking garage in the building is available for a fee. Food and drink are not permitted outside the hall. Neither smoking nor amplified music is permitted.

LEAD TIME FOR RESERVATIONS
Call as soon as possible.

RATES
Full day (8:00 A.M. to 4:00 P.M.), $1,000; half day (four hours), $600; luncheons, $600; evenings (6:00 to 9:00 P.M.), $1,000. The entire estimated rental cost must be paid fifteen days prior to the event. Additional expenses may include a $150-per-hour charge for each hour beyond the agreed-upon time, $30 per hour for a National Guard Association representative to be on site after 5:00 P.M., and fees for parking, tables, tablecloths, and microphones.

WASHINGTON INTERNATIONAL SCHOOL

3100 Macomb Street, NW
Washington, DC 20008
202/243-1810
www.wis.edu/rentals

A mansion in a woods in Cleveland Park

The architect who designed the Smithsonian's Freer Gallery of Art and the west wing of the Corcoran Gallery also designed this mansion. Completed in 1912, the house and its twenty acres eventually became the residence of Marjorie Merriweather Post and her husband, Ambassador Joseph Davies, who lived here in the 1940s. The Washington International School, a multilingual, multicultural day school, set up shop on this woodsy Cleveland Park campus in 1972.

On weekends, in the evenings, and during school breaks, you may reserve the mansion's handsome, yellow-pine-paneled reception chamber, whose French doors open to a large, awning-covered terrace that overlooks a sloping encampment of trees. This elegant room has a fireplace, beautiful moldings, and built-in bookcases. Also available in the mansion is Davies Hall, another paneled room with a fireplace, this one with arched floor-to-ceiling windows and a wooden floor.

Two light-filled classrooms are available in a building known as the Greenhouse. You may also rent a portion of the grounds, like the Dacha Garden, a truly lovely area just outside the Greenhouse set off by brick walls and backing up against the school's library (called the Dacha). Or, you may reserve the grounds at large.

CAPACITY

Reception: 175 in the mansion, 350 on the grounds
Banquet: 100 in the mansion

Meeting: 20 in each of the Greenhouse classrooms

LOCATION
In the northwest Washington neighborhood of Cleveland Park, a few blocks up from Connecticut Avenue. There is ample free parking on the grounds.

FOOD/BEVERAGE
The site works exclusively with one caterer. There are no formal kitchens, but there are work spaces that the caterer can use for preparation purposes. Alcohol is allowed, but cash bars are not.

LIMITATIONS/RESTRICTIONS
The school is available on weekends, evenings, and during school breaks.

LEAD TIME FOR RESERVATIONS
Call for availability.

RATES
Mansion: $1,600 for a nine-hour event, with an overtime charge of $200 per hour
Greenhouse: $100 per hour
Grounds: $400 for six hours

FACILITIES FOR THE PHYSICALLY DISABLED? Some
There is a ramp for wheelchairs at the entrance to the mansion.

WASHINGTON NATIONAL CATHEDRAL
Massachusetts and Wisconsin Avenues, NW
Washington, DC 20016-5098
202/537-5581 (cathedral), 202/537-6383 (College of Preachers)
www.cathedral.org/cathedral

You can't go any higher in Washington (without the aid of an airplane) than the Pilgrim Observation Gallery in the west tower of the Washington National Cathedral. The cathedral takes up fifty-seven acres of the loftiest place in the city, and when you gather in the tower, you are at the height of this highest ground.

The gallery works best as a foil to the view. The walls are oak-paneled, the floor plain linoleum; overhead is Gothic ribbed stone vaulting. To glory in the vaunted panorama of the city and its environs, you must actually leave the oddly shaped reception space and proceed to the surrounding arcade. This is an enclosed stone passageway whose seventy windows reveal close-ups of gargoyles, grotesques, and other wondrous elements of the cathedral's Gothic architecture, as well as more distant views of Sugarloaf Mountain, the Potomac River, the Washington Monument, and other area landmarks.

The Observation Gallery extends to a central reception area and back to a small space where the history of the cathedral is on display. A two-hundred-seat auditorium is also on this floor. Other marvelous rental areas include the Churchill Porch, a high-ceilinged, interior space just off the cathedral's main floor; a handsome library holding a mammoth dining table (with seats for thirty); and the Garth, an outdoor courtyard enclosed by stone walls. Last but not least are the truly delightful offerings of the College of Preachers: the Tudor-style dining room, complete with an impressive fireplace and a LeCompte, triple lancet stained-glass window; a peaceful garden in the cloistered courtyard; conference rooms, such as the paneled library overlooking the garden; and twenty-six bedrooms, one of which is a suite in the college tower with views of Washington and the cathedral.

Oh, yes, you can also tent the lawn.

A tour of the cathedral is included when you hold an event here, although an additional fee is charged for a docent-guided tour of the gardens and for lectures/performances by the cathedral's master stonemason, organist, gardener, and so on.

CAPACITY

Reception: 160 in the observation gallery, though this can vary from event to event; 20 to 150 in the College of Preachers dining hall; 300 on the tented lawn; 150 in the Garth

Banquet: 125 in the observation gallery, 20 to 64 in the College of Preachers dining hall, 300 on the tented lawn, 100 in the Garth, 30 in the cathedral's library

Meeting: 10 (in a College of Preachers conference room) to 200 (in the observation gallery's auditorium)

Overnight accommodations: 26 rooms provide lodging for up to 33 people

LOCATION

At the intersection of Massachusetts and Wisconsin Avenues, NW.

FOOD/BEVERAGE

For gatherings in the observation gallery and other cathedral locations, you must choose from the cathedral's list of approved caterers. There is no kitchen facility in the west tower. For events held in the College of Preachers quarters, which include a full-service kitchen, you use the in-house catering service.

LIMITATIONS/RESTRICTIONS

Use of the observation gallery is open to all, but only after cathedral hours. Private, worship-related events, such as wedding ceremonies, are not permitted in the gallery, nor are smoking and amplified music. Wine and beer are the only forms of alcohol permitted. Dancing is limited. Two elevators at the west entrance of the cathedral can each transport twelve people at a time to the gallery.

Use of the College of Preachers is open to all, anytime, subject to the college's own schedule. The college exercises case-by-case discretion regarding guests under eighteen. Smoking is permitted only in the dining room. Liquor is prohibited, but beer and wine are allowed. Dancing is limited. Amplified music is not encouraged.

LEAD TIME FOR RESERVATIONS

Call for availability.

RATES

Observation gallery, $2,000; Churchill Porch, $600; cathedral library, $1,500; Garth, $2,400; grounds, upwards of $4,000, depending upon the size of the group.

Rental of the College of Preachers meeting rooms starts at $45 for a half day's use of a small chamber to $250 for a full day's use of the largest one. Lodging rates run from $70 per night for a single to $145 per night for a suite. Catering fees run from $10 per person for breakfast to $20 per person for dinner. Call for rental fees for reception spaces.

FACILITIES FOR THE PHYSICALLY DISABLED? Some

WHITEHALL

18301 Whitehall Estate Lane, off Route 7
Bluemont, VA 20135
703/716-9700
703/716-7400 (fax)
www.goldgrape.com
whitehall@goldgrape.com

Federal manor house in Virginia hunt country

Fifty acres at the foot of the Blue Ridge Mountains, with an antebellum mansion in the middle—that's Whitehall. Among your options: a grand gala for 180 in the ballrooms, with pretty views of the meadow, elegant ivory and white appurtenances, and a garden terrace, or a full-blown corporate picnic for three thousand around the grounds.

You enter Whitehall's ballroom through French doors set within a majestic, four-columned, porticoed entrance. A raised stage, fluted columns, long windows, and grand fireplace are the hall's main features. Up a short set of stairs, through a vestibule, and to the left is a formal dining room with an off-center Italian marble fireplace and a Victorian chandelier. Beyond the dining room are twin parlors connected by a foyer. Porches and verandas with wicker furniture and rocking chairs lie off each of these reception rooms.

CAPACITY
Reception: 200 in the ballroom, 300 throughout the manor house
Banquet: 180 in the ballroom, 250 throughout the manor house
Picnics and outings: 3,000 throughout the property
Meeting: 25 to 200

LOCATION
From the Beltway (I-495), take the Dulles Toll Road to the Dulles Greenway (Route 267). At the end of the Greenway, proceed west onto Route 7 toward Winchester. Drive about seventeen miles, passing the exits for Hamilton, Purcellville, and Round Hill. Pass Hill High Orchards and get in the left lane; make a U-turn at Route 760 (Clayton Hall Road) and immediately turn right onto the Whitehall property.

FOOD/BEVERAGE
A catering and special events firm owns and operates Whitehall and will handle all your food and beverage requirements. A large kitchen provides plenty of counter space, a refrigerator, and other equipment.

LIMITATIONS/RESTRICTIONS
Whitehall is available weekdays and weekends, March through December. Smoking is prohibited inside. Amplified music is allowed but should be played at a reasonable level.

LEAD TIME FOR RESERVATIONS
Call for availability. Whitehall accepts reservations up to fifteen months in advance.

RATES
Social functions: $3,000 on Saturday, $2,500 on Sunday, and $950 on weekdays. These rates cover an eight-hour period; additional time is billed at $175 per half hour.

Conferences: $500 on weekdays. Nonprofit organizations receive special rates. Catering fees for a sit-down or buffet dinner with an open bar average $70 to $95 per person.

FACILITIES FOR THE PHYSICALLY DISABLED? Yes

WHITE-MEYER HOUSE

1624 Crescent Place, NW
Washington, DC 20009
202/939-5592
www.meridian.org/facility

Meridian House's Georgian neighbor

This redbrick Georgian mansion is next-door neighbors with Meridian House (see page 172). Meridian International Center actually owns and operates the White-Meyer House as an extension of its activities in the field of international culture and educational exchange. Together, the two properties occupy an entire city block, which means that when you rent both houses for an event you're essentially throwing a block party—albeit a very exclusive and refined one.

Most people find that just one of these mansions will satisfy their event requirements. When the choice is the White-Meyer House, you're entitled to use five spacious rooms, as well as the terrace and garden, all on the first floor. The layout of the house leads guests through mammoth wooden double doors from the marble-floored entry hall to the white-paneled sitting room, where host and hostess wait to greet them; to the largest area, the drawing room, with its many long windows overlooking the gardens; to the library, paneled in black walnut and opening onto the terrace; and to the light-filled dining room, also adjoining the terrace. Wood panels separating the library and dining room can slide back to create an expansive chamber that advances through French doors to the terrace. In each room you find high ceilings, marble fireplaces, parquet floors, and, very often, art exhibits sponsored by Meridian International Center. Renovation work has restored architectural details to rooms and made possible the installation of such modern features as track lighting, air-conditioning, and a sophisticated security system.

One other space is for rent here: a small, paneled study said to have been used by Henry White, the house's original owner and a distinguished career diplomat, as a refuge from both worldly and domestic woes. The house was later the childhood home of Washington Post chairman of the board Katherine Graham.

CAPACITY
Reception: 350
Banquet: 70 to 110
Meeting: 100 theater-style, 35 conference-style

LOCATION
From downtown Washington, head north on 16th Street, NW, to Belmont Road. Turn left and follow the street around as it curves. Turn right on Crescent Place.

FOOD/BEVERAGE
The staff prefers that you choose a caterer with demonstrated experience at Meridian House. A catering kitchen is equipped with ample work space, a

refrigerator, warming ovens, and a microwave.

LIMITATIONS/RESTRICTIONS
All red-staining foods, including red wine, are prohibited. Smoking is prohibited inside. Fund-raising is not allowed. Floral arrangements must arrive prepared.

LEAD TIME FOR RESERVATIONS
Call for availability.

RATES
Daytime functions: whole day/whole floor, $1,500; whole day/one room, $1,000; half day/whole floor, $1,000; half day/one room, $500.
Evening functions: whole floor, $3,500; one room, $1,000.
Wedding receptions: $6,000 for the use of the entire floor. Call for additional information.

FACILITIES FOR THE PHYSICALLY DISABLED? No

THE WOMAN'S CLUB OF CHEVY CHASE, MARYLAND, INC.
7931 Connecticut Avenue
Chevy Chase, MD 20815
301/652-8480 (phone and fax)

Handsome clubhouse welcomes nonmembers

The Woman's Club of Chevy Chase was founded in 1913 and, with its current roster of four hundred women, is still going strong. (There's a Junior Woman's Club, too, for the under-forty set.) But if age and membership size aren't enough to convince you of the club's vitality, all you need do is take a peek at the classy quarters the club has kept for some sixty-two years. The white-painted brick building houses one large "auditorium," a South Wing (added in

1967), and an upstairs denlike boardroom.

The auditorium is so named because of its large stage, with Carolina pine flooring and heavy flanking curtains. At the other end of the room, under an overhang, is the library, a paneled area with full bookshelves, a pair of fireplaces, and sets of furniture arranged just so. The library may be set off from the rest of the room by a partition.

The entire expanse of the auditorium, including the library, measures fifty by seventy feet. In between lie an oak floor, knotty-pine-paneled columns and wainscoting, French doors along one side leading to the garden, and a high ceiling. You'll notice the musicians' balcony above you, which you can use for its intended purpose or for taking pictures of the party below. Behind the balcony is the boardroom, a sort of funky space, but hey, it's got a table, it's private, and there's a very nice powder room up there.

The South Wing has less character but is pleasant, with peachy walls, paneled windows, chandelier lighting, and plants.

CAPACITY

Reception: 400 in the whole clubhouse, 85 in the South Wing

Banquet: 250 without dancing or 200 with dancing in the whole clubhouse, 50 in the South Wing

Meeting: 200 in the auditorium, 50 in the South Wing

LOCATION

From the Beltway (I-495), take the Connecticut Avenue exit, headed toward Chevy Chase. The club is located about one mile south of the Beltway exit on your left.

FOOD/BEVERAGE

The club has a list of suggested caterers, but you may choose your own licensed and insured caterer, subject to the manager's approval. Use of the full-service kitchen costs extra. The club can offer you the use of some forty rectangular tables and two hundred chairs.

LIMITATIONS/RESTRICTIONS

The clubhouse is available year-round, subject to the club's own schedule. For instance, from October through May, Monday through Thursday rentals must take place after 5:00 P.M. Decorations may not be nailed or tacked to the walls. Events must end by 1:00 A.M. There are ninety parking spaces in the club's lot; neighboring church and library properties may be available to provide additional spots. When you rent the clubhouse on the weekend, you must pay for a minimum of eight hours.

LEAD TIME FOR RESERVATIONS

For Saturday functions, call at least one year in advance; for functions on other days, call six months ahead.

RATES

Rates range from $300 for five hours' weekday use of the South Wing, without the kitchen facility, to $1,700 for Friday through Sunday use of the whole clubhouse, including the kitchen, for eight hours. Additional costs include a $200 damage fee (due with the initial deposit and applied to your balance if there's no damage) and fees for use of microphones and coffee urns.

FACILITIES FOR THE PHYSICALLY DISABLED? No

THE WOMAN'S NATIONAL DEMOCRATIC CLUB

1526 New Hampshire Avenue, NW
Washington, DC 20036
202/232-7363
womansndc@aol.com

A jewel of a clubhouse

You'd be hard pressed to find a more gracious meeting place than this clubhouse. Once the home of a well-to-do opera singer, the mansion now has other purposes, one of which is to be "a place of tolerance, where minds may meet." Certainly the club's finely appointed interior and genial atmosphere create the appropriate setting.

With its peaked turret and many-sided shape, the club's exterior resembles a small castle. Ten rooms on two floors, as well as a garden, are available for functions. Each room is furnished with portraits, paintings, antiques, and political memorabilia donated by members, distinguished Democrats, and friends.

Perhaps the most notable of these rooms, for meeting purposes, are the Marjorie Merriweather Post Parlor, the Adlai Stevenson Room, and the Sam Rayburn Lounge. The parlor is furnished with antique furniture, a piano, and an Oriental rug and makes an inviting reception area. For larger luncheons, meetings, and dinners, you'll want to use the Stevenson Room, which is a pleasant and large space with a raised stage and all sorts of meeting accoutrements. The Rayburn Lounge serves mostly as a cocktail and luncheon room and has a bar at one end. Its walls are hung with pictures, cartoons, and documents dramatizing historic moments in Speaker Rayburn's career.

The other rooms and the garden are choice spots for small meetings or for catching moments of repose. Don't miss the library, an engaging room filled with books by and about prominent Democrats; the Daisy Harriman Room, named for one of the club's famous founders and furnished with art and drawing room pieces from her estate; and the lovely brick-paved and enclosed garden.

CAPACITY
Reception: 350 to 400
Banquet: 225
Meeting: 200

LOCATION
In the Dupont Circle area of northwest Washington, one block northwest of the Dupont Circle stop on Metro's red line.

FOOD/BEVERAGE
The club has its own in-house catering service and prepares all food but will work with you to plan your meals.

LIMITATIONS/RESTRICTIONS

Birdseed and rice throwing are prohibited. Smoking is allowed only on the balcony and on the patio.

LEAD TIME FOR RESERVATIONS

The staff recommends that you call for availability.

RATES

Members: $1,500 for four hours, plus $500 for each additional hour
Nonmembers: $3,000 for four hours, plus $500 for each additional hour

FACILITIES FOR THE PHYSICALLY DISABLED? Yes

WOODLAWN MANOR HOUSE

16501 Norwood Road
Sandy Spring, MD 20860
301/299-5026

A nineteenth-century gem set in Maryland countryside

At first sight of the Woodlawn Manor House and surrounding grounds, you notice that the estate has a welcoming appearance rather than an imposing one. The house is large, but not huge. Its architecture is simple Georgian brick with some Victorian touches; it's not bedecked with columns and porticoes. And though wide-open green pastures encircle the house, a private garden embraces the manor close up, beckoning you to enter. Woodlawn is a gracious host of a house awaiting your arrival.

The restored home offers five rooms on two floors for functions. First-floor rooms include a dining room decorated in nineteenth-century style; a cozy family room with a large brick hearth and fireplace, original exposed beams, and comfortable furniture; and a long double parlor painted Jamestown blue and white, with brass chandeliers and windows overlooking the lawn. Upstairs are two sitting rooms decorated in the Williamsburg mode.

Outside, you'll find trees shading the house on all sides. Use of the building includes use of the garden, which is enclosed by a hedge of boxwoods and bordered on the inside by rows of multicolored flowers. A white gazebo provides the perfect covered spot for the band or the bar. The surrounding grounds are available as well. Of interest, too, are several old outbuildings: a log cabin, a late-1800s tenant house, and a stone meat house and dairy.

Woodlawn was built around 1800 by the Thomases, a Quaker family that ran a small boarding school here. The Maryland-National Capital Park and Planning Commission now owns the site.

CAPACITY
Reception: 125 inside, 300 or more outside
Banquet: 40
Lawn party: 300 or more
Meeting: 7 to 40 in one room

LOCATION
From the Beltway (I-495) north of Washington, take the White Oak exit, which leads you to New Hampshire Avenue. Follow New Hampshire Avenue approximately seven miles to Norwood Road. Turn left on Norwood Road, go two miles, and turn right onto the Woodlawn property.

FOOD/BEVERAGE
You must choose a caterer from Woodlawn's approved list. The house has a kitchen equipped with a warming oven, triple sink, refrigerator, and freezer.

LIMITATIONS/RESTRICTIONS
Smoking is prohibited inside the mansion, and tents are prohibited in the garden/gazebo area. Tents are required on the grounds when your party includes more than 125 people.

LEAD TIME FOR RESERVATIONS
Three weeks for weekday and evening events and for weekend events taking place from November through March; nine months for weekend events scheduled for April through October.

RATES
Meetings: $50 per hour, Monday through Friday, from 8:00 A.M. to 5:00 P.M.
    The rate covers the use of the house and grounds for an entire working day.
Social functions: Friday, Sunday, and holidays, $800; Saturday, $900; Monday
    through Thursday, $600. These rates cover the use of the house and grounds
    for a seven-hour period; the overtime charge is $200 per hour.

FACILITIES FOR THE PHYSICALLY DISABLED? Yes

WOODROW WILSON HOUSE

2340 S Street, NW
Washington, DC 20008
202/387-4062
www.woodrowwilsonhouse.org

Home to Wilson after the White House

Picture this: Woodrow Wilson skipping down the aisle of a train on his honeymoon night whistling the early-1900s tune "Oh You Beautiful Doll." It isn't a very presidential image, but it certainly is an endearing one. It shows the personal side of our twenty-eighth president, which you learn about when you rent the house to which he retired at the end of his second term.

This redbrick, Georgian Revival town house offers you the use of five rooms, a terrace, and the garden, all much as they were when the Wilsons lived here in the 1920s. You can hold intimate banquets in the same room where Wilson dined (but only when he was properly attired in a dinner jacket). After dinner, you may want to stroll out to the red tile terrace for a little night air or retire to the library for some quiet business talk. The library is a dark, cozy room filled with books and mementos of Wilson's hobbies and presidency.

Or maybe you'd like to hold court in the drawing room, where Wilson stood at the window to acknowledge the crowd that had gathered to honor him on Armistice Day in 1923. Many of the drawing room's furnishings were wedding gifts, including a French Gobelin tapestry from the French ambassador and a marble mosaic from the Vatican.

The charming solarium completes the suite of rooms available for events on the main floor. A large interior window overlooks the house's central stairway while the solarium's other windows provide a view of the garden.

The two-level garden area, enclosed by a stone wall, is a spacious place in which to gather for receptions and banquets during the warmer months. A modern conference room is available on the house's first floor for small meetings, lunches, and dinners.

CAPACITY

Reception: 175 in the house alone, 300 in the house and garden
Banquet: 36 in the house alone, 150 in the house and garden
Garden party: 200
Meeting: 45

LOCATION

One block off Embassy Row (Massachusetts Avenue) in northwest Washington.

FOOD/BEVERAGE

You must choose a caterer from the museum's approved list. The site does not have kitchen facilities, only a small pantry with a microwave oven.

LIMITATIONS/RESTRICTIONS

You can rent the conference room for daytime functions, but the other rentable areas are available only in the evening. Evening functions must end by 11:00 P.M. The house is not air-conditioned, and smoking, red wine, dancing, and amplified music are prohibited inside.

LEAD TIME FOR RESERVATIONS

One to six months, depending on the season. Fall and spring are the busiest times.

RATES

Main floor and terrace, $3,000; main floor and garden, $5,000; main floor dining room, $2,500; main floor, $2,000; conference room, $500. A $100 membership fee is also requested. These rates cover a maximum of four hours' use.

FACILITIES FOR THE PHYSICALLY DISABLED? Some

The first floor, including a rest room, is wheelchair accessible.

Sites for
500 to 1,000 people

THE CAPITAL CHILDREN'S MUSEUM

800 3rd Street, NE
Washington, DC 20002
202/675-4120, ext. 4149
www.ccm.org

A wonderland for children of all ages

Pack your curiosity and your sense of wonder and you're all set to have fun at the Capital Children's Museum. Here you'll discover exhibits that are just as fascinating for adults as they are for children.

You can rent the whole museum or parts of it for use after public hours, and portions of it for use during the day.

The *Chuck Jones, An Animated Life* Hall is a great place to get your colleagues to loosen up. The exhibit features walk-through sets from some of the greatest classic cartoons; an Animation Hall of Fame, with walls of famous cartoon characters; a Make-It-Move Hall, with hands-on demonstrations of animation techniques; the Observe and Draw section, where you draw your own cartoon classics; and Sound Town, where you add sound effects and dialogue to your cartoons.

Other exhibits include those on the cultures of Japan (*Through the Eyes of a Child*) and Mexico, as well as a cave replicated from the Ice Age.

Four theme-decorated birthday party rooms (Winnie the Pooh, Birthday under the Big Top, Birthday on the Moon, and Birthday under the Sea) and the auditorium are available during regular museum hours, as are the special exhibit galleries when no exhibits are on display there. The auditorium features a stage, folding chairs, and minimal decorations.

If you rent one of these spaces for a daytime event, you can tour the museum after paying the admission charge. At night, however, you're entitled to tour only the space you've rented, so your best bet is to rent one or all of the exhibit areas. Inclusion of hands-on activities, however, will require staffing and additional fees.

CAPACITY
Reception: 500 in the entire museum
Banquet: 100 in one room
Meeting: 200 in the auditorium

LOCATION
One block from the back of Union Station and six blocks from the US Capitol.

FOOD/BEVERAGE
You're free to choose your own caterer. A small kitchen is available for warming and cooling foods.

LIMITATIONS/RESTRICTIONS
Rental is subject to the museum's schedule. The site is not available for weddings. There is limited parking available, although arrangements can be made to rent a parking lot directly across the street. Smoking is prohibited in the museum.

LEAD TIME FOR RESERVATIONS
At least sixty days, but call for availability.

RATES
Rates range from $200, for small birthday parties and meetings, and $500, for use of the auditorium during the day, to $6,000, for the entire museum.

FACILITIES FOR THE PHYSICALLY DISABLED? Yes

CERESVILLE MANSION

8529 Liberty Road
Frederick, MD 21701
301/694-5111
www.ceresville.com

A longtime site for entertaining

Ceresville Mansion was an anniversary present from Edward Shriner to his wife in 1888. The Shriners and subsequent owners have all loved to entertain here. These days, Frederick County and Washington-area residents continue the tradition, renting the site for wedding receptions, birthday celebrations, business events, and picnics.

You are welcome to roam all four floors and the nine thousand square feet of space that make up Ceresville, although the prime party rooms are on the first level. A large atrium-ballroom measures forty-eight by forty-five feet and leads to a lovely terrace with a pergola and reflecting pool backing up against woodlands. The ballroom is circular and has windows all around. It holds a center-wall fireplace, a set of columns, and a second-floor balcony. Off the ballroom lies the original portion of the house: a dining room whose walls are covered with a mural depicting an Italian villa, a center hall, twin parlors (mirror images of each other, down to the bow windows), and a library. Decorative features include large mirrors, sliding doors, wainscoting, and antique furnishings. The upstairs suite of four rooms and a long hall continues the old-fashioned feel.

Down the hill from the mansion are a meadow and pavilion, which are often used for picnics and family reunions.

CAPACITY

Reception: 225 inside, 350 with tenting on the terrace
Banquet: 170 in the ballroom with dancing and a head table, 200 in the ballroom
without dancing and a head table, 350 with tenting on the terrace
Meeting: 100 to 125
Company picnics: 600 in the meadow

LOCATION

Take I-270 north. Just south of Frederick, stay in either of the two left lanes. I-270 becomes Route 15 north, which you should follow four miles to the Route 26 east exit (Libertytown/Walkersville). Go about two miles—through three traffic lights and over a bridge—until you see the mansion on your right. Pass the mansion and turn right into the driveway.

FOOD/BEVERAGE

The mansion handles all your food and beverage requirements and will customize your menu.

LIMITATIONS/RESTRICTIONS

The house is available year-round. A minimum of 125 guests is required to reserve the mansion on a Saturday, and a minimum of 100 guests is required to reserve the mansion on a Friday or Sunday. Smoking is prohibited inside. Open flames are not allowed.

LEAD TIME FOR RESERVATIONS

Call a year in advance.

RATES

Rates vary depending on the time of year, number of guests, and day of the week. Count on spending $1,950 for a party of more than 125 on a Saturday evening in season (April through December). Rates include two hours for setup, four hours of event time, and one hour to clean up. Additional hours are billed at $500 per hour. Ceresville charges $375 for wedding ceremonies.

FACILITIES FOR THE PHYSICALLY DISABLED? Yes

The first floor, with a ramp and rest room, is fully wheelchair accessible.

THE CLUB AT FRANKLIN SQUARE

1300 I Street, NW
Washington, DC 20005
202/408-1300

Cozy pub and parkview clubroom

Washington has long been a city of clubs, from the politically oriented Capitol Hill and National Democratic Clubs to those catering to Washington's upper crust, like the Sulgrave. In the last decade, though, a fresh crop of city clubs has sprung up, alike both in the way they cater to the ranks of Washington professionals at large and in locating clubhouses within downtown office buildings. Less exclusive than many of the old-time, high-society types, the younger generation encourages the use of club facilities for special events by both members and nonmembers.

A perfect example is the Club at Franklin Square, housed within a modern, twelve-story office building on a quiet block of I Street. The club lies off the main lobby, a vast atrium of marble- and granite-inlaid floors and walls, a towering ceiling, and immense pillars. You can use the lobby (on weekends only) and more than double your event capacity.

The club occupies nearly ninety-one hundred square feet. At lobby level is the Parkview Room, overlooking Franklin Square Park and decorated in shades of dusty blue, with cherrywood furniture and Oriental ginger jars, lamp bases, and plant pots. This is the club's dining room, but tables and chairs may be moved to create more space. French doors can close off the far end of this room for a gathering of about sixty.

On this same level lie three handsome conference rooms, one with bloodred, pieced fabric wallpaper and all three displaying interesting artwork. Downstairs a cozy, forest-green-paneled pub with banquettes and booths wraps around to meet a British-style library complete with fireplace (decorative) and landscape paintings.

CAPACITY
Reception: 400 in the club, 1,000 using the lobby and club

Banquet: 130 in the club, 300 in the lobby

Meeting: 12 in a boardroom, 60 in the Parkview Room annex

LOCATION
On I Street, NW, between 13th and 14th Streets, directly across from Franklin Square Park. Parking in the building is unlimited after 5:00 P.M. on weekdays and all day on weekends; there is a fee.

FOOD/BEVERAGE
Except for wedding cakes, the club handles all food and beverage details. A commercial kitchen lies just off the main room.

LIMITATIONS/RESTRICTIONS
The club is available for functions after 3:30 P.M. on weekdays and anytime on weekends. The lobby is available weekends only, anytime. Nonmembers who are sponsored by a member may use the club; the club will help you obtain sponsorship. Smoking and red wine are prohibited in the lobby.

LEAD TIME FOR RESERVATIONS
Call at least three months in advance.

RATES
Members pay no rental fee; nonmembers pay $500 to rent the whole club, including the atrium-lobby. (Membership is by current member invitation only.) Catering fees vary. An average cocktail reception will cost between $30 and $50 per person, including drinks.

FACILITIES FOR THE PHYSICALLY DISABLED? Yes

CORCORAN GALLERY OF ART

17th Street and New York Avenue, NW

Washington, DC 20006

202/639-1781

www.corcoran.org

The only drawback to holding an event at the Corcoran Gallery of Art is that you eventually have to leave. The museum is a dreamlike palace of art, architecture, and atmosphere. Frank Lloyd Wright is said to have called it the best-designed building in Washington. After your event, you'll probably call it one of your favorite Washington sites.

Receptions and banquets take place in the double atrium and on the atrium bridge. The double atrium is the focal point of the museum—it's a two-story, templelike hall up a flight of stairs from the entrance. Fluted columns punctuate this great space, rising forty feet from the marble floor to the skylighted ceiling. The bridge, overhead, spans the middle of the atrium, gracefully distinguishing the second level from the first.

The wide, wide marble staircase that takes you to the upper atrium leads you first to a landing and the back part of the museum. Proceed through the spectacular rotunda and you arrive at the Clark Landing. This is a small, walnut-paneled room with enormous charm. A staircase winds up one side, a gallery overhangs—the perfect niche for a string quartet or harpist.

The Corcoran, which is most famous for its extensive collection of American masterpieces, will open some or all of its galleries for browsing, depending upon the type of event you're holding. The galleries are located all around the upstairs atrium and extend way beyond the south side of the building on both floors. You'll revel in such works as Frederic Remington's sculpture *Coming through the Rye* and Rembrandt Peale's huge portrait of George Washington, as well as modern art by Andy Warhol, Mark Rothko, and others.

An auditorium is also available for lectures, chamber music, and other small performances. This blue-tinted, semicircular room has a round stage, a concert grand Steinway piano, and a colonnade running along the back.

CAPACITY
Reception: 1,000
Banquet: 400
Auditorium: 193

LOCATION

Within walking distance of the White House, one block west. The museum faces the Ellipse.

FOOD/BEVERAGE

You must choose from the Corcoran's list of approved caterers.

LIMITATIONS/RESTRICTIONS

Events in the gallery may take place at any time on Tuesday and from 6:30 P.M. to midnight any other day except Thursday. Events may be held in the auditorium at any time, subject to the Corcoran's schedule. (The Corcoran School of Art frequently uses the auditorium, especially during the day.) The director of special events reviews each request for use of the Corcoran. Cash balls and ticketed events are not permitted; red wine, fund-raising, and smoking are prohibited. You must arrange for a certificate of insurance from your own insurance carrier for the use of the museum.

LEAD TIME FOR RESERVATIONS

Four to twelve months is recommended.

RATES

The gallery is made available to corporations that make a donation of $9,000, $7,500 of which is tax-deductible. The rate for nonprofit groups is $7,500. Wedding ceremonies and/or receptions are allowed; the cost for ceremony and reception is $15,000, of which $12,000 is tax-deductible, and the cost for a reception alone is $12,000, of which $10,000 is tax-deductible. The following service fees are charged after the event: $750 for operations, $3 per person for security, and an overtime charge of $1,500 for each hour beyond five hours.

The auditorium may be leased for $1,800, with additional charges of $150 for operations and $150 for security.

FACILITIES FOR THE PHYSICALLY DISABLED? Yes

DAR

THE NATIONAL HEADQUARTERS OF THE NATIONAL SOCIETY
DAUGHTERS OF THE AMERICAN REVOLUTION

1776 D Street, NW

Washington, DC 20006

202/879-3318

www.dar.org

Three beautiful, interconnected buildings taking up a city block

The covered portico of Memorial Continental Hall on C Street is a dead
ringer for the White House (and often serves as a stand-in for the real thing in
the television series the *West Wing*). The porticoed 17th Street entrance faces
the Ellipse. From either of these spots, you have a pretty peerless view of the
Washington Monument, the Ellipse, the White House, and other landmarks.

The interiors of DAR's three buildings are just as breathtaking. Most
Washingtonians are familiar with one of them, Constitution Hall, best known

as a superb concert hall. But few people know about Memorial Continental Hall's magnificent third-floor banquet room, with its hardwood floor, antique furnishings, and grand chandeliers. And then there's the grand O'Byrne Gallery, with high ceilings and French doors leading to the covered portico and terrace. This newly remodeled gallery is creamy white and has lots of moldings and herringbone-patterned hardwood floors. Your party easily flows from here into the skylighted library or to the expansive, marble-floored Pennsylvania Foyer. You have to come and see for yourself these and countless other perfect places to gather.

Inaugural event schedulers and others planning functions for more than one thousand people should consider Constitution Hall, which can hold quite a crowd (see capacity information below).

CAPACITY
Memorial Continental Hall: 12 (seated in the Kemper Executive Conference Room) to 121 (seated in the third-floor banquet hall). The largest space for a stand-up reception is the library, a beautiful, skylighted gallery that can hold up to 200.

Administration Building: 40 (seated in the President General's Assembly Room) to 380 (standing in the O'Byrne Gallery and flowing out to the covered terrace)

Constitution Hall: 180 seated, 225 standing in the lounge; 500 to 700 seated, 1,200 to 1,500 standing in the lobby; 3,702 seated theater-style, 720 for banquets in the auditorium (auditorium seats can be removed, if necessary)

LOCATION
DAR Headquarters occupies the block between 17th, 18th, C, and D Streets, NW, near the White House. Farragut West, at 17th and I Streets, NW, is the closest Metro station. Parking is on the street, or you can contact nearby garages to coordinate parking for your event.

FOOD/BEVERAGE
The site has a list of preferred caterers, though you may choose another as long as the caterer possesses a valid license. A kitchen in Memorial Continental Hall is available for prep work and is equipped with a stove, sink, microwave, refrigerator,

freezer, and pantry. Staging areas are available throughout all three buildings.

LIMITATIONS/RESTRICTIONS
You may rent areas in these buildings anytime, though additional rental fees apply for after-hours events. The DAR Museum and its thirty-three period rooms may be toured during your function. Red wine and other staining drinks are not allowed. Smoking is not permitted.

LEAD TIME FOR RESERVATIONS
Call for availability.

RATES
Fees vary based upon the scope of the event, but count on paying a minimum of $420 per hour, with a minimum four-hour rental, for any single space in Memorial Continental Hall or in the Administration Building. The rental fee for Constitution Hall is $5,000 for evening events and $3,000 for government groups and daytime events. Additional fees include charges for security and staffing.

FACILITIES FOR THE PHYSICALLY DISABLED? Yes

FRYING PAN PARK
2709 West Ox Road
Herndon, VA 22071
703/437-9101

Historic landmark in a park

Funny name, Frying Pan. One story has it that early pioneers searching for gold in a creek came upon some Indians frying up meat in a pan stolen from the pioneers. The settlers killed the Indians, retrieved their pan, and appended the name "frying pan" to the creek and the surrounding land.

Frying Pan Park offers two facilities for events: the Activity Center and an outdoor riding ring. The Activity Center's main feature is its sand-floor riding arena, which seats eight hundred people and is equipped with a public address system. The center is best suited for such activities as soccer games, chili cook-offs, and horse-and-dog shows, whereas the outdoor equestrian center is strictly for horse riding. The park grounds, which are mostly open, unshaded pastures, are available as well.

Within Frying Pan Park lies Kidwell Farm, a dominant property in Fairfax County in the 1920s. The forty-five-acre, working farm demonstrates the country ways of decades past.

CAPACITY
Park picnic: 50 to 75
Activity Center: 800

LOCATION
From the Beltway (I-495), take Exit 9 or 9A (Route 66 west) to Route 50 west. Follow Route 50 west to a right on Fairfax County Parkway. Take a left onto West Ox Road; the park entrance is on the right.

FOOD/BEVERAGE
You make your own food and beverage arrangements. A food vendor is on site during special events on the weekends.

LIMITATIONS/RESTRICTIONS
The Activity Center is available year-round, every day. An alcoholic beverage use permit is required to serve alcohol.

LEAD TIME FOR RESERVATIONS
Call as much as a year in advance for the Activity Center. The site is popular year-round.

RATES
The fee structure for the Activity Center varies widely, depending upon its use

and the length of time for which it is rented; call for those rates.

FACILITIES FOR THE PHYSICALLY DISABLED? Yes

THE GALLERIA AT LAFAYETTE CENTRE

1155 21st Street, NW
Washington, DC 20036
202/835-0093

A palatial ballroom amidst office buildings

It's not hard to imagine oneself in a fairy tale—the ballroom scene in Cinderella, for example—when one entertains at the Galleria. The atrium has all the dimensions and trimmings of a palace ballroom. It's a twelve-thousand-square-foot space with a floor of coral, green, and black Italian marble. Four stories up is the ceiling, a clear and rose-tinted glass dome crisscrossed with girders. An arcade stretches along one side of the atrium, enabling guests to amble amiably away from center stage for more intimate conversation or a private dance. But the decorative element that clinches the fairy-tale feel is the staircase. Guests enter the Galleria on the mezzanine level and discover themselves on view at the head of a wide marble stairway. (Fantasize a blare of trumpets and a footman announcing your arrival.) The stairs descend to a landing overlooking the hall and then arch right and left into a double staircase.

Other design features confirm that the Galleria was built specifically to hold special events. The mezzanine, which encircles the atrium at street level, is ideal as a cocktail reception area when you're having a sit-down dinner below. The stairway, as it unfolds in an arc to the coral marble floor, creates a niche inside the arc that's perfect for a bar, a ceremony, or the musical entertainment. Track lighting has been installed in the ceiling grids, and there is a built-in sound system.

CAPACITY

Reception: 750

Banquet: 400 with a dance floor

Conference: 400 seated theater-style

LOCATION

In downtown Washington, on 21st Street, NW, between L and M Streets, in the courtyard of Lafayette Centre.

FOOD/BEVERAGE

You may choose a caterer from the Galleria's approved list. There is a preparation space for caterers but no kitchen equipment.

LIMITATIONS/RESTRICTIONS

The Galleria handles one event per day. Weekday parties may not take place before 5:00 P.M., although you can start setting up before then. Guests must be gone by 1:30 A.M.

LEAD TIME FOR RESERVATIONS

Weekends, six months; weekdays, one to two months.

RATES

Thursday through Sunday, $5,000; Monday through Wednesday, $3,700. Add $500 for wedding ceremonies. Nonprofit groups receive a $1,000 discount.

FACILITIES FOR THE PHYSICALLY DISABLED? Yes

GUNSTON HALL PLANTATION

Mason Neck, VA 22079
703/550-9220
http://gunstonhall.org
events@gunstonhall.org

Meet at the home of a founding father

One of the things you learn when you tour George Mason's spectacular estate is that the statesman, who was instrumental in shaping our Constitution and is known as the father of the Bill of Rights, rarely joined in the fray. He preferred, instead, to work at home, and who can blame him? Gunston Hall is a garden of paradise along the Potomac River.

Mason's Georgian-style mansion sits on 550 acres that include extensive formal gardens, nature trails, outbuildings, an herb garden, meadows, and the contemporary Ann Mason Visitors Center. Available for rent are a modern meeting room in the Ann Mason building and a designated outdoor area, usually the tree-lined meadow, on the grounds.

The meeting room boasts a cathedral ceiling and brick walls. You can hold a meeting here using the facility's podium, microphone, screen and projector, then clear away all evidence of business and start partying. Glass doors lead to a brick-paved inner courtyard where, in warm months, you can set up a bar around the center fountain or in one of the tree-shaded corners. There is also a small private garden for ceremonies.

Whether or not you rent the grounds, you really must take a stroll outdoors. The wonderful gardens contain only plants found in colonial days; the twelve-foot-high English boxwoods that form a center allée were planted by Mason himself. You can hike the mile to the Potomac River via a nature trail.

Rental of the Ann Mason room or the grounds includes a guided tour of Mason's mansion. Built in 1755, the building is a masterpiece of architectural symmetry. Its interior is furnished as historians believe it would have been in Mason's day, and some of its original features still remain. Note especially the beautiful, hand-carved woodwork in the formal parlor and, in the study, the writing table on which Mason composed the Virginia Declaration of Rights, which became the model for the US Bill of Rights.

CAPACITY

Reception: 225 in the Ann Mason room and courtyard, 100 in the Regents'
 Garden
Banquet: 150 in the Ann Mason room and courtyard
Meeting/lecture: 150 to 175 in the Ann Mason room and courtyard
Ceremony: 150 in the Regents' Garden
Meadow party: 1,000

LOCATION

From Washington, travel south on I-95 to Exit 163 (Lorton). Follow the signs to Gunston Hall. From points south, go north on I-95 to Exit 161 (Gunston Hall/Ft. Belvoir/Mt. Vernon).

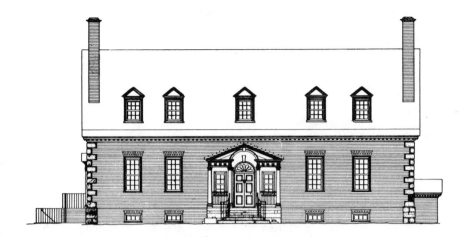

FOOD/BEVERAGE

Gunston Hall has an in-house caterer whom you must use. The site has a full kitchen and provides rental equipment if needed.

LIMITATIONS/RESTRICTIONS

Events cannot take place in the mansion, and food and beverage are prohibited there. If your party exceeds the capacity of the Ann Mason room, you must rent the grounds. Although a tent is not required with the use of the grounds, the staff strongly advises you to rent one, in case of inclement weather. Amplified music is allowed after 5:00 P.M.

LEAD TIME FOR RESERVATIONS

For weekend events, call a year in advance. For weekday events, call one to two months in advance.

RATES

Call for rates.

FACILITIES FOR THE PHYSICALLY DISABLED? Yes

LA MAISON FRANÇAISE

4101 Reservoir Road, NW
Washington, DC 20007
202/944-6090
www.info-france-usa.org/fculture.htm

The French Embassy's center for arts and entertainment

The great gates open and a guard waves you through the entrance and up the driveway when you attend an event at the French Embassy's magnificent performing arts and cultural center. While the embassy uses La Maison Française for its own diplomatic, cultural, and social events, it allows outside groups—but not individuals—to rent the facility for functions.

The marble building's design creates a bright and light-filled space, with twenty-foot-high ceilings, glass walls overlooking the landscaped grounds, and a skylighted lobby. In all, there are 8,850 square feet of reception space, including a carpeted ballroom, an adjacent indoor patio, an exhibit space with lowered ceiling, a marble bar, a seven-foot grand concert piano, and a curving vestibule. Sliding oak panels can close or open to accommodate the size of your group. An adjacent 285-seat auditorium features a wood-tiled stage, interpreters' booths, and state-of-the-art sound and lighting systems. In fact, the site provides most of the modern equipment you can think of.

Throughout the complex hangs the embassy's permanent modern art collection, including a tapestry by Fernand Léger, a painting by Olivier Debre, and a sculpture by Ipousteguy, which graces the front entrance.

CAPACITY

Meeting: 40 to 200 classroom-style
Reception: 800
Banquet: 600
Auditorium: 285

LOCATION

In Georgetown's western pocket, directly across the street from Georgetown University Hospital. The complex offers underground parking for as many as 250 cars.

FOOD/BEVERAGE

The in-house caterer (French, *bien sur*) handles all of your food and beverage requirements. Although items like mousselines and terrines and noisettes and tartelettes (is your mouth watering?) are, of course, the specialty here, less-French selections are available if you so desire.

LIMITATIONS/RESTRICTIONS

La Maison Française is available for daytime and evening events every day. Any organization, profit or nonprofit, that expresses an interest in or shares a connection with France is eligible to reserve the complex. Private functions for individuals are not permitted. Events must end by midnight.

LEAD TIME FOR RESERVATIONS

Call for availability before requesting the use of the space in writing.

RATES

Available upon request.

FACILITIES FOR THE PHYSICALLY DISABLED? Yes

LANSDOWNE RESORT

44050 Woodridge Parkway
Leesburg, VA 22075
703/729-8440 or 800/541-4801
703/729-4096 (fax)
www.lansdowneresort.com

Secluded luxury for both meetings and social events

Eight miles from Dulles Airport, on 205 acres fronting the Potomac River, is Lansdowne Resort, whose deluxe attractions make it a perfect choice for conferences and social gatherings alike. Though located on the increasingly busy Route 7, Lansdowne lies at the end of a winding boulevard, way back from the road, and is well shielded by dense woods; traffic sights and sounds never penetrate.

Beautiful landscaping is a key feature at Lansdowne; a series of terraces work to incorporate the resort into the lush natural environment. A portion of the ballroom terrace was designed to accommodate a fifty-two-inch-diameter oak tree with a one-hundred-foot spread. Lansdowne is also known for its eighteen-hole Robert Trent Jones Jr. golf course, whose well-manicured greens can be viewed from several spots on the property.

A rose-colored brick and glass building provides 330,000 square feet of space in the form of a nine-story guest room tower flanked by two five-story wings, twenty-five meeting rooms of varying sizes, a tiered amphitheater, two restaurants, and a lounge. Decorative features throughout include mahogany paneling, marble accents, and dramatic artwork by local artists.

As luxurious as Lansdowne is, the overall feel is of spaciousness, due in part to the many windows overlooking the grounds, and comfort, thanks to its overstuffed chairs and sofas. The resort offers a full range of meeting support and audiovisual services. Recreational amenities include the championship golf course, tennis courts, squash and racquetball courts, exercise facilities, jogging trails, and pools.

CAPACITY
Reception: 800
Banquet: 20 to 720, depending on the room
Meeting: 10 (in the smallest room) to 800 (theater-style in the largest)
Lodging: 305 guest rooms

LOCATION
Follow Route 7 west toward Leesburg and turn right onto Lansdowne Boulevard. Follow the boulevard to Woodridge Parkway. Make a right onto Woodridge and the first left into the resort.

FOOD/BEVERAGE
Lansdowne handles all of your catering needs. Its restaurants feature regional American cuisine. The kitchen is equipped with a smokehouse and bakery.

LIMITATIONS/RESTRICTIONS
No set restrictions; call with your specific requirements.

LEAD TIME FOR RESERVATIONS
Call a year ahead.

RATES
Rates vary seasonally. Call for more exact information.

FACILITIES FOR THE PHYSICALLY DISABLED? Yes

ODYSSEY III

600 Water Street, SW
Berthed at Gangplank Marina
Washington, DC 20024
202/488-6010
www.odysseycruises.com

For high-class cruising on the Potomac

This wide-bodied, streamlined, allover glass bullet of a boat enables you to get married "at sea" or celebrate other momentous occasions as it gently cruises the Potomac River. *Odyssey III* (*Odysseys I* and *II* are in Boston and Chicago) was designed specifically to accommodate the river's bridges, so its 240-foot length reaches long and low across the water.

Inside the gliding glass bubble is a three-part dining room, two parts of which have their own dance floor, stage, and piano. Each section has a bar of imported marble and white tile, green and blue carpeting, and comfortable blue- and green-cushioned chairs pushed up against tables set with white linens. You can reserve one, two, or all three sections; the rooms can be partitioned so that more than one event can take place simultaneously. In fact, you can reserve a portion of the outside deck encircling the vessel if yours is a small party.

The view is everything, though, and *Odyssey's* glass ceiling and wraparound glass walls allow every guest, at every moment, unobstructed sightings of the Lincoln Memorial, Georgetown, the Washington Monument, and other landmarks.

CAPACITY
Reception or banquet: 240, 220, and 140 in each of the three dining rooms; 600 throughout

LOCATION
Board *Odyssey III* on Washington's waterfront, at the Gangplank Marina, 6th and Water Streets, SW.

FOOD/BEVERAGE
Odyssey prepares all food fresh on board.

LIMITATIONS/RESTRICTIONS
Odyssey cruises year-round with certain restrictions; staff members will help you plan your event. You may bring your own entertainment. Smoking is permitted on the outside deck only.

Odyssey cruises north along the Potomac toward Georgetown, gliding beneath the bridges. At times, when certain winds and tide conditions prevail, the ship takes an alternate route, traveling south past historic Old Town Alexandria.

LEAD TIME FOR RESERVATIONS
Staff recommends that you call several months in advance and even further ahead for holiday events.

RATES
Wedding packages range from $74 to $140 per person and include the meal, cruise, live entertainment, bar package, wedding cake, tax, fees, and gratuity. Call for rates for other functions.

FACILITIES FOR THE PHYSICALLY DISABLED? Yes

PAVILIONS OF TURKEY RUN
6310 Georgetown Pike
McLean, VA 22201
703/893-6545

Shaded pavilions, fabulous location

Across from the CIA, on National Park Service land bordering the Claude Moore Colonial Farm, is a great outdoor spot for informal functions. You head down a tree-lined gravel road to the wide circle of pasture, a totally private field shielded by woods. A portion of the field is used for parking; the rest holds sand volleyball courts, a softball field, and horseshoe pits. (The site provides volleyballs and horseshoes.) Off to the right is a wooded path that leads to three open-sided pavilions. Each has a concrete floor and benches and tables; one has a stone fireplace. The smaller center pavilion is used by the on-site caterer for grilling and serving food (Colonial Caterers handles all your food and beverage needs).

A brick building beyond the pavilions houses rest rooms. Off to one side is a nature trail, and off to another is a path leading to the Claude Moore Colonial Farm, an authentic 1771 working farm whose crops and farm animals are tended by a family that actually lives in the log cabin you see here. Guests of the pavilions can visit the farm at no charge.

CAPACITY
Reception or any kind of stand-up function: 1,000
Banquet or seated function: 250 in the largest pavilion, 200 in the medium
    pavilion, and 150 in the smallest pavilion

LOCATION
From the Beltway (I-495), take Exit 13 (Route 193), and head east toward Langley, traveling about two miles. Turn left onto Colonial Farm Road (shortly before the intersection of Routes 193 and 123) and left again when you see the sign for the pavilions.

From the District, follow M Street, NW, west from Georgetown past the intersection with Wisconsin Avenue, continuing until you reach the junction with Canal Road. Take Canal Road until you reach Chain Bridge; turn left and cross the bridge. On the other side, turn right onto Route 123 (Chain Bridge Road) and follow the road until you reach Route 193 (Old Georgetown Pike). Turn right and right again onto Colonial Farm Road. Turn left when you see the sign for the pavilions.

FOOD/BEVERAGE
Colonial Caterers handles all catering arrangements, cooking the food on site and

providing all beverages, including beer and wine, if desired. Barbecue fare is the specialty, but the caterer will tailor the menu to your specified theme. You are not permitted to bring any other food or drinks onto the property. Colonial Caterers sets up the pavilion—including plastic table covers, centerpieces, and beverage service—ahead of time. Call for specific menus.

LIMITATIONS/RESTRICTIONS
The pavilions are available May through October. Weekend rentals take place between 11:30 A.M. and 11:00 P.M.; weekday hours may be more flexible. More than one event may be going on at a time, so if you want exclusive use of the property, you must rent all three pavilions and have a minimum of four hundred guests. Amplified music, balloons, and pets are not allowed. You are entirely responsible for cleanup.

LEAD TIME FOR RESERVATIONS
The pavilions are rented on a rolling basis, first come first served. June and September dates fill up first.

RATES
Large pavilion, $550; medium pavilion plus tented area, $450; small pavilion, $350; all three pavilions, $1,150 (minimum 400 guests). Food prices start at $17.95 per person plus 16% service charge and 4.5% tax for a full-fare menu including nonalcoholic beverages.

FACILITIES FOR THE PHYSICALLY DISABLED? No

THE SPHINX CLUB AT ALMAS TEMPLE
1315 K Street, NW
Washington, DC 20005-3307
202/898-1688
202/789-1148 (fax)

Wedged between an office building and a hotel, the Sphinx Club catches your eye. Its four-story façade is a mosaic of blue, rust, and white tiles enunciating an Arabic theme, its triple-arched entryway echoing the look of Aladdin's palace, perhaps.

The building is the property and temple of the Ancient Arabic Noble Order of the Mystic Shrine, or Shriners for short. But the group's schedule and the facility's size allow for plenty of use by non-Shriners. Inside, the temple is not very templelike.

On lobby level are three rooms that connect or partition, as you like. One is a dark chamber with a bar, another is filled with great looping archways and wrought-iron chandeliers, and the third is your standard conference room. The best room in the temple lies on the lower level, which you reach by descending a wide, mahogany-railed double staircase. The immense, seven-thousand-square-foot grand ballroom has wall-to-wall carpeting that repeats the colors and pattern of the mosaic on the building's façade. Other things to note are the movable stage and dance floor and state-of-the-art audiovisual equipment, including four built-in video cameras, individually controlled lighting, and one built-in projection screen television. Encircling the top half of the ballroom is a twenty-three-hundred-square-foot mezzanine, off which lie four small meeting rooms; two of these link by floating wall.

CAPACITY

Reception: 700 using the ballroom and mezzanine
Banquet: 525 without dancing, 400-plus with dancing
Meeting: 20 (in a single conference room) to 575 (theater-style in the ballroom)

LOCATION

The club is located between 13th and 14 Streets, NW, across from Franklin Square Park in downtown Washington. The McPherson Square Metro station is within walking distance. On evenings and weekends, parking is available at One Franklin Square, whose garage has an entrance right into the ballroom.

FOOD/BEVERAGE

You may choose from the club's approved list of caterers or use the in-house service.

LIMITATIONS/RESTRICTIONS

The club is a no-smoking building.

LEAD TIME FOR RESERVATIONS

Call as soon as possible.

RATES

Rates are negotiated on a case-by-case basis.

FACILITIES FOR THE PHYSICALLY DISABLED? Yes

THE SPIRIT OF WASHINGTON AND *THE POTOMAC SPIRIT*

At Pier 4
6th and Water Streets, SW
Washington, DC 20024
202/554-8013
www.spiritcruises.com

Make waves at your next event

Watch as your group unwinds aboard a ship that cruises the Potomac. The *Spirit of Washington* encapsulates the experience of an oceangoing luxury liner in a few pleasurable, memorable hours on the river.

From the streamlined vessel's open-air decks and the three-windowed lower decks, you have a clear view of Washington's monuments and Old Town Alexandria's colonial homes. Meanwhile, the boat's galley is sending up a feast, the bar is serving up drinks, and two live bands are serenading you with songs from the last four decades. During dinner cruises, a talented troupe of performers stages a musical revue. And, oh yes, there's dancing.

Designed inside to resemble a deep-sea cruise ship, the *Spirit of Washington* has dark blue carpeting and comfy cushioned seats. You can rent just a deck or the whole boat for a brunch, lunch, dinner, dance cruise, or even a meeting.

The *Potomac Spirit*, like the *Spirit of Washington*, has two fully enclosed decks with panoramic windows, plus a third open deck. This vessel cruises to Mount Vernon.

CAPACITY

Reception: 350 (*Potomac Spirit*), 600 (*Spirit of Washington*)
Banquet: 270 (*Potomac Spirit*), 558 (*Spirit of Washington*)

LOCATION

On Water Street at Pier 4 on the waterfront in southwest Washington, a short walk from the Waterfront on the Metro's green line.

FOOD/BEVERAGE

The *Spirit of Washington* and the *Potomac Spirit* cater their own events. For a deck or full-ship charter, you can request a menu suited to your group's tastes. Otherwise, the *Spirit of Washington* has a set menu that includes a choice of chicken, fish, or beef; rice, potatoes, green beans, salad, rolls, dessert, and coffee. The *Potomac Spirit* offers several food packages.

LIMITATIONS/RESTRICTIONS

Call to discuss your specific requirements.

LEAD TIME FOR RESERVATIONS

Three months is recommended, but call for availability.

RATES

The *Spirit of Washington*: A minimum of 120 people is required to reserve one deck, 500 people to reserve the entire boat. The group rates per person run from $29.95 for a weekday lunch cruise to $69.95 (Friday) and $75.95 (Saturday) for an evening dinner cruise.

The *Potomac Spirit*: A minimum of 120 people is required to reserve one deck, 270 people to reserve the entire boat. *Potomac Spirit* offers the same rate packages as *Spirit of Washington*.

FACILITIES FOR THE PHYSICALLY DISABLED? Yes

THE STATE THEATRE

220 North Washington Street
Falls Church, VA 22046
703/237-0300
703/237-5717 (fax)
www.thestatetheatre.com

Hold your event in a concert hall

A 1936 art deco–ish movie theater has taken on new life in the twenty-first century, staging concerts by favorite local bands, like the Cravin' Dogs, as well as nationally known groups, such as Jefferson Starship. The State Theatre's owners recognize that the same features that recommend the hall as a concert venue also make it a great place to hold a party, so they've made the theater available for everything from weddings to political fund-raisers.

The two-story theater has four bars—one in the spacious, first-floor lobby, two in the main room, and one in the second-floor lobby. Beyond the first-floor lobby is the hall, which slopes gradually down three levels from the entrance to the dance floor and the proscenium. The floor throughout most of the hall is a burnished oak, good for dancing no matter where you stand. The hall's multilevel design enables you to set up tables all in one room and within view of each other, with railings separating one level from the next. Overhanging part of the main floor is the balcony, whose original seating has been completely refurbished. The balcony and its adjoining lobby are available with the rental of the theater. You may also arrange to use the state-of-the-art sound and lighting system.

CAPACITY

Reception: 500 or 700 with balcony

Banquet: 250

Meeting: 200

LOCATION

From Washington or the Beltway (I-495), take Route I-66 to Exit 69. From the exit, take a right onto Sycamore Street, your first left onto Washington Boulevard, and your first left again onto Lee Highway, which becomes Washington Street. Follow Washington Street to the theater, on your left, turning just past the theater into the driveway that leads to the parking lot. The parking lot has one hundred parking spaces, and many other lots are available in the neighborhood.

FOOD/BEVERAGE

The State Theatre furnishes all alcohol and bartenders and provides its own catering service. Its chef can customize your menu. The full-service kitchen features a smoker, which can turn out anything from barbecued ribs to smoked salmon. You may choose to go with an outside caterer for an additional fee.

LIMITATIONS/RESTRICTIONS

The theater is available daily, year-round.

LEAD TIME FOR RESERVATIONS

Call for availability.

RATES

Rates are negotiable. The theater prefers that you call for further information.

FACILITIES FOR THE PHYSICALLY DISABLED? Yes

WOODLAWN PLANTATION

9000 Richmond Highway
Alexandria, VA 22309
703/780-4000
www.nationaltrust.org

A picturesque site near the Potomac

If you'd visited here in the early 1800s, you would have seen acres and acres of plantation fields being worked by slaves. A servant would have ushered you into the long hallway, where Nelly Custis Lewis, George Washington's foster daughter and the mistress of the mansion, would have greeted you. After dinner, the Lewis family would have entertained you in the parlor by playing the pianoforte, harps, guitars, and other instruments.

When you visit Woodlawn today, you see acres and acres of beautifully landscaped grounds that include century-old boxwoods, oak and Osage orange trees, a collection of nineteenth-century roses, two parterres, and nature trails. Now, you can entertain up to eight hundred of your closest colleagues here by holding a tented garden party.

Or you can hold smaller receptions, banquets, or meetings in the mansion's two "hyphens," known as the Reception and Underwood Rooms. The Underwood Room, named for the Alabama senator who lived here in the 1920s, has formal furnishings and a working fireplace. The Reception Room is a more casual space with off-white and Williamsburg blue walls. Both rooms give onto the carriage circle.

Still another space available for small luncheons and meetings is the downstairs Pub, a rustic room with painted brick walls and exposed beams.

Guides will be in the mansion during your event to explain the history of Woodlawn, including the fact that the plantation was George Washington's gift to Nelly Custis and Lawrence Lewis, his nephew, upon their wedding. You'll see Nelly's own needlework, vases that were gifts from Lafayette, the house's original Virginia pine floors, and a lot more.

CAPACITY

Reception: 100
Banquet: 50
Garden party: 800
Meeting/luncheon: 40 to 50

LOCATION

Fourteen miles south of Washington, on Route 1.

FOOD/BEVERAGE

You must choose a caterer from Woodlawn's approved list and purchase all your alcoholic beverages from the site.

LIMITATIONS/RESTRICTIONS

Smoking is permitted outside only. Dancing and amplified music are prohibited in the mansion. You must tent the grounds when the number of your party exceeds the mansion's capacity.

LEAD TIME FOR RESERVATIONS

Call for availability.

RATES

Rates vary depending on time of day, number of people, and space used for your event. Here's an example: An evening function on the tented lawn for five hundred people will cost $2,150, covering a five-hour period and a tour of the house.

FACILITIES FOR THE PHYSICALLY DISABLED? Some

The first floor of the house is wheelchair accessible.

Sites for more than 1,000 people

EMBASSY OF THE RUSSIAN FEDERATION
2650 Wisconsin Avenue, NW
Washington, DC 20007
202/546-6717

Formidable exterior hides glorious ballroom

The secret is out: The Russian Embassy on Wisconsin Avenue holds one of the most stunning ballrooms in Washington.

Behind the imposing iron gates and guardhouse is a stolid-looking white marble building. Make your way inside and you find more marble: The large foyer is covered in beautiful Italian stone, from floor to walls to pillars. At the rear of the room, a wall of windows overlooks a courtyard. Framed against the glass is a flowing double staircase, which takes you to the reception rooms.

At center stage is the spectacular main ballroom, whose floor measures 650 square meters (about 7,276 square feet) and whose ceiling stands high at 8 meters (about 26 feet). On the ceiling are painted the seals of different Russian cities (Moscow's is St. George the Conqueror killing the dragon). A colorful, golden ring enamel artwork by Zurab Tsereteli depicting Russian Orthodox churches in major Russian cities covers a good portion of one wall. A modern mural on the opposite wall depicts cities in the former republics of the Soviet Union. Interspersed between long windows on a third side are large mirrors and cushioned benches. Other sumptuous touches include inlaid parquet floors, chandeliers, and lush folds of golden damask fabric stretched decoratively over sections of wall.

Off the ballroom are other luxurious salons, each with walls covered in richly colored, embossed silk: a deep yellow room and its olive-green antechamber, a brilliant aqua room and its adjoining, ruby sitting area. Beyond the ruby room lies a stately dining room with a coffered ceiling, long windows, and an enormous dining table that seats thirty. This floor also holds an auditorium with

271

a platform stage and two hundred plush, camel-colored, cushioned seats. In fair weather, the embassy's landscaped courtyard may be used, as well.

CAPACITY
Reception: 75 (in one of the smaller rooms) to 1,200 (using every space, including the courtyard)
Banquet: 30 (in the dining room) to 530 (using the ballroom and its adjoining chambers)
Meeting: 200 in the auditorium, 30 in the dining room

LOCATION
Just north of Georgetown, on Wisconsin Avenue.

FOOD/BEVERAGE
Occasions is the preferred caterer, although you may choose another subject to embassy approval. The embassy has two kitchens, one on each level.

LIMITATIONS/RESTRICTIONS

The site is available subject to its own schedule; the embassy would like to restrict the number of rentals to no more than three or four per month. Use is limited to nonprofit and corporate organizations. You must submit a letter of application to the ambassador to make a site inspection and to receive permission to rent the facility.

Smoking is permitted outside only. The embassy recommends that you reserve a nearby parking lot and arrange for valet parking.

LEAD TIME FOR RESERVATIONS

Call as soon as you have a date in mind for your event.

RATES

Rates vary depending on the rooms reserved and the type of group renting the site. It's best to call for this information.

FACILITIES FOR THE PHYSICALLY DISABLED? No

GEORGETOWN UNIVERSITY CONFERENCE CENTER

3800 Reservoir Road, NW
Washington, DC 20057
202/687-3242

Confer in a ballroom, have a ball in a conference room

This new building on Georgetown University's old campus contains a wonderfully versatile space that contracts, expands, and breaks apart to suit the size and purpose of your function. At the heart of the facility is the Grand Ballroom and adjoining Salons A through H, which provide a total square footage of 10,500. Interesting, crested glass light fixtures illuminate this elegant, floral-carpeted space, which includes a portable dance floor. The ceiling stands high at twelve feet. You can partition any or all of the salons, which range in size from 760 to 3,510 square feet.

Six smaller conference rooms lie on the periphery. The Executive Board Room is both the nicest and the largest of these, encompassing 750 square feet and offering stained-wood chair rails and crown moldings, a dropped ceiling, and a fine oak expandable conference table that seats fourteen (the room accommodates as many as seventy, seated theater-style). Each room in the conference center is equipped with the latest audiovisual, teleconferencing, and sound system technologies.

Other features recommend the center: a sunny, windowed arcade known as the South Gallery, which parallels the ballroom and overlooks the campus and the Potomac River; a rooftop, grass-covered esplanade, also with a great view; and the 146 well-appointed guest rooms.

CAPACITY

Reception: 50 (in the smallest meeting room) to 1,000 (in the Grand Ballroom)
Banquet: 10 (in the smallest meeting room) to 900 (in the Grand Ballroom)
Conference: 10 to 416 seated theater-style in a salon or conference room, 1,200 seated theater-style in the Grand Ballroom
Lodging: 146 guest rooms

LOCATION

On the campus of Georgetown University, adjacent to Georgetown Hospital, on Reservoir Road, NW. Parking is free on Saturdays and Sundays in the center's garage.

FOOD/BEVERAGE

The center's on-site caterer handles all your food and beverage requirements.

LIMITATIONS/RESTRICTIONS

The center is available for functions year-round. Call to discuss your specific requests. Smoking is prohibited inside the center.

LEAD TIME FOR RESERVATIONS
Call for availability.

RATES
Rates vary depending on the type of function. Conference room rentals run about $15 per person. Catered lunches start at $17.95 per person, and catered dinners start at $25.50 per person. An all-inclusive wedding package costs $80 to $95 per person and covers room rental, one hour of hors d'oeuvres, four hours of an open bar, a three-course meal, and other items. Overnight accommodations run $99 to $165.

FACILITIES FOR THE PHYSICALLY DISABLED? Yes

HIGH POINT FARM
Route 355
Clarksburg, MD 20871
301/428-0650
www.highpointfarm.net

Fun and games on 150 acres

This property is so big that it can host five huge parties simultaneously, and they won't interfere with each other. High Point Farm is located on the highest point in Montgomery County between Washington and Frederick, hence the name. The land has been an active farm since the 1700s, and there's an old 1791 farmhouse on the property to prove it. These 150 acres now belong to Egan Barbecuers, a family catering firm in business for more than thirty years. The Egans have added a dimension to their catering business by allowing the rental of High Point Farm.

Five individual event sites, four with a pavilion, are scattered over the property. Each location is private, and huge tents are on hand should it rain. High Point furnishes what you need for volleyball, horseshoes, tetherball, hiking, sack races, softball, football, and Frisbee and offers other attractions, like a petting zoo and tractor rides, if you're interested. The farm lies right across Route 355 from the entrance to Little Bennett Regional Park, which has miles of hiking trails.

Watching the on-site cooking is part of the fun. Egan Barbecuers does do barbecue, of course, but also all kinds of food cooked over wood or charcoal fires.

CAPACITY
50 to 6,000

LOCATION
From the Beltway (I-495), pick up Route 270 north and take Exit 18 (Route 121 north) toward Clarksburg. Follow Route 121 half a mile and turn left on Route 355. When you see the entrance to Little Bennett Regional Park on your right, look left, and you'll see the driveway to High Point Farm. Turn left and follow the driveway to the farm. There is plenty of parking.

FOOD/BEVERAGE
Egan Barbecuers caters all events and will work with you to plan your menu. Alcohol is allowed.

LIMITATIONS/RESTRICTIONS

There are few restrictions here. Animals are not allowed on the property, and glass bottles and other containers are not allowed.

LEAD TIME FOR RESERVATIONS

Call for availability.

RATES

Use of High Point Farm costs a flat fee of $375. Count on paying catering costs of $13 to $20 per person, which covers both food and drinks.

FACILITIES FOR THE PHYSICALLY DISABLED? Yes

HISTORIC CAR BARN OF GEORGETOWN

3600 M Street, NW
Washington, DC 20007
202/333-6784
202/342-1486 (fax)
www.robertcummings.com/carbarn

Two rooms with a view

If you've already searched for unusual rental locations that present dramatic and sweeping views of Washington, you know they almost don't exist. And then there's the Historic Car Barn of Georgetown. You want a sight of the Potomac? You got it. The Washington Monument? There it is, off to your left. The Watergate, the Kennedy Center, the Lincoln Memorial, Key Bridge, Georgetown—all of these landmarks and others lie before you, through the panoramic windows of the Historic Car Barn's penthouse and from its pavilion.

The Historic Car Barn is a brick structure built into a hill in Georgetown. If you enter at ground level, you're on M Street; if you enter at the fourth (penthouse) level, you're on Prospect Street, a stone's throw from Georgetown University. Back in 1761, this was the site of a tobacco warehouse, whose foundation still supports the current building. Eventually, the barn was used to quarter horses and trolley cars, hence its name.

The penthouse is one large room, with hardwood floors and windows all the way around. When you rent the penthouse, you have access to the terrace, which is laid with large, red clay tiles and crowned at center with a large pavilion (a favorite spot for ceremonies). The terrace can be tented.

CAPACITY

Meeting: 350

Reception: 550 in the penthouse, 600 on the terrace, 1,100 using both the penthouse and terrace

Banquet: 270 in the penthouse, 200 on the terrace, 470 using both terrace and penthouse

LOCATION

In Georgetown, directly across from Key Bridge. You may enter on Prospect or M Street, NW. There is space within the building for 120 cars.

FOOD/BEVERAGE

You must choose a caterer from the Car Barn's approved list. There is a kitchen.

LIMITATIONS/RESTRICTIONS

The site is available all day, year-round, and allows only one event to take place at one time in the penthouse. Amplified music is prohibited outside. You must arrange for valet parking.

LEAD TIME FOR RESERVATIONS

The Car Barn accepts reservations up to two years in advance but recommends that you call for availability.

RATES

Weekdays, $5,500; Friday and Sunday, $6,000; Saturday, $7,000.

FACILITIES FOR THE PHYSICALLY DISABLED? Some

The Prospect Street entrance and penthouse rest rooms are wheelchair accessible; the M Street entrance and first-floor rest rooms are not.

J. R.'S FESTIVAL LAKES

Fort Evans Road
Leesburg, VA 22075
703/821-0545

Mailing address: 8130 Watson Street
McLean, VA 22102

A barn for business, picnic areas for pleasure

Tired of meeting in windowless conference rooms? Bored at the thought of another office party in the company cafeteria or at the same old bar down the street? If you want to add some pizzazz to your function, take your group to J. R.'s, which can accommodate as many as five thousand conferees (or wedding guests).

J. R.'s lies at the end of a country road in a private, wooded setting with lakes. You can kick off your meeting, sales presentation, or seminar in the renovated Club Barn. The barn is open on three sides and houses tables and benches, a stage, a public address system, and lighting that can be dimmed for audiovisual presentations. Horseshoes, a wood-chip floor, and bales of hay scattered about reinforce the rustic atmosphere.

At the close of the meeting, you can get down to the more serious business of having fun. J. R.'s offers just about every kind of outdoor activity you can imagine: volleyball, badminton, horseshoes, swimming, fishing, golfing, hiking, and boating. The site is so large that tractor-drawn wagons transport you from one activity area to another.

J. R.'s helps you plan your event by providing you with artwork for invitations, promotional material, lists of activities, maps, menus, and names of recreational vendors. They help arrange entertainment acts for you as well.

CAPACITY
Reception: 5,000
Banquet: 1,500 in the barn and an adjoining area that can be tented
Meeting: 1,500 in the barn and an adjoining area that can be tented
Picnic: 6,000

LOCATION
From the Beltway (I-495), take Exit 10 west to Route 7 west. Go twenty-one miles on Route 7 to Route 15 north toward Frederick. Travel .3 mile and exit right to Fort Evans Road. Go 1.4 miles and turn left into J. R.'s.

FOOD/BEVERAGE
J. R.'s rustles up barbecue-style feasts for most functions, although other menus are available upon request.

LIMITATIONS/RESTRICTIONS
Use is seasonal, from April through October. A minimum of one hundred persons per group is required to reserve the site.

LEAD TIME FOR RESERVATIONS
Call for availability. Weekdays and evenings are usually easier to reserve.

RATES
Rates range from $17 to $25 per person, depending upon the menu selection. Food and beverage costs cover the use of the entire site. Media equipment is available at an extra cost.

FACILITIES FOR THE PHYSICALLY DISABLED? Some
The barn and its rest room are wheelchair accessible.

MARRIOTT RANCH

5305 Marriott Lane
Hume, VA 22639
540/364-2627
540/364-3564 (fax)
www.marriottranch.com
info@marriottranch.com

Git along, all you cowboys!

The West comes east at this forty-two-hundred-acre spread of working cattle ranch and horse farm, located in the foothills of the Blue Ridge Mountains. Owned and operated by Marriott International since 1951, the ranch opened its gates as a special event site in 1989.

Marriott Ranch defines three separate spaces as possible event locations. For festival and picnic gatherings of up to as many as three thousand people, the farm offers the Pavilion and surrounding grounds. The rustic wooden structure overlooks Virginia countryside and mountains and is surrounded by slopes of grassy lawn.

A hay wagon or horseback ride away, nestled in a wooded section of the property, lies Marriott Forks, a setting meant to evoke the feeling of a frontier town. On the way, you'll notice the herd of Texas Longhorns roaming the grounds, although they won't intrude upon your event. Hitching posts, a saloon front, and the smell of barbecue contribute to the Wild West atmosphere.

The ranch's third and most formal facility is the Inn at Fairfield, also known as the Manor House, which dates from 1814. The inn now operates as a bed-and-breakfast and has four large bedrooms for overnight guests. Its first floor holds a suite of reception rooms that have high ceilings, triple-hung windows, and comfortable furnishings. You may hold parties outside the house, too; sweeping lawns are dotted with large oak and hickory trees and offer pastoral views as far as the eye can see.

Marriott Ranch hosts all kinds of events and is able to enliven your affair with horseback riding, chuck-wagon dinner theater, cattle drives, hay wagon rides, country music, campfires, country-western dance lessons, barbecues, and anything else that makes for a successful hoedown.

CAPACITY

Reception or banquet: 50 to 2,000 at the Pavilion, 50 to 275 at Marriott Forks, and 50 (inside the Manor House) to 400 (on its lawn). When you have more than 50 people at the Manor House you must tent the lawn.

LOCATION

Marriott Ranch is located about sixty minutes from Washington. Follow Route 66 west to Exit 18 (Markham). At the end of the exit ramp, turn left. Go .1 mile to the stop sign on Route 55, continue another hundred yards to the dead end, and turn right onto Route 688. Follow Route 688 for 5.5 miles to Hume. Turn right onto Route 635 and continue for 3.3 miles to the ranch's main entrance, on the left.

FOOD/BEVERAGE

Marriott Ranch caters your event. The Manor House and Pavilion both offer limited kitchen space.

LIMITATIONS/RESTRICTIONS

The ranch's event season generally runs from April through November, with some exceptions. In season, the site is available for all sorts of functions every day, anytime. Because of its size, the ranch may be hosting more than one event at a time. The bed-and-breakfast is open year-round.

The site has designated smoking and nonsmoking areas. Audiovisual and other business equipment is available. The staff can arrange for any entertainment you desire, from a moonbounce to an orchestra.

LEAD TIME FOR RESERVATIONS

Call as soon as possible.

RATES

The Manor House and lawn rent for $1,450 on weekdays and $2,000 on weekends. The Pavilion and Marriott Forks each rent for $1,000 at all times. The catering rate for a large picnic will run about $25 to $30 per person, not including alcohol. Call for other food and beverage options. Bed-and-breakfast rates range from $125 to $195.

FACILITIES FOR THE PHYSICALLY DISABLED? Some

The Pavilion is wheelchair accessible, and the Manor House has a ramp.

NATIONAL AIR AND SPACE MUSEUM

Smithsonian Institution
Independence Avenue at 6th Street, SW
Washington, DC 20560-0310
202/357-4022
202/357-2426 (fax)
www.nasm.edu/nasm/spevents
special.events@nasm.si.edu

Have a high-flying event in the museum that celebrates flight

Everyone wants to tour the Smithsonian's National Air and Space Museum—so many people, in fact, that the museum logs in a total of nine million visitors each year, making it the most popular museum in the world. A lot of people would like to hold a special event here, too, and a lucky few are able to do so.

If you are lucky enough to host a party or be feted here, you will have twenty-three exhibit areas to explore, which means that you and your party can get a good look at the Wright brothers' original 1903 flier or Charles Lindbergh's *Spirit of St. Louis.* You can touch a four-billion-year-old moon rock, climb inside a space shuttle, study the profiles of the pioneers of flight, and just generally walk around and be amazed at this hall of flying machines, each representing a devel-

opment in the ongoing story of manned flight. Should you wish to view one of the IMAX movies or venture into the Einstein Planetarium to study the stars, that's possible, too.

CAPACITY

The museum can accommodate small dinners for ten, sumptuous banquets for more than one thousand, and lavish cocktail receptions for three thousand. There are seven individual galleries, whose capacities range from fifty seated and seventy-five standing (in the Early Flight Gallery) to seven hundred standing (in the Milestones of Flight Gallery).

LOCATION

The museum is located on the National Mall, in the shadow of the US Capitol. Complimentary parking is available for evening events.

FOOD/BEVERAGE

You must choose from a list of preferred caterers.

LIMITATIONS/RESTRICTIONS

All events are cosponsored with the museum and must either be related to the museum's mission or hosted by a contributing sponsor of activities at the museum. Fund-raisers and private social events for individuals are not allowed. Smoking is prohibited.

LEAD TIME FOR RESERVATIONS

Call for availability.

RATES

The museum requests that you make a contribution but prefers to discuss the matter with individual clients.

FACILITIES FOR THE PHYSICALLY DISABLED? Yes

NATIONAL BUILDING MUSEUM

401 F Street, NW, at Judiciary Square
Washington, DC 20001
202/272-2448
www.nbm.org

Grand place to have a ball, inaugural or otherwise

You don't have to be an architect to appreciate the masterful design of the National Building Museum. Look at its exterior—the building stretches beyond the length of a football field, and its redbrick façade gleams as if the bricks were laid just yesterday. Now regard the interior. An Italian Renaissance courtyard takes up almost the entire first floor of the building, and a peaked roof encloses the court 159 feet above your head.

The Great Hall, as the courtyard is called, is the museum's main rental space. Its vast dimensions translate into a dramatic setting for large receptions, dinners, and other gala events. The hall's staggeringly beautiful features heighten

the drama. Eight marbleized Corinthian columns face each other across the court's central fountain. The columns, measuring eight feet across and seventy-five feet high, are among the largest interior columns in the world. All four floors look onto this magnificent space—via arcaded loggias on the first and second floors, a parapet on the third floor, and a wrought-iron balcony on the top floor.

Washingtonians know the National Building Museum as the old Pension Building because it was built between 1882 and 1887 to house Pension Bureau offices. From the interconnecting rooms off the central court, clerks dispensed funds to wounded veterans and their survivors of the American Revolution, War of 1812, Civil War, Spanish-American War, and World War I. If it seems an unlikely office building, that's because the architect, Montgomery Meigs, had an enlightened view of construction. In modeling the building after an Italian palace, Meigs had two purposes in mind: to create an open, airy, light-filled, and healthful working environment, and to provide the capital with a grand space for entertaining. Starting with Grover Cleveland's inaugural ball, held here in 1885 even before the building was completed, the site has hosted some of the biggest and best parties in town.

The structure opened as the National Building Museum in 1985. The museum is free and open to the public from 10:00 A.M. to 4:00 P.M. Monday through Saturday and noon to 4:00 P.M. Sundays and holidays.

CAPACITY
Reception: 1,600
Banquet: 1,600
You may be able to arrange for larger parties, but expect additional costs.

LOCATION
In downtown Washington, on F Street between 4th and 5th Streets, NW, directly across from the Judiciary Square Metro station, National Building Museum exit.

FOOD/BEVERAGE
You may choose your own caterer, subject to the museum's approval. There is a space available for caterers to use.

LIMITATIONS/RESTRICTIONS
To reserve the museum for an event requires the approval of the National Building Museum's special events office. Smoking is prohibited.

LEAD TIME FOR RESERVATIONS
At least six months, but call for availability.

RATES

Rates start at $11,000 and increase when you want access to the building before 4:00 P.M. There are additional charges for such services as security and cleanup.

FACILITIES FOR THE PHYSICALLY DISABLED? Yes

NATIONAL MUSEUM OF AMERICAN HISTORY

Smithsonian Institution
14th Street and Constitution Avenue, NW
Washington, DC 20560
202/357-3306
http://americanhistory.si.edu

Toast America's heritage in "the nation's attic"

Throughout its three vast floors, the National Museum of American History displays three centuries of our country's artifacts. Many of the treasures are one-of-a-kind, like the First Ladies' gowns and the John Bull locomotive. All are fascinating for the understanding they bring of the ways Americans have lived since our country's inception.

The National Museum of American History wants to make it clear that, "while the museum does not rent its space, events related to the museum's mission that are cosponsored with the museum may be held there. In addition, financial contributors to the museum may be invited to cosponsor a special celebratory event at the museum." Such a special event at the museum is unbeatable. Who could lack for conversation while standing, say, in the exhibit called *A Material World*? Surrounded by hundreds of objects, hand-crafted or machine-made, you turn your attention to a dangling surfboard, a cable from the George Washington Bridge, a classic jukebox. The exhibit evokes a mix of nostalgia and appreciation for American ingenuity. (A new exhibit, *American Legacies*, is slated to replace *A Material World* sometime in the next year or so; *American Legacies* will tell stories with artifacts and explore what it means to be an American.)

A *Material World* frequently serves as an icebreaking location, where guests gather for cocktails or a buffet. From this circular and central position, they can wander to other exhibits, which on this floor include everything from robotics in *Information Age* to the *Hands on Science* laboratory and a 280-ton steam locomotive on view in Railroad Hall. The first floor also holds a 275-seat auditorium and the Presidential Reception Suite, perfect for small dinners. The Palm Court, also on this level, may be used for dancing.

On the second floor, you will find the huge (thirty-by-forty-two-foot), original Star-Spangled Banner on view—not hanging up, but laid flat behind glass in a specially designed lab where, by day, expert textile conservationists painstakingly work to restore it. This is the very flag that inspired Francis Scott Key to write the US national anthem in 1814. (Restoration work will continue through 2002.) The second floor is also the site of *Field to Factory*, which tells the story of Afro-American migration, south to north, between 1915 and 1940; *From Parlor to Politics*, which depicts a different migration: of women, from domestic to political and professional pursuits; *First Ladies: Political Role and Public Image*, one of the most popular exhibits at the Smithsonian; and a three-hundred-year-old house, transplanted from Ipswich, Massachusetts, and an accompanying exhibit that traces and interprets the lives of the people who lived in it.

Try to get up to the third floor. Although food and beverage are not allowed here, it's worth visiting. This level features displays of ceramics, textiles, and military memorabilia, as well as an exciting new exhibit: *The Presidency: An American Institution*, which chronicles two hundred years of America's presidents, exploring the nature of the office and the personalities of the men who have held it.

CAPACITY

Reception: 10 to 3,500
Banquet: 10 to 300
Auditorium: 275

LOCATION

At 14th Street and Constitution Avenue, NW, bordering the National Mall. Street parking is available. In the evening, the building can offer free parking for about one hundred cars. The closest Metro stations are the Smithsonian and Federal Triangle stops.

FOOD/BEVERAGE
You may choose the caterer, whose insurance policy must meet the museum's requirements. Museum staff will help you coordinate your arrangements with caterers. The museum's first floor holds a full kitchen.

LIMITATIONS/RESTRICTIONS
Social events of a personal nature are not allowed, nor are fund-raising, product marketing, or political events. Functions must always be cosponsored with the museum—that is, the event must be demonstrably related to the museum's mission or hosted by a contributing sponsor of the museum. The museum must authorize in advance such things as the guest list, printed and promotional materials, and speakers or performers. Smoking is not permitted.

LEAD TIME FOR RESERVATIONS
At least two months, but events are frequently booked a year in advance.

RATES
The museum cosponsors events in celebration of donations and prefers to discuss this matter with individual cosponsors.

FACILITIES FOR THE PHYSICALLY DISABLED? Yes

NATIONAL MUSEUM OF NATURAL HISTORY
Smithsonian Institution
Constitution Avenue at 10th Street, NW
Washington, DC 20560
202/357-1650
www.mnh.si.edu/specialevents

Entertaining within view of dinosaurs and mastodons

It's the museum where a mammoth African bush elephant presides over the entrance hall. You know it, right? Everyone has visited the wonderful National Museum of Natural History and seen that famous elephant and countless other natural wonders, from the Hope Diamond to the trunk of the oldest known tree, collected by the Smithsonian and displayed for public enjoyment and edification. As the world's largest natural history museum, this monumental structure has great halls and exhibit areas in which to house its vast collections. And somewhere along the line some wise museum official realized that these spaces would be great for entertaining purposes, as well.

Now, not everyone is eligible to use the museum, and you can't hold weddings, birthday parties for old dinosaurs, or that sort of thing here (read Limitations/Restrictions, below). But if you are one of the blessed, here's what you need to know.

It's possible to reserve the entire museum or just a portion of it. The main individual spaces include the Baird Auditorium, the Rotunda, the Dinosaur Hall, the Janet Annenberg Hall of Geology, Gems, and Minerals, and the new Discovery Center. The Baird Auditorium, at ground level, is the largest auditorium on the National Mall. It has plush mauve seats, an audiovisual booth, a twenty-four-foot projection screen that rolls down to the stage, and front/rear screen video projection. The Discovery Center holds the Atrium Caf and a state-of-the-art IMAX 2-D and 3-D theater, where you can arrange to view current offerings, such as *Galapagos* or another selection from the museum's film library, during your event.

Directly above the auditorium on the first floor is the Rotunda (site of the elephant). Towering above the elephant is the grand dome, which creates an atrium of the two-level gallery below. Columns in the marble and granite Rotunda mark entryways to exhibit areas on both its first and second levels. One offshoot is the Dinosaur Hall, where skeletons of the giant reptiles stand for all to admire. An arcade encircles the second floor of the gallery. Highlights of the renovated Geology, Gems, and Minerals Hall include the Hope Diamond and National Gem Collection, moon rocks, fluorescent minerals, and a replica of a mine. With its world-class gems and rare geologic specimens glittering in the background, this area provides an especially dramatic atmosphere for events.

CAPACITY

Reception: 1,000 (in the Rotunda and adjoining Dinosaur Hall) to 3,000 (throughout the museum)

Banquet: 350 in the Rotunda

Auditorium: 565

IMAX Theater: 487 for 2-D films, 427 for 3-D films

LOCATION

Constitution Avenue, at 10th Street, NW, across the National Mall from the

Smithsonian Castle. Parking is on the street and in nearby lots. In the evening, the building can offer limited free parking on a space-available basis.

FOOD/BEVERAGE

The museum prefers that you choose a caterer from its list and that the caterers come self-contained, not needing any equipment. The museum provides setup areas for caterers but not a kitchen. An in-house caterer is also available.

LIMITATIONS/RESTRICTIONS

Social events of a purely personal nature are not allowed, nor is smoking. Functions must be cosponsored with the museum—that is, the event must be demonstrably related to the museum's mission or hosted by a contributing sponsor of activities at the museum. Fund-raisers are not permitted.

The Baird Auditorium is available every day at any time, year-round; the other spaces in the museum are available for evening functions only, year-round, except Christmas Day.

RATES

The museum requests that you make a contribution but prefers to discuss this matter with individual clients.

FACILITIES FOR THE PHYSICALLY DISABLED? Yes

The Baird Auditorium, however, rakes so steeply that it is better to keep wheelchairs stationed at the back of the room rather than attempt to roll them down the sharp incline.

NATIONAL MUSEUM OF WOMEN IN THE ARTS

1250 New York Avenue, NW
Washington, DC 20005
202/783-7366
www.nmwa.org

A museum made for entertaining

Even before it opened in April 1987, the National Museum of Women in the Arts stirred up controversy: Will a separate showcase bring long-deserved recognition to women artists, or will art segregated from works by men be taken less seriously? Whichever opinion you hold, one thing's indisputable: The museum itself seems made for entertaining.

Housed within a huge Renaissance Revival–style structure are four spaces for renting: the Lockheed Martin Great Hall, located on the first floor and mezzanine; third-floor galleries and reception room; a fourth-floor boardroom; and a fifth-floor performance hall.

The lofty Great Hall is a masterpiece of tricolored marble brought over from Turkey and laid down by Turkish workers. The hall's eleven-thousand-square-foot floor is all marble, and so is the sweeping double staircase that leads to the mezzanine. Three immense, cut-crystal chandeliers brilliantly illuminate the hall for banquets and receptions.

The third-floor gallery area and reception room are available for smaller affairs. Here resides the museum's permanent collection of more than fifteen hundred works by women—paintings, sculptures, graphic arts, and photography from the sixteenth century to the present.

Given the way exhibit rooms break up the space, these spots work best for receptions and small dinners.

The performance hall has mauve, gray, and rose furnishings and features a two-story-high ceiling, marvelous acoustics, state-of-the-art audiovisual equipment, and a platform stage framed within a wide arch.

The boardroom is furnished simply for business use and holds approximately twenty people for a luncheon.

CAPACITY

Reception: 85 to 1,200 in the Great Hall and mezzanine, 20 to 300 in the
third-floor galleries, 100 in the reception room

Banquet: 560 in the Great Hall and mezzanine, 125 in the third-floor galleries,
60 in the reception room

Meeting: 35 in the boardroom, 197 in the performance hall

Performance: 197 in the performance hall

LOCATION

In downtown Washington, two blocks from the White House, at the corner of
13th Street and New York Avenue. The museum is one block from the Metro
Center Metro station and within walking distance of the DC Convention
Center.

FOOD/BEVERAGE

The museum has a list of caterers, which it strongly recommends you use. A full
caterer's kitchen is accessed easily from the loading dock and freight elevators.

LIMITATIONS/RESTRICTIONS

The Great Hall and mezzanine area and the galleries are available for evening
events only. The performance hall and boardroom are available for daytime and
evening events. Smoking is not permitted.

LEAD TIME FOR RESERVATIONS

Rental is subject to the museum's own schedule. Call for availability.

RATES

Great Hall and mezzanine, $9,000 to $12,000; Great Hall, mezzanine, and upper
galleries, $11,000 to $14,000; third-floor galleries, $3,500; performance hall,
$800 to $1,250, depending on the type of organization renting; reception room,
$1,250 to $2,500.

FACILITIES FOR THE PHYSICALLY DISABLED? Yes

NATIONAL PRESS CLUB

529 14th Street, NW, 13th Floor
Washington, DC 20045
202/662-7522

High up in the heart of Washington

It's arguable that there's no better place to put your finger on the pulse of Washington, or the pulse of the country for that matter, than at the National Press Club. On any given day, you'll see the people you have just read about in the morning newspaper, or people you're going to read about in tomorrow's. All kinds of famous figures, including US presidents, world leaders, and media personalities, use the Press Club as a forum, and the world's best journalists are here to cover them.

Aside from the celebrity scenery, the club's quarters are sensational. Wrapped around an atrium on the thirteenth floor of the National Press Building are handsomely furnished rooms accented with marble, mahogany, and brass. Available for events are four meeting rooms (also used for press conferences), two lounges, and a ballroom. Each of the rooms can serve many purposes.

The meeting rooms are located along a hall that overlooks the atrium. Each is named for a distinguished American journalist and is equipped with communications and audiovisual systems. Three of the rooms can be joined or used individually.

On the other side of the atrium lie the areas best suited for social events. You can hold a lunch, dinner, or reception in the newly renovated First Amendment Lounge, from which you have a view of the White House and the Washington Monument year-round.

The Main Lounge is more formal but comfortable, furnished with overstuffed sofas, a grand working fireplace, and mahogany bars on both sides. This room works well as is for a reception or, with the furniture removed, for a banquet and dancing.

Finally, there's the ballroom, a huge hall with two large balconies and an undulating, two-story-high, paneled ceiling. The ballroom can be partitioned into three separate sections.

CAPACITY

Reception: 15 to 1,200

Banquet: 5 to 450

Conference: 5 to 450

LOCATION

Two blocks east of the White House and one block west of the Metro Center Metro station, at the corner of F and 14th Streets, NW.

FOOD/BEVERAGE

The club caters all meals and will work with you to plan your menu.

LIMITATIONS/RESTRICTIONS

No specific restrictions—call to discuss your requirements.

LEAD TIME FOR RESERVATIONS

About six months, but call for availability.

RATES

Rates vary based on the room rented and food and beverages purchased.

FACILITIES FOR THE PHYSICALLY DISABLED? Yes

NATIONAL ZOOLOGICAL PARK

3001 Connecticut Ave, NW

Washington, DC 20008

202/673-7835

www.si.edu/natzoo/hilights/spevents

Everything's happening at the zoo

Maybe you didn't know it, but the National Zoo allows you to take tea with the orangutans, sip a glass of wine while strolling through the Amazonia Rain Forest, or even munch on lunch while all about you pandas, lions, spectacled bears, and other assorted wildlife are munching theirs.

In fact, you can reserve the entire zoo for an event, though most people settle for just a portion of the 163-acre park. Amazonia is a favorite spot for functions. Here you can walk along dark winding paths overgrown with lush vegetation, behind which you might spy a monkey, macaw, or sloth peering out at you. Hummingbirds sing, a waterfall gently cascades, and riverfish, turtles, and piranhas keep pace with you, swimming behind the glass of a large underwater tank. The rain forest leads to the Science Gallery, another popular site that's often used for dining. Other areas include the great meadow, lion-tiger hill, the elephant house, the birdhouse—you name it!

CAPACITY

The National Zoo can accommodate almost any size function, from 25 for a meeting to 15,000 for a stand-up reception.

LOCATION

In upper northwest Washington, a short walk from both the National Zoo/Woodley Park and Cleveland Park Metro stations. The zoo has parking for eight hundred, which you may use when you hold an event here after hours.

FOOD/BEVERAGE

You may choose your own caterer or use the zoo's in-house barbecue/picnic food service for casual events. The zoo does not offer kitchen facilities for caterers.

LIMITATIONS/RESTRICTIONS

Use of the zoo for special events is restricted to corporations, associations, and others who make unrestricted gifts to the zoo and to those who cosponsor, with the zoo, an event related to the zoo's mission. Cosponsored events must have a clear commonality of interest or a direct connection. Social events of a personal nature, fund-raising, product marketing, religious events, and political functions are not permitted. Corporations and nonprofit organizations may use the conference rooms, classrooms, and auditorium.

The zoo is available for indoor events in the evenings only and outdoor events anytime. The site strongly recommends that you rent a tent for outdoor events. Smoking is prohibited indoors. Balloons are not allowed.

LEAD TIME FOR RESERVATIONS

The site prefers that you book your event two to four months in advance but advises you always to call for availability.

RATES

Donations vary and range from $600 for use of a conference room for the day to $2,500 for a daytime picnic and a minimum of $5,000 for an evening event.

FACILITIES FOR THE PHYSICALLY DISABLED? Yes

THE OLD POST OFFICE PAVILION

1100 Pennsylvania Avenue, NW
Washington, DC 20004
202/289-4224
www.oldpostofficedc.com

For dancing, dining, and socializing

Used to be that on New Year's Eve at the Pavilion, you'd find yourself in a crowd of thousands ringing in the new year. The Pavilion no longer hosts that party, but it may be just the spot for your crowd to ring in a new product, a merger, or a new president (the Pavilion has been the site of an inaugural dinner or two).

As you might have guessed, the old post office has plenty of space. It's an imposing neo-Romanesque structure, nine stories high. Inside, an enormous inner atrium shoots up to the roof. It is surrounded by offices at the upper levels and a festival marketplace with specialty retail stores, restaurants, and an international food court at the lower levels. When you rent the Pavilion, the stores and restaurants are usually closed, and your event takes place in the common area on the bottom two floors.

The lower levels are open areas; from any one of these floors you can see to the next, and wide marble central stairs connect the levels. When you look above the third floor, you see the vaulted glass roof and the original steel girders put in place when the building was constructed in 1899 as the first federal post office. Through the glass roof you might notice the Clock Tower, rising 315 feet on the outside. The tower offers one of the highest views of the city, second only to the Washington Monument's. From April 2 through Labor Day, it is open from 8:00 A.M. to 10:45 P.M.; from Labor Day through April 1, it is open 10:00 A.M. to 5:45 P.M.

When you rent the Pavilion, you get to use its stage, dance floor, piano, and powerful sound systems.

CAPACITY
Reception: 1,900
Banquet: 225
Theater-style event: 550

LOCATION
Halfway between the White House and the US Capitol on Pennsylvania Avenue, only two blocks from the National Mall and five blocks from the DC Convention Center.

FOOD/BEVERAGE
You can arrange for catering through the Pavilion restaurants or use the site's preferred caterers list. There is no kitchen, but preparation areas are available.

LIMITATIONS/RESTRICTIONS
The Pavilion is usually available for events in the evenings.

LEAD TIME FOR RESERVATIONS
A couple of months, but call for availability.

RATES

$15,000, plus costs for security and janitorial services. This rate covers the use of the lower two levels. A $7,500 deposit is partially refundable.

FACILITIES FOR THE PHYSICALLY DISABLED? Yes

POSTAL SQUARE

2 Massachusetts Avenue, NE
Washington, DC 20013
202/484-8181
202/484-0579 (fax)

Washington's old post office opens its doors for parties

You may have posted a letter or two here, at the imposing Beaux Arts building that from 1914 until 1986 served as Washington's central post office. If you did, no doubt you were impressed by the structure's stunning white, granite façade and monumental proportions.

A twenty-two-month renovation begun in 1990 gives you reason to marvel over the old post office's interior as well. Only now, it won't be while you're queuing for stamps. With post office functions transferred to another section of the building, Postal Square's historic lobby now is available for receptions and banquets.

The fourteen-thousand-square-foot hall has been restored to its 1914 grandeur. The spectacular coffered plaster ceiling stands three stories overhead. Everything is marble—floors, walls, and the set of three ponderous tables breaking up the space down the middle of the long corridor. A marble ledge once leaned upon by customers while conducting business with mail clerks stationed at windows works admirably as a place to set drinks or an elbow while chatting with pals during an event. Bronze detailing decorates portions of the walls. And there are fantastic granite columns at the entrances and a series of handsome chandeliers above. Scattered along both sides of the chamber are twenty-four tall alabaster torchères, with spiral bronze stems set on marble pedestals.

It's possible to arrange to use the National Postal Museum, on the lower level, in conjunction with your Postal Square event. See the entry for the National Postal Museum for details.

CAPACITY
Reception: 1,200
Banquet: 400

LOCATION
On Massachusetts Avenue, right next to Union Station, between 1st and North Capitol Streets, NE. You can park at Union Station or on the street.

FOOD/BEVERAGE
You may choose your own caterer, subject to the site's approval.

LIMITATIONS/RESTRICTIONS
Postal Square is available mostly for evening functions, though daytime use is sometimes allowed. If your party numbers more than five hundred people and you're having dancing, you must arrange for a dance floor. Red wine is not allowed. Your choices of decoration and menu must be pre-approved. Security, cleaners, and an engineer under contract with Postal Square management must be on site during your event.

LEAD TIME FOR RESERVATIONS
Call as soon as possible to reserve a date.

RATES
Specific rental rates vary, depending upon the type of event and the kind of organization renting; call for further information. Operating expenses for janitorial, engineering, and security services are additional.

FACILITIES FOR THE PHYSICALLY DISABLED? Yes

POTOMAC VALLEY LODGE
16601 West Willard Road
PO Box 199
Poolesville, MD 20837
301/428-8283
301/972-7396 (fax)

250 secluded acres and clubhouse ballroom

Potomac Valley Lodge, once a country club, offers clubhouse facilities and a variety of outdoor activities to those who hold functions here. You'll find the lodge at the end of a tree-lined driveway, off a country road in the historic White's Ferry area of Maryland. In spring and summer especially, thick rows of evergreens, dogwood, and cherry blossom trees shield the site.

The 250 acres include the eighteen-hole Poolesville Golf Course (a separate entity); four tennis courts; provisions for softball, horseshoes, badminton, volleyball, and basketball; playgrounds with sandboxes; and two covered pavilions equipped with picnic tables and benches, water and electricity. Although the grounds are nicely landscaped, much of it is open pasture, excellent for sizable picnics.

A circular green and a covered driveway front the lodge, separating it from the immense parking lot. You enter the building through a white-paneled foyer and go up a short flight to the central log cabin room, which holds an original, working stone fireplace, exposed beams, and low-hanging wagon-wheel chandeliers. At one end is a small grouping of sofa, chairs, and piano. Windows look onto the carriage room, which holds a bar, and an awning-covered deck outside. Down some steps from the log cabin room is the ballroom: large and airy, with white walls, oak parquet floor, and sliding glass windows overlooking the golf course.

CAPACITY

Ballroom: 200 for meetings, receptions, and banquets
Grounds: 4,000 for picnics and outdoor functions
Pavilion I: 700
Pavilion II: 500

LOCATION

From Washington, follow River Road north through Potomac Village, until the road dead-ends at a stop sign. Turn left and continue on River Road (Route 112), traveling five miles to West Willard Road. Turn right on West Willard Road and go about five more miles to the Potomac Valley Lodge entrance, on the right. The site has parking space for two thousand cars.

FOOD/BEVERAGE

The lodge caters all events here and offers menus for picnics, barbecues (including pig and bull roasts), and golf outings, as well as menus for cocktail receptions (for example, pâté or crabmeat balls), weddings, and formal parties (beef stroganoff, prime rib, and the like).

LIMITATIONS/RESTRICTIONS

The ballroom is available year-round for events; the grounds are available as the seasons permit. Although the Potomac Valley Lodge caters golfing parties, the lodge does not actually own the golf course, so you must reserve tee times, the driving range, pull carts, and riding carts through the Poolesville Golf Course and Pro Shop (call 301/428-8143). The lodge serves alcohol, but it is against the law for you to bring your own alcoholic beverages onto the premises. Picnics with alcoholic beverage service end at 7:00 P.M. unless you make special arrangements with the lodge. Pets are not allowed.

LEAD TIME FOR RESERVATIONS

Call as soon as possible to reserve a pavilion and its grounds. Call nine to twelve months ahead to reserve the ballroom. June and September are the site's busiest months.

RATES

To reserve the ballroom for a golfing banquet costs $500. Otherwise, the lodge charges only for catering, not rental, when you have an event here. Catering rates range from $4 per person for a continental breakfast to $19.95 per person for a steak cookout, exclusive of bar, service, and sales charges. Food service is for three hours, all you can eat. Company picnics for fewer than 150 adults incur a "use-of-site" fee of $200; catered golf outings incur an extra $200 use-of-site fee when there are fewer than one hundred golfers and an extra $300 when there are fewer than seventy-five golfers. Certain discounted prices apply for children—ask about these.

FACILITIES FOR THE PHYSICALLY DISABLED? Some

Each of the pavilions has one wheelchair-accessible outdoor bathroom; the lodge is not specially equipped.

ROSECROFT RACEWAY

6336 Rosecroft Drive
Fort Washington, MD 20744
301/567-4000

Put your event on the right track

And they're off! Take your group to the races and watch your event come out a winner.

You find Rosecroft nestled in the hills at the end of a winding, tree-lined road. The clubhouse is an enclosed structure whose three levels offer reception space for thousands. In spite of its size, Rosecroft has a warm, clubby feel to it.

The club's prime attraction is its Terrace Dining Room, on the second and third floors. With room for twelve hundred, seated, it's one of the largest banquet spaces in the capital area. The huge, glass-fronted room has tiered seating and overlooks the home stretch, so everyone has a great view of the harnessed trotters and pacers as they strain for the finish line. Every table has its own ten-inch color television, which further ensures that you don't miss the action. Doors on the first floor of the club lead to outdoor seating by the rail. Open year-round, Rosecroft is a pretty, secluded spot in which to hold a function.

CAPACITY

Reception: 5,000 (when all three floors are rented)
Banquet: 30 to 600 in third-floor banquet rooms, 1,200 seated in the Terrace
   Dining Room, 3,000 seated on all three floors

LOCATION

From the Beltway (I-495), take Exit 4A and follow the signs for Rosecroft.

FOOD/BEVERAGE

The clubhouse caters all functions. It offers a varied menu featuring mostly American and Maryland favorites, such as prime rib and crab cakes, but the staff will work with you to customize your menu.

LIMITATIONS/RESTRICTIONS

Live races take place during the evenings only (post time is 7:20 P.M.), Thursday through Saturday; simulcast racing can be viewed Wednesday through Monday.

LEAD TIME FOR RESERVATIONS

Two to four weeks.

RATES

Group buffet dinners start at $23 per person; group sit-down dinners start at $24.95 per person. A minimum of twenty-five people is required for group rates, which cover admission, programs, seating, dinner, dessert, beverage, taxes, and gratuities.

FACILITIES FOR THE PHYSICALLY DISABLED? Yes

SMOKEY GLEN FARM

16407 Riffleford Road
Gaithersburg, MD 20878
301/948-1518
www.smokeyglenfarm.com
jsweet@smokeyglenfarm.com

Get down to the serious business of barbecue

The barbecue you taste at Smokey Glen Farm has been more than forty-five years in the making. It all started in the 1950s, when a man named Sweet had a swell idea: Why not sell barbecued chicken at University of Maryland football games? The idea took off, and by 1958 Sweet was not just seriously into barbecuing, but into the barbecue outing business.

Smokey Glen Farm is a social site as well as a business. Located on ninety-three acres of rolling and wooded hills that back up to Seneca Creek State Park, Smokey Glen is the perfect setting for an outing. There are three picnic areas on the property: the Meadow, the Grove, and the Pavilion, each featuring open-air pavilions for seating and athletic facilities for horseshoes, volleyball, basketball, softball, miniature golf, and other games. In addition, the site helps you arrange for a host of other activities, from pie-eating contests to hayrides and square dances.

The staff coordinates your whole barbecue shebang, including—and this is most important—the preparation of the feast. Charcoal-roasted chicken, prime rib, spare ribs, pig, corn on the cob, and lobster, as well as charcoal-baked breads and desserts, are just some of the farm's sumptuous specialties.

CAPACITY
Daytime picnics and evening parties: 120 (minimum) to 5,000
Lobster bakes, business meetings, and special-menu events: 50 (minimum) to 250

LOCATION
From the Beltway (I-495), take the I-270 north exit toward Frederick. Follow I-270 to Exit 6B (Darnestown/Route 28); go west on Route 28 toward Darnestown for 5.5 miles. Turn right onto Riffleford Road and right again into Smokey Glen Farm.

FOOD/BEVERAGE
Smokey Glen handles all food and beverage arrangements.

LIMITATIONS/RESTRICTIONS
Gambling is prohibited. For daytime events, the serving of alcohol is limited to beer and wine for no more than six hours. Bar service for evening parties may include hard liquor in addition to beer and wine but must end by 11:45 P.M.

LEAD TIME FOR RESERVATIONS
Call for availability. Weekday events are usually easier to schedule. The site starts taking reservations in January for the remainder of the year. Repeat customers get first priority.

RATES

Rates range from $19.65 per adult for a daytime picnic to $34.45 per adult for a daytime lobster bake and food, beverage, and the use of the site. Many additional food items are available at an extra charge. There is a $300 service charge for groups numbering fewer than 250 for daytime picnics and for groups under 120 for business meetings.

FACILITIES FOR THE PHYSICALLY DISABLED? Some

The pavilions and some rest rooms, parking facilities, and picnic tables are wheelchair accessible.

SPECIAL EVENTS AT UNION STATION

50 Massachusetts Avenue, NE
Washington, DC 20002
202/289-8300
202/289-7268 (fax)
www.unionstationevents.com

A capital entertaining spot in view of the Capitol

When it was designed, at the beginning of the twentieth century, Union Station's mission was to serve as the "great and impressive vestibule to Washington." And despite its size, the Beaux Arts building has always managed to fulfill this purpose with aplomb and graciousness, shepherding presidents and commuters alike through its arched portals and along its marble floors.

A restoration completed in 1988 gave new life to the station and made perfectly evident what might have been hinted at before: As a special event site, Union Station is a natural. Take the Main Hall. Modeled after the Roman public baths of Diocletian, its barrel-vaulted, coffered ceilings are ninety-six feet up from the Italian marble floor. Light streams in through the large front entryways and from the clerestory windows in the ceiling. The hall is 225 feet long and 125 feet wide.

The East Hall was once a dining room for travelers but now may be used separately or with the Columbus Club and/or Main Hall for functions. Here you'll find flat skylights in the alcoves of the north and south walls and hand-stenciled clerestory walls trimmed with gold leaf.

Finally, Union Station's most intimate area is the Columbus Club, a private chamber located up an Italian marble staircase from the Main Hall. No longer the station's "fancy soda fountain," the Columbus Club is a favorite party site these days, admired for its ornamental plaster ceilings and molded cornices emblazoned with Pompeiian flourishes of red, green, and gold.

CAPACITY
Columbus Club: 225 for a banquet, 450 for a reception
East Hall: 450 for a banquet, 800 for a reception
Main Hall: 1,650 for a banquet, 3,500 for a reception
Throughout: more than 2,000 for a banquet, 10,000 for a reception

LOCATION
On Massachusetts Avenue, NE, a couple of blocks from the US Capitol.

FOOD/BEVERAGE
Special Events at Union Station functions as a full-service event site, managing all of your menu and beverage requirements and, as desired, audiovisual, entertainment, security, and other arrangements.

LIMITATIONS/RESTRICTIONS
The East and Main Halls are available for evening rentals only. The Columbus Club is available all day, every day.

LEAD TIME FOR RESERVATIONS
It's recommended that you call at least ninety days in advance to reserve the Main Hall. Call at least thirty days ahead to reserve the East Hall and Columbus Club.

RATES

Rates start at $750 for a half-day, weekday rental of the Columbus Club and go up from there, depending upon the site, size, and nature of your event, as well as what support services you require.

FACILITIES FOR THE PHYSICALLY DISABLED? Yes

TARARA VINEYARDS

13648 Tarara Lane
Leesburg, VA 22075
703/771-7100 or 703/478-8161 (metro area)
www.tarara.com

The setting is ideal: 475 acres fronting the Potomac, out in the country not far from Leesburg. That's what Tarara Vineyards's owners, Whitie and Margaret Hubert, thought when they purchased the property in 1985 to start their wine business. (To date, the couple has planted fifty acres of grapes.) You are likely to find the spot heavenly, too, if you're looking for a peaceful, bucolic place suitable for a meeting, a company outing, or a family function.

In the winery, adjoining the tasting room, is the space for seminars. This area is pretty businesslike, with grayish tan wall-to-wall carpeting, white walls, artwork, round tables, and padded conference chairs. There are no windows to distract you from the matters at hand—and that's probably a good thing, given the scenery. Just outside the winery, built out from a bluff, is the deck, from which you can see the flood plain, the Potomac River, Sugar Loaf Mountain, and maybe some deer frolicking below. Up the hill is a large wooden pavilion, thirty-two by sixty-four feet, equipped with electric and water sources and furnished with picnic tables that can seat 250 people. Around the property are numerous recreational options, including softball fields, volleyball courts, horseshoe pits, hiking trails, and a children's playground. Last but not least are the wine caves, which the Huberts blasted out of a rock hill. You can arrange to tour these and taste Tarara's award-winning wines during your event.

Note: Tarara also operates a B and B above the winery. Three bedrooms and one suite all have private baths and views of mountains and lakes.

CAPACITY
Reception: 2,500 using the pavilion and fields, 75 in the winery, 100 using the winery and deck
Banquet: 250 in the pavilion, 75 in the winery, 130 using the winery and deck
Meeting: 250 in the pavilion, 40 in the winery, 75 using the winery and deck
Lodging: 3 rooms, 1 suite, all with private bath

LOCATION
Follow Route 7 in Virginia to Leesburg. Go north on Route 15 approximately eight miles to Lucketts, and then go right on Route 662. Follow Route 662 three

miles to the Tarara sign, and turn left into the driveway. Proceed all the way back, following the signs to the parking area. There's plenty of parking available.

FOOD/BEVERAGE

You may choose your own caterer. The winery has a large kitchen area equipped with a sink, refrigerators, a dishwasher, and plenty of setup space. All wines served during your event will be Tarara's.

LIMITATIONS/RESTRICTIONS

The vineyards are available for events every day at any time, all year long. There are no specific restrictions.

LEAD TIME FOR RESERVATIONS

The owners recommend that you book four months ahead, but call for availability.

RATES

Rates vary depending on the size of the crowd, the day of your event, and the area you're renting, but they generally range from $600 (for up to 50 guests) to $1,750 (for up to 125 guests attending a Saturday wedding). Call about picnic rates for large crowds.

Lodging costs $120 for each of the bedrooms and $135 for the suite.

FACILITIES FOR THE PHYSICALLY DISABLED? No

WESTFIELDS MARRIOTT AND CONFERENCE CENTER

14750 Conference Center Drive
Chantilly, VA 20151
703/818-0300 or 800/635-5666
703/818-3655 (fax)
www.marriott.com

From the custom-designed, three-and-one-half-ton bronze doors at its grand entrance to the marble-covered Rotunda, rising twenty-two feet to its copper dome, and the ergonomic meeting room chairs, Westfields is out to bowl you over. This is not your average conference center.

The U-shaped brick building's exterior resembles an immense English manor, complete with front courtyard. Through those bronze doors is a two-level complex holding twenty-eight conference rooms that you can partition or enlarge to accommodate your group, 335 guest rooms and suites, a state-of-the-art auditorium, a high-tech media center (equipped with high-speed Internet access T1 lines), a series of public rooms, a pub, three dining rooms, and recreational facilities that range from an indoor lap pool and Jacuzzi to an outdoor pool, Jacuzzi, and tennis and volleyball courts. The conference center also has a fine golf course and a clubhouse located seven miles away; shuttles ferry you there.

What you need to know is that Westfields exudes elegance. The place is resplendent with art and antiques. Decorating is done on a grand scale: Twenty specially designed, delicately crafted chandeliers hang throughout the center; classic white marble columns frame the central Rotunda; antique billiard tables and brocaded walls embellish the pub; and a nine-and-a-half-foot Bosendorfer grand piano graces the upper Rotunda.

Those attending conferences at Westfields will find the meeting rooms attractive and well equipped with a range of business services that include state-of-the-art audiovisual systems. Those attending wedding receptions and other social functions will rhapsodize over the abundance of beautiful touches, from generous displays of fresh flowers to the fine art found throughout.

CAPACITY

Reception: more than 1,000 in the largest room, with other rooms accommodating smaller parties. The conference center can handle 4,500 throughout.
Banquet: 800 in the largest room. Other rooms accommodate smaller parties.
Meeting: 10 (in a small conference suite) to 1,200 (in the ballroom)
Auditorium: 200
Lodging: 335 guest rooms

LOCATION

Westfields is seven miles south of Dulles Airport and twenty-five minutes from Washington. From Washington, take I-66 west to Route 28 north, toward Dulles Airport. Follow Route 28 two miles to Westfields Boulevard, where you turn left. At the first intersection, turn right onto Stonecroft Boulevard; go to the first traffic light and turn left on Conference Center Drive. Westfields is on the left.

FOOD/BEVERAGE

Westfields caters all conferences and other functions held here. If yours is a business event, you may opt for the Complete Meeting Package Plan, which includes all three meals served in the Fairfax Dining Room, or choose from Westfields's other offerings: the Palm Court restaurant, Wellington's Pub, private dining rooms, or room service. If you are planning a wedding or social affair at Westfields, staff will help you plan a menu to please.

LIMITATIONS/RESTRICTIONS

Smoking is restricted to certain areas. There are no other specific restrictions—call with your requirements.

LEAD TIME FOR RESERVATIONS

Call no sooner than a month ahead for a daytime meeting; call as soon as you have a date for overnight conferences. If you're planning a wedding reception, call six months to a year in advance. Westfields books wedding receptions no earlier than a year in advance.

RATES

Call for specific rates, which vary by season. Count on costs in the ballpark of $245 to $425 per person, per night for a complete meeting package, which includes meeting room use, setup fee, standard gratuities, all three meals, lodging, and continuous coffee breaks. An evening wedding averages $80 to $125 per person. None of these rates include bar charges.

FACILITIES FOR THE PHYSICALLY DISABLED? Yes

How to book group seating
for theater performances

After a busy day of staging your own events, you and your associates might like nothing better than to sit back and watch a fine performance at one of Washington's wonderful theaters. Here are a few tips about how to book groups of seats for performances.

Maybe you don't care whether your group sits together; maybe you do. Either way, according to staff at each theater, your best bet for reserving the number of seats you want is simply to make reservations early, weeks in advance if possible. Even so, you may be out of luck; popular shows are often sold out way ahead of time. Since most theaters now have their own Web sites, you can also book seats online. At the sites listed below you can not only make reservations but get information about upcoming performances, ticket prices, and seating charts.

Some theaters may require immediate, full payment to confirm reservations; others may require a twenty percent deposit. Groups of twenty or more may qualify for a group discount, although each theater has its own criteria. The Shakespeare Theatre, for example, gives groups of ten or more discounts as great as forty-five percent. Rates can be affected by any number of factors: the type of your organization, the number of tickets you want, the seats and performance day you're reserving, and the policy of the show's producer or promoter. Sometimes no discounts are available. The Kennedy Center, for example, seldom discounts tickets for Friday and Saturday night performances. If your group is eligible for a reduced price at any of the theaters, you can expect it to start at about ten percent.

Many Washington-area theaters ask that you call a specific number if you want to book seats for a group. Below are group phone numbers and Web sites for the major theaters in town.

Arena Stage: 202/488-4380, www.arenastage.org
Ford's Theatre: 202/638-2367 or 800/899-2367, www.fordstheatre.org

Kennedy Center for the Performing Arts: 202/416-8400 or 800/444-1324, www.kennedy-center.org

National Theater: 202/628-6166 or 800/432-7780, www.nationaltheatre.org

Shakespeare Theatre: 202/547-1122, www.shakespearedc.org

The Source Theatre Company: 202/462-1073, www.dcmdva-arts.org/sourceth

The Studio Theatre: 202/232-7267, www.studiotheatre.org

The Warner Theatre: 202/783-4000

Wolf Trap: 703/255-1851, www.wolf-trap.org

Woolly Mammoth Theatre Company: 202/393-3939, www.woollymammoth.net.

How to arrange special tours of the White House and official briefings at the White House or on Capitol Hill

The first thing you want to do to arrange a special tour of the White House, a briefing by White House officials, or a briefing on Capitol Hill is to call your company's or association's government relations office in Washington and ask staff members to handle the matter. It is their daily business to represent your organization's interests before Congress and the Executive Branch, and they are usually familiar with congressional and White House procedures.

If your organization doesn't have a Washington office, the tips below may help.

Special White House Tours

To arrange a special tour of the White House for your organization, get in touch with the office of your senator or representative. Describe your organization and tell the office how many tickets you need. Each member's office has its own procedure for requesting and disbursing tickets, but this much holds true for all:

♦ Special White House tours are very popular—the White House fields more than five hundred requests daily—so you should try to make your arrangements months in advance and at least six months ahead for spring and summer tours. It is nearly impossible to schedule a special White House viewing in the summer because of all the tourists visiting Washington with the same idea.

♦ The White House allots each congressman's and senator's office no more than ten tickets weekly, and sometimes fewer, so the chances are that your group won't be allowed to exceed that number.

♦ The White House conducts four special tours each morning at 8:15 A.M. with fifty people in each group, which means that you'll probably be joined by other "special" viewers.

Briefings by White House Officials

Briefings by White House officials can be difficult to arrange. According to the White House's Office of Public Liaison, the procedure for scheduling briefings changes so often that any published information would quickly become out of date. That office recommends that you call the main number at the White House (202/456-1414) and ask to speak to the scheduling office of the administration official(s) with whom you'd like to meet. The switchboard will then put you in touch with the right office. Be prepared to explain what your organization is and the issue you'd like to discuss. You can expect to be asked to submit your request in writing.

Briefings on Capitol Hill

The way in which you arrange briefings on Capitol Hill depends on whom you want to meet, how many people are involved, and whether there's a particular issue you'd like to discuss. If there are just a few of you and you want to meet with one particular congressman or senator, call that member's office and set up an appointment. If there are more than a few of you or you want to meet with several congressional members, call each of the members' offices directly to arrange a meeting. You then work with one member's office to reserve a conference room on the Hill. (You're much more likely to get the biggest turnout of members if you hold your event on the Hill.)

Finally, if your group wants to brief or be briefed by members on a particular topic, call the congressional committee that has jurisdiction over that issue. Then you request that a briefing be arranged between your organization and committee members in a conference room on the Hill. For example, if the American Medical Association wishes to inform congressional members of its concerns regarding Medicare, the association would need to call the Committee on Health and Human Services, among others.

If you don't know which committees handle your issue, call the office of the congressman or senator representing your area and ask. You can get the office numbers of congressional members and committees by calling the main number at the US Capitol: 202/224-3121.

If your aim is to acquaint as many congressional members as possible with your views on an issue, your best bet is to arrange the briefing through the office of a senator or representative from your area or with whom you share a common interest in the issue. Those members can reserve a conference room and might also agree to send invitations to the House or Senate at large.

There are some marvelous meeting sites on Capitol Hill. They can be reserved only when the event you're holding is a congressionally related activity—that is, sponsored by a congressional member. Two popular spots are the Mike Mansfield Room in the US Capitol Building and the Cannon Caucus Room in the Cannon House Office Building.

The Mike Mansfield Room is a paneled chamber that can accommodate 120 people seated in rows of chairs (theater-style) or 100 people seated around conference tables. The Cannon Caucus Room is huge, elaborate, and furnished with chandeliers and red carpeting. It can accommodate 350 people seated or 550 people standing for a meeting, 250 people seated for a banquet, and 450 people for a stand-up reception.

You might also inquire about the US Botanic Gardens, which reopened to the public in the fall of 2000 after an extensive renovation. The remarkable conservatory used to be available for receptions and banquets; it might be so again, but at this writing details are not available. Check out its Web site, www.nationalgarden.org, to learn more.

Ask congressional staff for other meeting place recommendations on the Hill.

Topical Cross-Reference

Clubs

Halls

Historic Sites

Inns and Overnight Conference Centers

Mansions about One Hundred Years Old

Mostly for Meetings

Museums

Picnic Sites

Private Homes

Geographic Index

Old Town and Other Parts of Alexandria

Upper Northwest Washington

Virginia Countryside

Alphabetic Index

About the Author

Elise Hartman Ford has been a freelance writer in the Washington, DC, area since 1985. She contributes regularly to such newspapers and magazines as the *Washington Post* and the *Washingtonian*. She is the author of *Frommer's Guide to Washington, DC* and *Frommer's Washington, DC, from $70 a Day*, as well as other books in the Frommer's series. She resides in Chevy Chase, Maryland, with her husband, Jim, and their daughters, Caitlin and Lucy.